HOL

MERIDIAN

Crossing Aesthetics

Werner Hamacher

Editor

Stanford
University
Press

─────────────

Stanford
California

HOUSING PROBLEMS

Writing and Architecture in
Goethe, Walpole, Freud, and Heidegger

Susan Bernstein

Stanford University Press
Stanford, California

Publication assistance for this book was provided by
Brown University.

Printed in the United States of America on acid-free, archival-
quality paper

Library of Congress Cataloging-in-Publication Data

Bernstein, Susan, 1957-
  Housing problems : writing and architecture in Goethe, Walpole, Freud, and Heidegger / Susan Bernstein.
      p. cm.--(Meridian, crossing aesthetics)
  Includes bibliographical references and index.
  ISBN 978-0-8047-5854-3 (cloth : alk. paper)--ISBN 978-0-8047-
5855-0 (pbk. : alk. paper)
  1. Architecture in literature. 2. Architecture, Gothic, in literature. 3. Architecture and literature. 4. Architecture and philosophy. I. Title. II. Series: Meridian (Stanford, Calif.)
  PN56.A73B47 2008
  809'.93357--dc22   2008006694

Typeset by Bruce Lundquist in 10.9/13 Adobe Garamond

For A

Contents

Acknowledgments

Thanks to the many institutions that supported this work in progress: the Fulbright Senior Scholar Program, Brown University, the Stiftung Weimarer Klassik, the Goethehaus (Weimar), the Freud Museum (London), das Freud Museum Wien (special thanks to Inge Scholz-Strasser), and St. Mary's College, Twickenham (Strawberry Hill).

Much gratitude and appreciation to Suzanne Doppelt, whose collaboration and cotourism doubled the scope of this book.

Thanks to the many friends and colleagues who read the manuscript in progress for their invaluable comments, critique, and support: Popahna Brandes, Paul Fleming, Forrest Gander, Michael Gizzi, Werner Hamacher, Philippe Lacoue-Labarthe, Karen Newman, Avital Ronell, Zachary Sng, Jeffrey Wallen, Samuel Weber, and Susan White.

Thanks to the many students at Brown University, New York University, and the Technische Universität Berlin whose participation in seminars helped develop the arguments of this book.

Thanks to all Bernsteins for their support, especially to Molly Bernstein and Philip Dolin, who are my mainstay, and to my Dharma family.

Many thanks to Denise Davis for her meticulous attention to the manuscript and her abiding friendship

Exceptional thanks to Kevin McLaughlin for his critical insight and unfaltering confidence.

Abbreviations

BT	Heidegger, *Being and Time*
BW	Heidegger, *Basic Writings*
GS	Benjamin, *Gesammelte Schriften*
GW	Freud, *Gesammelte Werke*
HA	*Goethes Werke—Hamburger Ausgabe*
ID	Heidegger, *Identity and Difference*
IuD	Heidegger, *Identität und Differenz*
NCP	Oppen, *New Collected Poems*
PLT	Heidegger, *Poetry, Language, Thought*
SE	Freud, *Standard Edition*
SL	Oppen, *Selected Letters*
SuZ	Heidegger, *Sein und Zeit*
VuA	Heidegger, *Vorträge und Aufsätze*
W	Heidegger, *Wemarken*

HOUSING PROBLEMS

Introduction

SALVE. These letters, wrought of inlaid wood, lie at the threshold of Johann Wolfgang von Goethe's house in Weimar, Germany. A few steps beyond, the often-photographed vista through Goethe's rooms comes into view. Goethe's inscription marks the spot from which the classicizing vision of his home begins to open up, a vision aligning doorways to suggest a symmetry belied by the irregular wood patterns of the floors and the slightly twisting angles of this baroque house's layout. But Goethe's greeting comes a bit late. For one encounters the Roman salutation only after already having passed through the portal from the street, turned to the right, and climbed the long and stately staircase that Goethe himself designed to take up an inordinate amount of space—a use of space indicating wealth and grandeur. After visiting Goethe, Jean Paul remarked: "His house is striking: it is the only one in Weimar in the Italian taste, with such a staircase."[1] Goethe's house impresses even before one can begin to read it; the gesture towards unity and containment through inscription and design is exceeded by the materiality that supports it. The building cannot quite contain the experience of it; the very inscription of initiation points to an edge beyond itself, a falling-off into an uncharted priority or shadow-exterior.

The difficulty of the doorway or the threshold is the difficulty of beginning. The narrator of Kafka's late story "Der Bau" ["The Burrow"] is famously afflicted by this problem. The entrance remains an eyesore throughout the story, for it is a constant reminder of the persistence of a hostile exterior. The narrator begins: "I have completed the construction of my burrow and it seems to be successful."[2] The verb *scheinen* (seems) immediately sheds doubt on the status of the burrow. The next sentence directs our attention to the problem of the doorway, which turns out to be probably the grossest error of the burrow. At first we encounter a sort of trompe l'oeil: "All that can be seen from outside is a big hole; that, however, really leads nowhere" (325/359). While the narrator concedes that this deception is nothing but the remnant of uncompleted building efforts, the flaws surrounding the doorway point to the inevitable failures of finitude, the impossibility of conceiving and carrying out a totalizing plan, and the painful failure to secure an interior—a failure marked by the fact of a passageway. "At that one point in the dark moss I am mortal" (325, translation emended/360).

The entrance or beginning articulates the rupture between the architectural plan and its physical instantiation; it opens the gap between the synchrony of conception and its diachronous realization. The relation between experience and understanding stumbles over this threshold. For Jacques Derrida architecture punctuates experience not only as space but as spacing. It thus marks out a zone of experience that must always exceed, and thus elude, theoretical mastery: "We appear to ourselves only through an experience of spacing which is already marked by architecture. What happens through architecture both constructs and instructs this us. The latter finds itself engaged by architecture before it becomes the subject of it: master and possessor"(Leach, 324/*Psyché*, 478).

Efforts to theorize architecture and to lay out the architectonic continue to collide with or bring about the experience of the material resistance of the individual building. *Housing Problems* opens up over this threshold to explore what Bernard Tschumi calls a "disjunction," a fundamental paradox of architecture:

> A debate at a conceptual architecture conference in London (where the majority of contributors predictably concluded that "all architecture is conceptual") emphasized the strange paradox that seems to haunt architecture: namely, the impossibility of simultaneously questioning the nature of space and, at the same time, making or experiencing a real space. . . . This constant questioning about the nature of architecture only underlined the inevitable split between discourse and the domain of daily experience. . . . Again, *it was impossible to question the nature of space* and at the same time make or experience a real space. The complex opposition between ideal and real space was certainly not ideologically neutral, and the paradox it implied was fundamental. (67–70)

Tschumi points to the excess of building and experience that cannot be subsumed by concepts. "Caught, then, between sensuality and a search for rigor, between a perverse taste for seduction and a quest for the absolute, architecture seemed to be defined by the questions it raised. *Was architecture really made of two terms that were interdependent but mutually exclusive?* Did architecture constitute the reality of subjective experience while this reality got in the way of the overall concept?" (69). Tschumi concludes that this paradox is constitutive of architecture; it sets up a constant dynamic moving between discursive levels.

On the one hand, architecture and architectonics are rational processes that precede and ground any empirical building. In this schema a house would be a determinate end result of the architectural process, one that now stands apart and is of little interest. *Housing Problems* seeks to redirect interest to this excluded or marginalized house. For this reason the sphere of the "merely empirical" is given a place here. The actual houses of Goethe, Horace Walpole, and Sigmund Freud, mostly now museums, are studied here in a pseudopositivistic manner alongside textual articulations of architectonic problems. This empirical underpinning points to a random origin or ungrounded beginning within the sphere of buildings. On the other hand, the house brought under scrutiny always reveals itself to be another text, another inscribed surface. The effort here to link text and house brings into focus the historical tradition that has established a symmetry between design and instance, interior and exterior, author and house. *Housing Problems* takes as its point of departure Goethe's efforts to establish such a synthesis through the concept of *Bildung*: education, formation, edification. This tradition, marked by the effort to harmonize house and man, continues to shape literary research and is one of the unexamined fantasies of historicism. At the same time the interest here in architecture holds open the tension between the generalizing figures of architectonics and the singular quality of housing features. These continue to mark theoretical thinking even as they dissolve and withdraw. This movement of architecture is the focus of the final chapter, on Martin Heidegger's "house of Being" and George Oppen.

Architecture articulates both the plan of design and its realization, intimately related yet not reducible to a single entity, organized through spatialization and difference as well as through the legislative and controlling tendencies of the *arkhè*. Architecture can be understood as the art of beginning, of origination and foundation (*arkhè*, beginning or origin,

+ *tektōn*, master builder; related to *techné*, art or technique, both derived from *tiktōn*, to generate or create), and thus as the model of the law-giving and prescriptive function per se.³ As the possibility of transference or translation between sketch—*Grundriß*, design, plan—and building, architecture is determined as a teleological and law-giving art.⁴ This more general sense of architecture, or architectonic, contrasts with the specific art of architecture to which the word usually refers. The architectural plan produces a building that stands beyond it, solidified, stony, empirical. Architecture is therefore not only the originary art or art of origination; it is also a *constructum*: something already made and handed down, what it historically has been.⁵ It also produces the specific material structures that resist absorption into a unified plan and give rise to a sphere of experience that protrudes beyond the margins of the page. This book explores this relationship of disjunction between architectonic design and architectural instance, between the subject as master-designer and the experience of material walls, between the theory of architecture and the facticity of houses.

Combining the general sense of architectonic as an inaugural art and the limited sense of architecture as building, architecture installs a vertical hierarchy that insures the elevation of the idea or the concept and the subservience of material, the precedence of form and structure over ornament, detail, or part. Western philosophical discourse is deeply imbricated with architecture in that both fields are engaged in processes of establishment, setting up, institutionalization, edification, structuring, and construction. The opacity of architecture and its elements makes possible the erection of theoretical and systematic thinking, the laying of foundations, and the defining of the border between inside and outside. In this sense, building is constitutive of thought, for it supports the very laying out of exposition.⁶ René Descartes, for example, frequently invokes architectural images to establish this epistemological structure. In the *Discourse on Method*, Descartes compares his search for a firm foundation to an architectural project. Mathematics occupies pride of place as a solid foundation:

> Above all I enjoyed mathematics . . . [but] . . . I was astonished that on such firm and solid foundations nothing more exalted had been built, while on the other hand I compared the moral writings of the ancient pagans to the most proud and magnificent palaces built on nothing but sand and mud. . . . As

for the other sciences, in so far as they borrow their principles from philosophy, I considered that nothing solid could have been built on such shifting
foundations. (31–32/37–38)

Discourse itself is understood as an architectural structure with a foundation and an overlay. Sciences and humanities are unreliable because
they do not have a solid foundation; they are also conglomerate structures that connect parts horizontally rather than investigating and re-
structuring the foundation in a vertical direction. For Descartes the
installation of the foundation-superstructure model also implies the
privileging of a single subject as origin and author. A building based
on a unified and synchronous design is superior to buildings joined together through history:

> There is less perfection in works composed of several separate pieces and made
> by different masters, than in those at which only one person has worked. So it
> is that one sees that buildings undertaken and completed by a single architect
> are usually more beautiful and better ordered than those that several archi-
> tects have tried to put into shape, making use of old walls which were built
> for other purposes. So it is that these old cities which, originally only villages,
> have become, through the passage of time, great towns, are usually so badly
> proportioned in comparison with those orderly towns which an engineer de-
> signs at will on some plain that, although the buildings, taken separately,
> often display as much art as those of the planned towns or even more, nev-
> ertheless, seeing how they are places, with a big one here, a small one there,
> and how they cause the streets to bend and to be at different levels, one has
> the impression that they are more the product of chance than that of a human
> will operating according to reason. (35/41–42)

Rational construction based on a single conception is deemed more solid
and beautiful than aggregation through time and space. Architecture is
thus allied primarily with the unified blueprint or design, which ought
to be applied uniformly, creating a one-to-one correspondence between
rational design and material execution.

Immanuel Kant displays a similar predilection for the architectonic
design. In the penultimate section of the *Critique of Pure Reason*, Kant
presents the term "architectonic" as follows: "By an architectonic I understand the art of systems."[7] Architectonic unity, he explains, is characterized by rational necessity and is distinguished from technical unity,
or those general structures that are produced through aggregation or

empirical accumulation. This accumulation belongs to the sphere of the history of reason; history can be gathered up and reshaped, refigured and re-presented in a necessary and systematic form:

> It is unfortunate that only after we have spent much time rhapsodically collecting all sorts of stray bits of knowledge as building materials [*Bauzeug*], at the suggestion of an idea lying hidden in our minds, and after we have, indeed, over a long period assembled the materials in a merely technical manner, does it first become possible for us to discern the idea in a clearer light, and to devise a whole architectonically in accordance with the ends of reason. (655/2:697)

This architectonic projection or design does away with the haphazard quality of the *Bauzeug*, or construction materials. The recasting of knowledge according to a single idea picks up historical material; Kant remarks that much knowledge has already been amassed and thus makes possible "an architectonic of all human knowledge, which . . . in view of the great amount of material that has been collected, or which can be picked up from the ruins of old collapsed buildings [should not be difficult]" (655/2:698). Architectonics, then, marks a fold between induction and deduction, between the technical or rhapsodic gathering of the historical, and its recasting as a necessary system of relations. One might say the word "architectonic" is the transcendental correlate to the field of architecture; it enfolds and presents the rules of the buildings, ruins, and materials that architecture deploys. Architecture provides the constitutive elements of the articulation of architectonics; at the same time, it is put aside as extraneous matter that is merely empirical.[8]

This extraneous matter reemerges as the marginalized house. We can find it in Descartes, for example, if we consider the circumstances of his realizations about foundations and building in the passage quoted above. At the beginning of the second section of the *Discourse on Method*, we find that Descartes has withdrawn from his military activity because of the weather. Delayed by contingency, he relates:

> I was, at that time, in Germany, whither the wars, which have not yet finished there, had called me, and as I was returning from the coronation of the Emperor to join the army, the onset of winter held me up in quarters in which, finding no company to distract me, and having, fortunately, no cares or passions to disturb me, I spent the whole day shut up in a room heated

by an enclosed stove, where I had complete leisure to meditate on my own thoughts. (35/41)

The cozily heated room provides shelter from the violence of history and allows a temporary dissociation from empirical surroundings that takes the form of Descartes' thoughts. This room is not accounted for by Descartes' musings on building; we take it to be a random dwelling decked out empirically, in all the roughness and unevenness of the unplanned city. In the *Meditations*, Descartes classes this type of experience with those things that can be obliterated by doubt: "for example, that I am here, sitting by the fire, wearing a dressing-gown, with this paper in my hands" (96/69). The conditions of writing are denied through writing, the comforts of the room demolished by what the room allows Descartes to think. The disjunction between Descartes' architectural metaphors in the exposition of his method and the details of the setting of these meditations enacts the paradox Tschumi speaks of. It points also to the room, the house, the domestic interior, as a denied condition for theoretical thinking.

Let's go back for a moment to Tschumi's emphatic question: *Was architecture really made of two terms that were interdependent but mutually exclusive?* In Hegel's *Aesthetics* we find that this relationship obtains between architecture as the first symbolic art on the one hand and the "calling" of architecture to fulfill itself in the purposiveness of building shelters—in fact, the house "as a fundamental type"—on the other. Architectonic order and housing are mutually exclusive. This relationship comes out in the difficult relationship between the definitions of architecture as the first symbolic art and the story of its progress to the building of shelters as its true concept. Because art is defined in general as the mutual interpenetration of idea and *Gestaltung* (shape or formation), of interior and exterior, independent architecture as the first art ought to meet this same criterion. As the first symbolic art, however, architecture is defined as the predominance of a material exteriority insufficiently penetrated by spirit—as an exterior subsisting on its own, giving vague intimations of interiority or meaning, but remaining predominantly as unworked exteriority. Housing therefore cannot be an art, because it subordinates the exteriority of building to the function of shelter and surrounding for an interior that is the center of meaning. The building as house has its purpose (*Zweck*) outside itself in the interior it shelters and is no longer art. Originary architecture, in contrast, cannot yet be marked by that difference; instead, it would resemble sculpture. Hegel writes:

> But should there be absent at the beginning the difference between (a) the aim, explicitly present in man or the temple-image, of seeking an enclosure and (b) the building as the fulfillment of this aim, then we will have to look around for buildings which stand there independently in themselves, as it were like works of sculpture, and which carry their meaning in themselves and not in some external aim and need.[9]

The intrusion of purposiveness (*Zweckmäßigkeit*) into architecture implies a differentiation between means and ends following the organization of interior and exterior. As the means of building are subordinated to the purpose of shelter, the exterior of the house is seen as fully distinct from the interior spirit it shelters.

The first form of architecture—as an independent and free-standing art—is the building of towers that have as their function only the gathering of the people who build them, as in the construction of the Babylonian Tower (2:638/14:276–77).

This gathering is not purposive because it does not work with a dichotomy between inside and outside. The tower is itself the bond that it creates. At the same time such structures are ambivalently connected with symbolic meanings that go beyond them. The tower of Belus, for example, which Hegel hesitantly suggests may be connected to the tower in the Bible, stands symbolically in seven levels, massive and solid, probably following the pattern of the seven planets and spheres of the heavens (14:278).

Hegel's description of independent architecture is rather confused. While he states that the architectural function is the gathering of peoples, this function is basically dropped and does not make its way into the aesthetics of architecture. The artistic quality of independent architectonic features seems instead to have to do with geometrical relations obtaining between solid masses. This latter quality is developed in the exposition of architectural works "wavering between Architecture and Sculpture" (2:640/14:279). Although these may use sculptural forms—obelisks, sphinxes, etc.—Hegel argues that these are used in an independently architectural way. The purely architectonic has to do with positioning in space, especially of massive objects. The Memnon statues, according to Hegel, actually function more architecturally—or to be more precise, architectonically—than sculpturally because they are not focused on the distinction between inside and outside that properly belongs to sculpture:

> These were two colossal human figures, seated, in their grandiose and massive character more inorganic and architectural than sculptural; after all, Memnon columns occur in rows and, since they have their worth only in such a regular order and size, descend from the aim of sculpture altogether to that of architecture. (2:643/14:282)[10]

Despite the architectonic claims of the *Aesthetics*, which should find a symmetrical triad in each art form (symbolic, classical, romantic) and thus in each particular art, it seems impossible to find a simple beginning for the first art; it can only be described through a comparison with sculpture, a later art form, and seems to have no identity of its own.[11]

The architectonic is allied with the mathematical eurythmy that must remain somewhat mysterious. Free-standing, that is, nonfunctional, architecture can include architectural elements such as doors, gates, and walls, as long as these are not there to enclose a space and make a house. Following Strabo, Hegel describes this phenomenon:

> Then follows a huge ceremonial entrance . . . narrower above than below, with pylons, and pillars of prodigious size . . . some of them standing free and independently, others grouped in walls or as magnificent jambs; these being likewise broader at the base than above, rise in a slant, freely, and independently to the height of fifty or sixty feet; they are unconnected with transverse walls and carry no beams and so do not form a house. (2:644–45/14:284)

The resistance to the right angle and the straight line prevent symbolic architecture from falling into the fundamental architectural type of the house—that is, they preserve an architecture that is no architecture.

Architecture progresses to fulfill its calling as a building that cannot properly be considered an independent art:

> For its vocation lies precisely in fashioning external nature as an enclosure shaped into beauty by art out of the resources of the spirit itself, and fashioning it for the spirit already explicitly present, for man, or for the divine images which he has framed and set up as objects. Its meaning this enclosure does not carry in itself but finds in something else, in man and his needs and aims in family life, the state, or religion, etc., and therefore the independence of the buildings is sacrificed. (2:633/14:270)

For Hegel art cannot be structured by this kind of functionality in which the *Gestaltung* has its meaning outside of itself. Building, epitomized by the sheltering function of the house, has already surpassed art. Thus the middle of architecture, the house, is an empty point that is no longer art but rather a surrounding for the sculpture, the human figure, as classical art, which has now moved into the center. Such architecture is no longer art and also not yet art; the architectural will progress into the Romantic form, which ought to unify the two previous forms and reinstall the independent and free excess over the function of shelter characteristic of the Gothic cathedral. The house is thus both the essence and the absence of architecture. In Hegel we might say that the relation between the architectonic and housing is one of disjunction.

The problematic quality of the beginning of architecture, and the difficulty about the structure of a properly independent architecture understood as architectonic, points to the more general difficulty of beginning or grounding the Hegelian exposition.[12]

The art of building in fact underlies the exposition of Hegel's *Aesthetics* itself, emerging to contain the very Idea of the beautiful. The figure of the Pantheon emerges as Hegel describes the self-articulating unity of art: "Now, therefore, what the particular arts realize in individual works of art is, according to the Concept of art, only the universal forms of the self-unfolding Idea of beauty. It is as the external actualization of this Idea that the wide Pantheon of art is rising. Its architect and builder is the self-comprehending spirit of beauty" (1:90/13:124). The difficulty in defining and describing the architectural strikes at the very possibility of the theoretical exposition. As a symbolic art, architecture must exceed mere spatial organization and suggest some kind of indeterminate meaning. The trouble is that the structure of meaning itself is allied not with architectonics, which must evade or defer meaning, but with housing, thus with a form already past that of art: "That is to say, on the one hand, the work of art, present to sense, should *give lodgement* [*beherbergen*] to an inner content" (2:635/14:272, my emphasis). Independent and free-standing architecture is thus called upon to signify without signifying, to house without sheltering. Tschumi's notion of disjunction suggests a gap between architectural design and empirical building or, as he writes, between "discourse and the domain of daily experience," or "*the nature of space* and . . . a real space" (69). With respect to Hegel we can conclude that it is impossible to theorize and expose the structures of containment in the same gesture that thematizes containment. Hegel's *Aesthetics* houses architecture but only by evading its own gesture of sheltering and containing.

Architecture loses its ground in Hegel's *Aesthetics* just as it is called in to ground its theoretical frame. This is possible because housing is conceived of as an opposition between an interior and an exterior. To avoid this binarism into which Hegel's writing draws us, we might turn to Heidegger's claim for the essential interrelatedness in his essay "Bauen Wohnen Denken," "Building Dwelling Thinking," in which building, dwelling, and thinking are simply different aspects of the same. Heidegger's interpretation of building here combines the two aspects of architectonic and function that Hegel separates in the itinerary of architecture. Rejecting the separation of means and end (*Mittel* and *Zweck*), Heidegger proposes a view of building as both a gathering (*Versammlung*) and a sheltering or protecting that is a fundamental trait (*Grundzug*) of building and not a means to an end organized as interior and exterior.

Heidegger argues that the bridge considered as a thing[13] does not simply connect two river banks that are already there; instead "the banks emerge as banks only in the crossing over of the bridge *[im Übergang der Brücke]*. The bridge designedly causes them to lie across from each other. One side is set off against the other by the bridge" (*PLT* 152/ *VuA* 146.) The bridge gathers together (*sammelt* and *versammelt*) not only the people who build it, as for Hegel, but much more, it gathers together the entire landscape that is its surroundings. The bridge is a "place," an *Ort*, that gathers together what Heidegger calls the four or the fourfold, *das Geviert*: "As such a thing, it allows a space into which earth and heaven, divinities and mortals are admitted" (*PLT* 155/ *VuA* 147).

This gathering of the fourfold, mysterious as it is, allows the bridge to be crossed without separating means and end, without bringing in *Zweckmäßigkeit*. The crossing of the bridge crosses from the two banks to the broadest possible notion of crossing over:

> Now in a high arch, now in a low, the bridge vaults over glen and stream— whether mortals keep in mind this vaulting of the bridge's course or forget that they, always themselves on their way to the last bridge, are actually striving to surmount all that is common and unsound in them in order to bring themselves before the haleness of the divinities. The bridge *gathers*, as a passage that crosses, before the divinities. (*PLT* 153/ *VuA* 147)

The possibility that the bridge is "merely a bridge" (*bloßeine Brücke*) is derivative of this gathering sense of the bridge's crossing over. From the perspective of this alternative, we might still ask what happens to "the mere bridge." In the same essay, Heidegger brings up the specific empirical example of the bridge over the Neckar at Heidelberg. The thinking of the expanded crossing, of the bridge, itself bridges the distance between here and there or between signifier and referent:

> If all of us now think, from where we are right here, of the old bridge in Hei-delberg, this thinking toward that location is not a mere experience inside the persons present here; rather it belongs to the nature of our thinking *of* that bridge that *in itself* thinking gets through, persists through, the distance to that location. From this spot right here, we are there at the bridge—we are by no means at some representational content in our consciousness. From right here we may even be much nearer to that bridge and to what it makes room for than someone who uses it daily as an indifferent river crossing. (*PLT* 156–157/ *VuA* 151)

According to this passage, "we here" are able to overcome spatial and temporal limitations and make our way to the essence of the bridge. Think-ing itself functions like the bridge Heidegger describes, crossing from here to there, from this to that. Being in space is first of all a relatedness that undoes any simple binarism between presence and absence: "I am never here only, as this encapsulated body; rather, I am there, that is, I already pervade the room, and only thus can I go through it" (*PLT* 157/ *VuA* 152). But Heidegger introduces a hierarchy here: *nur so*, only thus; that is, the relatedness of place, *Ort*, makes possible or underlies the abstract relation-ship of space. In the same way, the bridge-thought sketches a ghost image of the unknowing feet treading the bridge day in and day out. The text produces an excluded and disparaged excess, here, in the tactile relation-ship to the bridge, generally connected to the merely functional aspect of architecture.[14] Derrida points to the way in which the theoretical orienta-tion of the term "architectonic" tends to overlook the resistance exerted by the specific art of architecture:

> On the one hand, this general architectonics *effaces* or *exceeds* the sharp speci-ficity of architecture; it is valid for other arts and regions of experience as well. On the other hand, architecture forms its most powerful metonymy; it gives it its most solid *consistency*, objective substance. By consistency, I do not mean only logical coherence, which implicates all dimensions of human experience

in the same network: there is no work of architecture without interpretation, or even economic, religious, political, aesthetic or philosophical decree. But by consistency I also mean duration, hardness, the monumental, mineral or ligneous subsistence, the hyletics of tradition. Hence the *resistance*: the resistance of materials. (Leach, 328/*Psyché*, 482)

Architecture's specificity is aligned with the materiality of both history and experience.

Housing Problems maintains the tension between the architectonic and the architectural and thus maintains a link between the theorization of architecture on the one hand and the usual sense of architecture on the other—*das Gewohnte*, or habitual. The habit of the literal is housed in the house, our usual dwelling, the unaccountable spaces and rooms through which even the most philosophical bodies pass. The juxtapositioning of the theoretical and the trivial is central to *Housing Problems*. The problem first posed itself to me—perhaps by chance—in Weimar, where the architectural structures of libraries and archives are barely distinguishable from those of tourist sites and domestic displays. The movement of scholarly research through archival spaces raises questions about the distinction between the necessary and the contingent, the scientific and the random.

According to the schema laid out above, a house would be a determinate end result of the architectural process, one that now stands apart. Not only a building with a problematic and perhaps disjunctive relationship to the art of architecture, the house also involves the specifics of bourgeois life.[15] As an unmoving relic, the house installs the inside/outside binary, the main terms of its "economy," the law of the house. The house thus conjoins the general solidifying feature of architecture as well as the function of containment.[16] The close relation between housing as a space of containment and preservation, and photography, marked especially by the word "camera," is also a theme of this book. The house and, even more forcefully, the room function by way of a quadrangle, the four walls that stake out and secure an interior. Yet the quadrangle is never secure; like the house it is haunted, it reverses itself, it opens outward. The frame of the quadrant opens up onto an endless and undefined field, a field of rubble where no identity is stable. In the house or room we take refuge and deny the unraveling at our edges. *Housing Problems* undertakes to mobilize the house into the gerund "housing" to open up this denial. More specific than architecture, it still engages architectural problems. The term "housing" continues to pose the question of the relation between architecture and building, or between thinking and the empirical. The facticity of the house points to a limit of thinking, an undercurrent of the untheorized and excluded materiality that is a condition of possibility of architecture, or writing. The desire and necessity to contain and control, "to house," continues to form us, despite the urge to erode its stability.[17]

The house-museum presents the reified moment in the problem of housing. The authorial house-museum, which came into vogue in Europe and the United States in the late nineteenth and early twentieth centuries, presents a late form of the house as fetish. The famous Goethe House in Weimar, for example, was one of the first to become a museum in the 1860s, thus continuing the tradition of visitation that Goethe himself had invited. The fetish quality of the house-museum comes to an extreme limit at the desk; paper and pen seem to suggest an opening to understanding, a direct link to the genesis of the literary masterpiece. From here it is a small step to both the fetish formations that Freud discusses in his essay on that topic and to the duplicates and multiplications of self-images meant to ward off death that he outlines in the essay "The Uncanny." In both cases the prostheses of the subject that stand in for it function to deny death or absence at the same time that they commemorate and thus underscore it. The idea that the house stands in for a self and tells its secret story, holding on to its owner as origin and spirit, is a myth.

"*Bildung* and Buildings in Classical Weimar," the first section of chapter 1, "Goethe's Architectonic," presents a reading of Goethe's writings about the Strasbourg Cathedral in terms of the concept of *Bildung*, a broad humanistic concept that includes education, formation, cultivation, and development that Goethe himself helped to develop. *Bildung* can be understood as the process by which a subject externalizes and realizes itself through its material productions and surroundings. This model presents a kind of utopia in which exterior signs would be perfectly transparent expressions of an interior self. In terms of Goethe's two texts on German architecture, separated by more than fifty years, I show how the maturation process is supposed to absorb and bring under control the architectural and rhetorical exuberance exhibited in his first essay of 1772. Similarly, certain houses and rooms in *Wilhelm Meisters Lehrjahre* (*Wilhelm Meister's Apprenticeship*) open the space in which the narrative is gathered together, identities are revealed and lessons learned. Through analysis of the grandfather's art collection, its loss and subsequent reappearance in the uncle's castle, I show how ordered display serves to appropriate space and express the unified identity of its owner. At the same time a bare housing continues to exceed the space of presentation appropriated by the narrative of *Bildung*, pointing to the persistent materiality of time and space beyond logical unification. Finally, I suggest that the description of the uncle's house and collections in fact duplicates the display of Goethe's own house in Weimar and recent touristic and historical descriptions of it. The capacity of the *Goethehaus* to stabilize and represent subjectivity, I argue, relies on the logic of *Bildung*. According to the same model, visitors to authors' homes can believe they are reabsorbing the authentic trace or the genuine exterior left by a life in the past. The absorption of these traces encourages visitors to internalize images of identity and national culture. This model of culture enables the cult of personality and place that surely contributed to Hitler's favoring of the city of Weimar, a stronghold of support for the Nazis and the place of the founding of the Hitler Youth. The location of Buchenwald eight kilometers outside the town testifies to the brutal failure of the logic of totalization.

I argue in this book that the experience of place is actually an opportunity to connect texts, images, recollections, and representations in a way that produces the sense we attribute to them. Taking Goethe and his home in Weimar as my point of departure, I show how depictions of house and home in his writings cooperate with material remains—from rock collections and garments to buildings and graves—to create what we think of as "historical reality." What we perceive as an extension of "presence" is a dense layering of texts that rhetorically produce certain effects of authenticity and connectedness.

Chapters 2 and 3 continue to develop the problematic relation among history, architecture, and narrative in a reading of Horace Walpole's *The Castle of Otranto*, Poe's stories "The Fall of the House of Usher" and "The Oval Portrait," and Jane Austen's *Northanger Abbey*. I argue that the prominent role of architecture in Gothic and uncanny literature can be understood in terms of a semiotic collapse between sign and referent characteristic of these genres. Building itself becomes language, and a language not controlled by a referential function. In *Otranto*, Alphonso, the disarticulated subject of ownership—literally the dismembered body parts of a ghostly giant—is scattered throughout the castle. Hallways and doors lead us through our reading and likewise withhold understanding to produce narrative tension. Architectural features function in the same way as the stuttering speech of the servants and the mute gestures of the visiting knights: irritating delays that in communicating delay communication. The eventual collapse of the castle and the restoration of the proper lineage reverse the semiotic reversal that the narrative has presented. Finally, the novel reinstalls the vertical hierarchy of ground and predicate, or subject-owner and property, that the Gothic seems to overturn. The preservation of order that seems to be subverted can also be seen in the realist effect not only of the narrative but also of the architectural experiments of Horace Walpole and his contemporaries known as Gothic revival: the construction of pseudo-Gothic buildings, *folies*, trompe-l'oeil facades, and towers connected to nothing. The readings of Poe's stories and Austen's novel show how the repetition of the Gothic exceeds the Gothic itself. In "The Fall of the House of Usher" the house collapses as a Gothic romance is read aloud. The duplication between signifier and referent, rather than leading to restoration as in Walpole, induces instead an excessive double that results in collapse. In Austen, of course, the effect is parodic.

Chapter 4 shows how Goethe's *Wahlverwandtschaften* (*Elective Affinities*), in contrast, tries over and over to follow a hermeneutic of the letter and the spirit similar to that of *The Castle of Otranto*, yet fails to build a unifying structure that would reveal the coherence of parts or progress towards resolution. The disappointment of the architectural can be read in the many stops and starts of building projects, restorations, and remodelings throughout the text. The "foundation stone" (*Grundstein*), of course, reveals its own fallibility, foreseeing its own demise even as it is supposed to extend the present into an indeterminately successful future. Likewise, in the scene of the laying of the foundation stone, Edward's reading of the preservation of the glass with the intertwining E and O remains an arbitrary interpretation, a projection whose ground is fictional and fragile. Interestingly, *Wahlverwandtschaften*, a work of high literature, subverts the architectural ordering of meaning much more than *Otranto*, part of a more popular tradition working through mechanics and claptrap, and drawing on obvious conventions.

Chapter 5 begins with a consideration of Freud's house in London, now a museum that commemorates both the founding of psychoanalysis and, less overtly, the Holocaust. This chapter seeks to understand the interrelation between the space of the house, Freud's notion of psychic topology (primarily in *The Interpretation of Dreams* and the essay on the uncanny), and the process of analysis. Derrida's *Archive Fever*, first given as a lecture at the Freud House, points to the role of the house in the establishment of memory and archives but does not say much about the actual house. Another entry to this story is gained through the American poet H.D.'s *Tribute to Freud,* one of the only texts that describes the residential situation and details of the house as part of her analytic experience with Freud in the 1920s. In this text personal memoir and literary allusions work together to create a textual network that stands in the place of an empirical place. H.D. gathers together her analytic experience through a reading of "Mignon's Song," Goethe's famous poem taken from *Wilhelm Meister's Apprenticeship,* that is centered around the image of a sheltering house. The place of this song leads into a reading of Gérard de Nerval's "Delfica," a poem fashioned after it, and the collapse of authorial identity it implies.

I compare Freud's abandoned home at Berggasse 19, Vienna, with the more fully furnished museum in London. Just as Freud's conception of the subject cannot be assured through an externalized presence but rather is originally articulated as a displaced mark, trace, or repeated recollection, in the same way, his housing brings to our attention the problems of instability and absence. The couch itself becomes the disappearing center of Freud's spaces. These homes can never communicate the reassuring groundedness lent to Goethe's residence in Weimar. The apartment in the Berggasse was emptied when the Freuds were compelled to flee Nazi-annexed Austria. It now contains little beyond an exhibit of a collection of photographs of the apartment taken by Edmund Engelman a few days before Freud's departure in 1938. Clearly Freud's students considered this documentation of place to be absolutely crucial to the future of psycho-analysis. This desire to fix a spatial origin suggests that Freud's thinking was necessarily linked to its surroundings—that furnishings and housing stand as silent records of the origin of thought. Interestingly, this drive is explicitly connected to photography, a medium that undermines the stability it strives to document. This chapter thus also includes a reflection on the medium of photography, the way in which it is thought to preserve a slice of the past, and its apparently indexical function. In contrast, Freud's home in London, the Freud Museum that contains most of Freud's personal possessions, his collection of antiquities and art pieces, and his original couch, reminds one constantly of its surrogate character.

Chapter 6 approaches the problem of the house in several texts by Martin Heidegger. The chapter traces alterations in the function of architectural elements and figures, which sometimes open up and sometimes restabilize the status of identity. The chapter begins with a study of *In-sein* in *Being and Time* (*Sein und Zeit*), which here is to be understood in terms other than those of spatial containment. *In-sein,* Being-in, instead characterizes the exposure of *Da-sein,* Being-there, in its finitude. Rooms, furniture, and domestic settings play an important role in Heidegger's exposition of *In-sein.* These install an ontic element in the exposition of the ontological trait of *In-sein* which, like Descartes' *poêle,* cannot be gotten rid of. In fact architectural surroundings make possible an orientation in space without taking recourse to an abstract and measurable empty geometrical space. But generally, housing becomes *unheimlich,* uncanny or unhomely, in concealing *Da-sein's* fundamental *Un-zuhause sein,* its not-being-at-home. A discussion of the "Letter on Humanism" traces out a double tendency of the essay. On the one hand, *in* continues to mark a hovering, unstable relationship between *Da-sein* and *Sein.* On the other hand, the language of "the house of Being" appropriates the architectural to allow Being to present itself. The house thus comes to stand as a hinge or joint between the ontic and the ontological. The chapter continues to consider the oscillation between stability and destabilization connected with housing and building in "Building Dwelling Thinking" and *Identity and Difference* ("Bauen Wohnen Denken" and *Identität und Differenz*). It concludes with a reading of "the event," *das Ereignis,* as it appears in *Identity and Difference,* and the reading of this text by American poet George Oppen. Through a coreading of Oppen and Heidegger, based on Oppen's citation of Heidegger and a fascinating diary entry about his relation to Heidegger, the text concludes with an opening up of the notion of building and a dual reading of subjectivity as stretched between *Dichten* und *Denken,* poetry and thinking, or Oppen and Heidegger.

Housing Problems interprets material practices of historical restoration and presentation together with fictional, autobiographical, and philosophical texts. While recent critical debates have pitted history and language against each other, this project takes them to be originally connected. The book includes work by photographer Suzanne Doppelt. Her nonrepresentational photographs work along with the text to critique the desire for containment and stability inherent in the theme of the house. This book takes up more general questions of the relation between literature and history in a way that is tangible to anyone who has pointed out the house of a person of renown. Literature informs this very pointing and the ways in which we presume that these houses form and cultivate us.

§1 Goethe's Architectonic

Bildung and Buildings in Classical Weimar

On March 19, 1999, the *New York Times* ran a long illustrated story on page A3 entitled "The Sorrows of Goethe: A Creepy East German Tale" with the subtitle: "It turns out the Communists just couldn't resist digging up the National Poet." This was the second time in recent years that Tischbein's famous portrait of Goethe in Italy was reprinted in the *Times*. This more recent article describes lugubriously a "secret operation" in 1970 in which "East German scientists exhumed the body of Goethe, loaded his corpse onto a cart, dragged it off to a nearby museum and worked on its preservation for three weeks. The remains were then returned to their crypt in the city of Weimar." The article describes the operation with gleefully lurid and repetitive language: "Seven people," it says, "carried out the work on Goethe's corpse. They loaded his body onto a cart as night fell on Nov. 2, 1970, and pulled the contraption the short distance to the Goethe museum." No great skill is needed to see the gothic language here. The article is also accompanied by a photograph of Goethe's empty coffin and one of his skull (both taken during the "operation"). Despite the obvious pleasure in the macabre, the narrative is clearly meant to provoke scandal around this unearthing and dismemberment of the poet's body. The impropriety of carting about his mortal remains is reinforced by the image of the gaping coffin revealing an empty space that ought to be filled and closed.

The *Times* article sets itself the multiple task of condemning this scandal and informing its readership about the status of Goethe in the

German tradition as well as the meaning of the choice of Weimar as the European Union's "cultural capital" for 1999. The article seeks to portray something of the German tradition and serves the same tradition by insisting upon the unity and stability of its greatest poet, objecting to his dismemberment and dislocation. Describing the crypt in Weimar shared by Goethe and Schiller, the article says: "It was widely believed until today that the repose of the poets, who both lived in Weimar, had been uninterrupted."

The remains were in fact moved several times, including during the early 1940s, when the two corpses were "evacuated" to a bunker in Jena to protect them from possible Allied bombing. The article clearly has an investment in the very belief it cites, for the qualities of wholeness and immobility—"permanence"—are constitutive of the concept of identity to which it subscribes. In 1 Corinthians 3, Paul writes the famous lines: "Do you not know that you are God's temple and that God's Spirit dwells in you? If any one destroys God's temple, God will destroy him. For God's temple is holy, and that temple you are." The construction of this temple distinguishes spirit from matter and creates a space in which spirit dwells. An unopened coffin or an intact crypt can create the same impression. But when it is opened, it releases not spirit, but decaying matter, not genius, but, as the *Times* reported of Goethe's brain, "a dust-like mass."

A second article on Goethe appeared in the *New York Times* in September 1997. In this case the paper printed a photograph of two girls gazing over a guard rope, peering into the bedroom in Goethe's house—one of the main tourist sites in the city of Weimar. The photo accompanied an article on K. H. Pruys's biography of Goethe suggesting that he was homosexual. The article explicitly posed questions about whether a changed understanding of Goethe's sexuality would fundamentally alter his identity. The image of the *Goethehaus* counteracts the anxiety surrounding this implied destablization of identity. The house is a secularized temple meant to stabilize, contain, and preserve the subject who inhabits it.

The house of a famous writer is a commonplace of tourism constructed on a familiar hermeneutic circle. Goethe formed and shaped his house, which outlives him as a kind of memorial that can help us to understand "Goethe" and his works. On the other hand, Goethe's literary remains house the understanding of the relationship between subject and its material container, the interaction between creative activity and works, or what we might also call the process of formation, or *Bildung*, thanks to which we can learn from the physical remains of his house. The house teaches us about the man, but the man teaches us about the relationship between man and house. In other words the house cannot really teach anything; it can only reiterate a program already articulated elsewhere. The notion that a house stands in for a self and tells its secret story, holding on to its owner as origin and spirit, is, to borrow Derrida's phrase, a "white mythology." Sabine Schirdewahn captured the fetishistic aspect of the exposition of the writer's room in an art installation at the Casa di Goethe in Rome entitled *Interieur III*.[1] The installation is an imitation of Goethe's work room containing a chair and table with ink pots and writing implements on it. The objects are made of white wood and cardboard and are covered with wax. The walls of the simple room are covered with cloth worked through with thick white paint. This embalmed scene of literary origin counteracts the "authenticity effect" when we see, for example, the window in this *Goethehaus* out of which Goethe leans in Tischbein's appealing drawing of his ass. Schirdewahn's installation exposes the ideology of the room as object of exposition. Nevertheless, it is constructed within the confines of the four walls of a room and housed in a museum setting in the Via del Corso. To break free from the confines of the house—of architecture—is not a simple matter.

On a more technical level most of what is said to be "authentic" in the *Goethehaus* museum (or generally) is based mostly on texts—*aus der Überlieferung*—handed down through written tradition. In museum talk *Überlieferung* is contrasted with the term *Musealisierung* or "musealization." When a historical house is presented as being exactly the way it was, this means that there is evidence *aus der Überlieferung* to support material reconstruction. Texts are consulted for remarks about shape, color, furnishings, etc. In this case the textual sources include Goethe's diaries, correspondence with contractors, bills for material and labor, and letters from visitors. The authentic positioning of a historical interior embodies or emplaces these textual remarks. Thus text is handed down to us in the form of a material house; indeed, how can a piece of furniture tell us of its own immobility? How can it persuade us that it has, in fact, stood in the same spot since Goethe's own time? When textual evidence is lacking, musealization steps in to supplement historical reconstruction. Musealization means the construction of a historical space as it might or could have been: that is, it is furnished with pieces from the same period and in the same style but without any claim of specific authenticity. (The Schiller House, for example, is largely musealized.) But the average tourist does not remark the difference between *Überlieferung* and *Musealisierung*, just as the intervention of reading and interpretation in the mise-en-scène of *Überlieferung* is unremarked and taken for immediacy.

The euphony of the title of this chapter, which links *Bildung* and buildings, is suggestive of the simultaneous interdependence and mutual exclusion of the architectural described by Bernard Tschumi between the unifying structure of *Bildung*, an organic model of self-formation and education, and buildings. Housing provides an inscriptional space that allows subjectivity to inscribe itself and externalize itself in its residence; at the same time, it produces merely empirical sites, hollow containers that cannot be included in the mirroring relation of inside and outside that allows a building to become meaningful. This architectural dialectic also structures the concept of *Bildung* articulated in the eighteenth century. While the resonance between *Bildung* and building may be specious, the connection between construction and (self-)formation can also be heard in the term "edification," from the Latin (*aedes*, temple or house, + *ficare*, to make). *Bildung* installs a certain architectonic of selfhood according to which a narrative unfolds, progressing through various stages of conflict and resolution that allow an interior to be distinguished from an exterior. The wall, the architectural boundary between the two, marks the blind spot or gap that divides the subjectivity that *Bildung* ought to render whole.

Bildung is generally understood to signify a process of self-production and reproduction that is supposed to integrate the individual into a social totality. Several studies have attended to the connection between the narrative of *Bildung* and what has come to be called "aesthetic ideology."[2] The terms *Bildung* and aesthetic ideology both imply a synthesis between an empirical or sensuous object or image and some kind of totalizing conceptual structure. In a temporal model the single experience or episode is taken up by a totalizing story constructing an overarching identity. Both *Bildung* and aesthetic ideology involve a moment of appropriation of sensuous material into a meaningful structure or one of the incarnation of meaning in a sensuous body. In *Phantom Formations—Aesthetic Ideology and the Bildungsroman*, Marc Redfield especially associates *Bildung* with Schiller's notion of aesthetic education, which he summarizes as "the progress from a naive, sensual aesthetic to a sentimental interiority" (21). Bill Readings's *The University in Ruins* gives a concise account of the notion of *Bildung* and the German Idealist construction of the university. In *The Postmodern Condition*, Jean-François Lyotard identifies *Bildung* as one of modernity's now obsolete master-narratives.[3] Similarly, Readings argues that as Excellence replaces the idea of culture, *Bildung* ceases to be an operative principle. Even if *Bildung* no longer commands the shape of the university, it nevertheless may still be at work in many of the ways in which national culture is popularized and transmitted. In recent years there has been a good deal of discussion about questions of cultural memory, restoration, and commemoration. Many of the questions concerning cultural presentation focus on issues of accessibility and how individual objects, displays, or texts can serve to inculcate, communicate, and perpetuate the formation of cultural subjects.

Readings stresses the way in which the university was meant to fulfill the project of *Bildung* by creating citizen-subjects able to participate in and reproduce the German state. The integration of general and particular through university education both creates and sustains national identity and culture. Readings also points astutely to the link between the constitution of material culture and the rise of tourism, describing how "literary culture" becomes "the site where the link forged between a people and its land becomes visible or expressed" (95). Touristic objects and places, he argues, may seem to offer easy access to culture, yet the structure of the meaning that has been attributed to them is already caught up in a larger system of economic exploitation. Despite changes in the universities of the twentieth century, practices of cultural tourism seem to be dominated still by the aesthetic logic of *Bildung*. *Bildung* produces a scission, a gap within the identity it is supposed to construct; it produces the same flaw as any structure of specular identity. Perhaps there is a structuring transition linking *Bildung* and buildings in a way that gathers both together. Similarly, such a reading would have to address the question of the "mere building" and consider how it might be gathered into the broader questions of construction and formation. In what follows I will begin to investigate the cooperation of *Bildung* and buildings in Goethe's essays "On German Architecture" ("Von deutscher Baukunst") and in *Wilhelm Meister's Apprenticeship*.

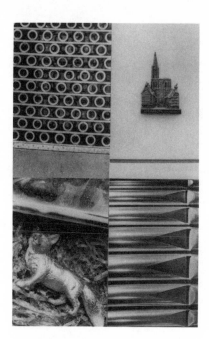

Goethe's Cathedral Pieces

Goethe wrote two essays entitled "Von deutscher Baukunst" ("On German Architecture") that span a time period of more than fifty years. The later text (1823) was written as an introduction to a reprint of the earlier text, which dates from 1772 and presents Goethe's experience of the Strasbourg Minster. Composed in several parts in 1771–72, the first essay is thought to have originated in Sesenheim and Frankfurt, where Goethe lived in his family home after completing his law studies in Strasbourg. The later essay, written during the mature era of the Goethe House in Weimar, proceeds systematically to delineate the rule of proportion governing the beauty of Gothic architecture, or what Goethe here calls *deutsche Baukunst*, German architecture. The text shows a learned aspect, quoting the French architect François Blondel, a vehement classicist, to assert the priority of proportion over detail: "All the pleasure we derive from artistic beauty depends on the observation of rule and measure: on proportion."[4] Like the other arts, architecture both reveals and conceals its mediated origins; Goethe says of German architecture: "It must thus embrace something great and fundamentally felt, something considered and developed, and it must both conceal and manifest proportions whose effect is irresistible" (118/*HA* 12:177).

The truth of a cathedral's proportion can be hidden in excessive detail, decoration, and seemingly random ornamentation, which also make possible the overwhelming effect of stony mass and enormous size. Commenting that he need not be embarrassed by this youthful text, Goethe attributes the overly enthusiastic style of his earlier essay to the enormity of the cathedral's immediate effect, an effect that overpowers the observer and forces its way to representation:

> Here we may recall somewhat earlier years, when the Strasbourg Minster had so great an effect on us that we could not help expressing our unsolicited delight. What the French architect had established by studious measurement and investigation came to us all unawares, and not everyone is asked to account for the impressions which astonish him. (118-20/*HA* 12:178)

The later essay describes an unconscious encounter with architecture that is legible though not, strictly speaking, understood in the first reading of the 1772 essay. Goethe attributes the same enthusiasm to the contemporary interest in Gothic architecture. Notice the collapse of exclamatory style and the resurrection of the past:

> How powerful has been their effect in recent times when feeling for them has been reawakened! Young and old, men and women, have been so overwhelmed [*übermannt*] and swept away [*hingerissen*] by such impressions that they have not only been refreshed and educated by the frequent examination, measurement and drawing of them, but have also adopted this style in new buildings destined for use. (120/*HA* 12:178)

The massive impression itself stimulates a process of reproduction and representation (mimesis) that sets in motion a certain development or edification (*sich erbauten*), but this does not counteract the utter self-loss in the perception of the Gothic indicated by the terms *übermannt* and *hingerissen*. This later essay, on the other hand, functions rather like an antidote to the total surrender to immediate sense perception; Goethe stresses the need "to feel and understand their value and the dignity in the proper—that is, the historical—way" (120/*HA* 12:178). The historical understanding developed in this essay, to which I will return below, supplements the immediate experience, completing it by means of a series of intermediary representations. The correct understanding demands distance and stability that masters and controls the architectural experience.

If the later essay is structured by a kind of representational mastery, the earlier one is characterized by a certain extravagance. The two essays can be polarized according to the familiar distinction of measure or proportion, a product of the spirit, versus the materiality of ornamentation and detail. The earlier essay takes up the postures of an extreme rhetoric of apostrophe and animation through which the boundaries between speaker and addressee, present and past, and life and death become confused. The text begins as a direct address to Erwin von Steinbach, a fourteenth-century builder of the Strasbourg Cathedral. Goethe first promises to build a memorial for Erwin but then exclaims: "Yet what need you a memorial! You have erected the most magnificent one for yourself" (103/*HA* 12:7). This address has two effects. On the one hand it positions the cathedral as the archive of history. Only when the Minster is identified as a monument, *Denkmal*, can architecture become a silent tradition that holds its secrets in an undeciphered language; in the later essay, Goethe says: "if these buildings stood for centuries like an old hand-me-down [*eine Überlieferung*: the Gage translation is "hangover"] from the past, without making any special impact on the ordinary man, the reason is not far to seek" (120/*HA* 12:178). On the other hand, through direct address Goethe erroneously reduces the history of the cathedral's construction, which of course extended over many centuries, to a single subject as its origin. At the same time the building itself is reinterpreted as an extension of its creator, commemorating its origin as its father. Goethe continues to throw his voice around in this essay, both addressing directly proponents of various other points of view and obliquely alluding to and paraphrasing other positions. The result is a heavily marked rhetorical speech full of exclamations in the place of argument and dramatized dialogue in the place of exposition: "'Puerilities,' babbles the Frenchman childishly after him, and triumphantly snaps open his snuffbox, *à la greque*. What have you done, that you should dare to look down your nose?" (105/*HA* 12:8). This bombast is supposed to embody the compulsive enthusiasm, the *Hingerissenheit* of the experience of the cathedral. Yet through the same rhetorical outlines the cathedral is thrown into relief as a mediator, a passageway for a prior subject or the harbinger of a historical understanding still to come.

Goethe describes the conventional evaluation of the Gothic style to which he at first also subscribed:

> The first time I went to the Minster, my head was full of the common notions of good taste. From hearsay I respected the harmony of mass, the purity of forms, and I was the sworn enemy of the confused caprices of Gothic ornament. Under the term Gothic I threw together all the synonymous misunderstandings, such as undefined, disorganized, unnatural, patched-together, tacked-on, overloaded, which had ever gone through my head. (107/ *HA* 12:10)

The proliferation of disconnected embellishments is a monstrosity: "Quite smothered with ornament!" Goethe cries, "And so I shuddered as I went, as if at the prospect of some misshapen, curly-bristled monster [*eines mißgeformten krausborstigen Ungeheuers*]" (107/ *HA* 12:11). Goethe turns away from this habitual knowledge—the repeated precepts of others—by turning towards his experience of the cathedral, again through exclamation: "How surprised I was when I was confronted by it!" This view (*Anblick*) presents an apparent immediacy, a sensation that lacks knowledge and understanding: "The impression which filled my soul was whole and large, and of a sort that (since it was composed of a thousand harmonizing details) I could relish and enjoy, but by no means identify and explain" (107/ *HA* 12:11). The young Goethe repeats this experiment, returning again and again to gaze at the cathedral. Gradually the image begins to blur as an architectural whole emerges and thus opens a way to knowledge: "How often has the evening twilight soothed with its friendly quiet my eyes, tired-out with questing, by blending the scattered parts into masses which now stood simple and large before my soul, and at once my powers unfolded rapturously to enjoy and to understand" (107/ *HA* 12:11). This is only possible, of course, because the material at hand has already been programmed to reveal its own order—the rational order Goethe originally secured by connecting the church to a singular creator (author).[5]

As Goethe noted, the *Bau* passes over into *Erbauung*, the edifice into the edification, as those enthusiasts gaze, sketch, and copy the image before them. The structure of the building thus holds together the cathedral and its visitors, stretching between them like a bridge; it does not belong to the cathedral as "object." As the necessary proportional rationality of the cathedral begins to clarify itself, the voice thrown out in the opening address to Erwin returns: "Then in hinted suggestions, the genius of the great Master of the Work revealed itself to me. 'Why are you so surprised?' he whispered to me. All these shapes were necessary ones" (107/*HA* 12:11). For a paragraph, the ghost of Erwin expounds to Goethe the structural principle of the cathedral, including the "five-pinnacled jewel" that was never completed. On the next morning the narrating Goethe can now perceive the cathedral as an organic whole: "How happily I could stretch out my arms towards it and gaze at the harmonious masses, alive with countless details. Just as in the eternal works of nature, everything is perfectly formed down to the meanest thread, and all contributing purposefully to the whole" (108/*HA* 12:12). The unity of the impression, however, can only be established through differentiation between origin and destination as embodied here in the figure of Erwin on the one hand and the building on the other. The notion of the building as memorial makes Erwin both present and absent, just as its solidity is shaken by its reinscription as *Überlieferung*. Likewise, there can only be what seems to be an immediate perception of architectural structure because the building is already a mediated expression. The duality of positions set up in the address to Erwin is duplicated towards the end of the essay, where Goethe addresses a newly appearing figure who actually seems to stand in for his own prior condition: "But it is with you, dearest youth, that I keep closest company, for, standing there, you are moved and cannot reconcile the conflicting feelings in your soul. At one moment you feel the irresistible power of this vast whole, and the next chide me for being a dreamer since I see beauty where you see only strength and rawness" (108/*HA* 12:13).

While Goethe places the emphasis on the whole as the source of the cathedral's beauty, this whole only peers forth through the gathering up of the many narrative angles and perspectives in the essay. These are never collected or ironed out—or at least not until 1823, in the later essay. This gathering is a primary component, though, of the effective formation of the architectural master who, Goethe writes, "first welded the scattered elements [*zerstreute Elemente*] into a living whole" (108/*HA* 12:12). In such a unity, springing from a single *Empfindung*, all elements are connected by a rational, if imperceptible, structural necessity. This organic whole, as in Herder, for example, is compared to a tree; Goethe compares Erwin's work to a "sublimely towering, wide-spreading tree of God which, with its thousand branches, millions of twigs and leaves more numerous than the sands of the sea, proclaims to the surrounding country the glory of its master, the Lord" (106/*HA* 12:10).

Oddly, this tree needs supplementation, just as the memory of Erwin and the resonance of his voice both need and do not need a memorial. While perhaps no monument is called for, no *Denkmal*, an articulated memory is needed. The two ends of this articulation are connected through the etymon *denken*, to think:

> It was given to but few to create such a Babel-thought [*einen Babelgedanke*] in their souls, whole, great, and with the beauty of necessity in every small-est part, as in God's trees. To even fewer has it been granted to encounter a thousand willing hands to carve out the rocky ground, to conjure up steps on it, and when they die, to tell their sons, "I am still with you in the creations of my spirit; complete what is begun, up to the clouds." (103/ *HA* 12:7)

The articulation of this *Babelgedanken* names both the original impos-sibility of completion and calls for its own future realization in the hands and mouths of others. Organic unity invisibly connects the past and the present, just as the structure of the whole permeates what seems to be a fragmentary and extravagantly ornate and unfinished mass. The sketch-ing of this conceptual completion is itself the fulfillment of the original design, not in the form of an actual building, but in the reception or representation of the fragment. Thus Goethe's repeated "What need you a memorial!" [*Was braucht's dir Denkmal!*]. The exclamation itself erects and memorializes what should already tower above the present. The thought-unity of the cathedral structures the history of its formation, or *Bildung*. Goethe contrasts the modish architecture of conglomeration based on imitation of classical rules with the inspirational exuberance of a self-generating structure. Addressing another imaginary interlocutor, Goethe says:

> If you had rather felt than measured, if the spirit of the pile you so admire had come upon you, you would not simply have imitated it because they did it and it is beautiful; you would have made your plans because of truth and necessity, and a living, creative beauty would have flowed from them. (105/ *HA* 12:8)

The architectural presents a mass out of which genius springs forth in a unified stroke connecting creator and observer through the unity of the plan. This distinguishes the Strasbourg Cathedral from contemporary imitations that only gather horizontally dispersed elements and patch them together randomly. A third type of collecting appears in Goethe's recharacterization of his own text. It cannot serve as a *Denkmal,* since none is needed; instead he claims to carve Erwin's name into a tree, like that of a beloved, and with reference to a biblical passage dedicates to it a cloth:

> It is not unlike the cloth that was let down to the Holy Apostle out of the clouds, full of clean and unclean beasts; also flowers, blossoms, leaves and dried grass and moss, and night-sprung toadstools—all of which I gathered, botanizing to pass the time, on a walk through some place or other, and now dedicate in your honour to their own rotting away. (104–5/*HA* 12:8)

This final simile is strange. The narrator himself appears to be a cold collector of random and meaningless items that, gathered together, present a memorial to decay. The comparison of the cathedral to a *Babelgedanken,* too, harbors a quiet criticism and fatality that doom it to incompletion and failure. Despite moments that clearly assert the dominance of organic and characteristic unity, the instability of the narrative line and the indirect assertions of the cathedral's inadequacies, imperfections, and illegibility obscure the point of this essay. Divided into sections and exposing the first person through multiple second-person addresses to created and often unidentified interlocutors, the essay follows no set pattern and reaches few conclusions. The final paragraph begins with what is probably self-praise of this same mobility: "Hail to you, youth, with your sharp eye for proportion, born to adapt yourself easily to all sorts of form!" (111/*HA* 12:15).

In the 1823 essay of the same title Goethe is more than aware of these qualities. The editors of the *Hamburger Ausgabe* mark it as written in the "dithyrambic style" of Herder and Hamann, thus including it is a literary historical trajectory that renders its strangeness uninteresting. In the later essay Goethe mostly masters his narrative extravagance, leaving his own speaker position only once to quote the French architect Blondel in support of the notion that Gothic architecture indeed follows proper rules of proportion, even if these are hidden by excessive ornament. While the perception of beauty may seem to come from the decoration, it originates in fact, says Blondel, in the structural harmony that shows through despite the excessive ornamentation. Just as the dialogical dimension of the earlier rhetorical ejaculations are flattened out and appear here as learned quotation, the three-dimensionality of the cathedral form is mastered through a series of two-dimensional representations. Goethe reports that he has come to master his early enthusiasm through various kinds of study, especially through his contact with the Boisserée brothers. The Boisserées' architectural studies of the Cologne Cathedral allow Goethe to get a handle on the overpowering structure of the cathedral itself. Studying the foundation unearthed by the Boisserées and their perspectival drawings and engravings, Goethe feels he can begin to trace the "first intentions" of the design. "Likewise," he writes, "the engraved proofs of the side elevation and the drawing of the front elevation went some way in helping me to construct [*auferbauen*] the image in my soul" (122/ *HA* 12:181). Goethe's remarks suggest the Kantian sublime, according to which an experience that exceeds the faculty of sense perception is then mastered by a representation.[6] Goethe himself admits:

> I cannot deny that the sight of the exterior of Cologne Cathedral aroused in me a certain indefinable apprehension. If an important ruin has something impressive about it, we sense, we see in it the conflict between an admirable work of man and time, still, mighty and wholly inconsiderate: here we are confronted with something at once incomplete and gigantic, whose very incompleteness reminds us of the inadequacy of man, the moment he undertakes something that is too big for him. (121/ *HA* 12:180)

The incomplete erection of the cathedral is supplemented by the mental erection that duplicates it; likewise, the two-dimensional depictions of the building allow its structure to appear, to be internalized and to contribute to the formation or edification of the maturing commentator. Through representation and explanation, the *Bild* is transformed into *Bildung.*[7]

Experience itself thus becomes a kind of architectural drawing, a compulsive tracing that deepens the two dimensions of the facade into the three dimensions of a building constructed in the cognitive articulation of its interrelations—its "plan." Perception opens in the to-and-fro between detail and whole:

> I had figured out the proper relationship among the larger divisions, the ingenious and rich ornamentation to the smallest point . . . but now I also came to understand the connection between these many decorations among themselves, the transition from one main segment to the next, the staggering of similar kinds of details that were yet very different in their images and shapes, from the saint to the monster, from the leaf to the crenature. The more I examined it, the greater my astonishment; the more I entertained and tired myself with measuring and drawing, the greater grew my admiration. I

spent a lot of time, partly studying what was there, partly reconstructing on paper and in thought what was missing or incomplete, especially the towers. (*Autobiography*, 419, translation emended / *HA* 9:385–86)

This visual supplementation will be facilitated even more through the architectural work of Sulpiz Boisserée, a young enthusiast who worked with his brother in search of the still missing unity of German culture.[8] Boisserée began his correspondence with Goethe in 1810. In the following years he continued to ask the venerable author's advice about his research into the Cologne Cathedral's history and about his various drawings and projections completing the cathedral, including technical advice about individual artists and various media. Working through the series of images the Boisserées provided, including also studies of other Gothic cathedrals on the basis of which historical generalization could provide material for supplementation, Goethe reaches a point of understanding that supersedes the first impression. In fact, with the publication and dissemination of the Boisserées' work, the idiosyncrasy of the first impression can be done away with altogether:

> But now that the Boisserées' work is nearing its end, the illustrations and their commentary will reach all amateurs, and the friend of art, even if he is far away, has the opportunity of completely convincing himself that this is the highest peak to which this style of architecture attained. For if, perhaps as a tourist, he should approach that miraculous spot, he will no longer be left to personal feeling, gloomy prejudice, or, on the other hand, to a hastily-formed dislike, but he will rather observe what is there and imagine what is not like someone who is knowledgeable, and is initiated into the secrets of the masons [*Hütengeheimnisse*]. (122/ *HA* 12:181)

The passage from the stone of the cathedral to its proportionate representation parallels the trajectory from the earlier to the later essay. Experience is archived; at the same time it produces an excess whose record is lost. Goethe concludes the later text with two contradictory references to the earlier one. On the one hand, he seeks to connect the two eras of experience by way of the organic metaphor. He is reprinting the earlier essay, he says, to show clearly the difference between the "first seeds" and the "final fruit" of his architectural vision. The plant metaphor allows experience to be conjoined, despite the emphasis on difference, into a model of growth and maturation, of development—of *Bildung*. The building stands as a cornerstone of *Bildung*, drawn to completion through the lines

connecting the *Blatt* (leaf) of the
Gothic decoration to the *Blatt* (leaf
or page) of Goethe's writing.[9]

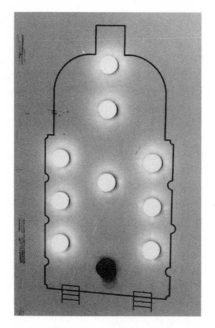

On the other hand, the "misshapen, curly-bristled monster"
Goethe first intimated in the
Gothic style does not disappear altogether. Claiming he has nothing
to be ashamed of or to apologize for
in the earlier essay, Goethe adds: "If
that essay has something amphigurical in its style, that may perhaps
be forgiven in such a case where
the inexpressible is to be expressed"
(122/12:181–82). The difficulty of
enunciation perhaps pertains most
accurately of all to this word itself:
amphigurisch, amphigurical, which,
according to the editors' note,
means "a piece of writing in which the sentences are unintentionally only
fragments of ideas and contain no reasonable meaning. Goethe often uses
Amphiguri, amphigurisch in the sense of a wordy veiling of the real ker-
nel of thought" (*HA* 12:637n). This editorial comment repeats Goethe's
organicizing gesture to cover up the uncontrollability or monstrosity of
the word itself—the unintentional fragment, the *Zierat* or ornament, that
speaks the unspeakable precisely because it has nothing to say, it has no
meaning to be rendered.

We find here an unavoidable alliance of writing and architecture,
whether as *Bruchstück* or *Denkmal*, construction or trace. The unifying
structures of *Bildung* and *Erbauung* allow architecture to pave the way
for an emerging subject. In this sense *Bildung* would function architectonically, that is, it would articulate the condition of possibility for
the appearance of the *Bild* that is constructed as a building. Building
emerges here along the contours of collection—both the gathering together of the disparate and distended portions of a line and the serial
display of individual moments in the Boisserées' images. The mediation of the collection plays an interesting role here. Notably Goethe almost never mentions any interior of the Strasbourg Cathedral and only

briefly treats that of the Cologne Cathedral. Instead, experience forms itself horizontally, through repeated readings and editions, through archivization and collection; *Bildung* and edification, then, would not be based on an interior/exterior model. Goethe shows us this possibility despite his organicizing and totalizing gestures. Moreover, understanding becomes a collective and collaborative effort between Goethe and the Boisserée brothers.

Goethehaus

As we have seen in relation to the cathedrals at Strasbourg and Cologne, perception, tracing, collation, and collection bring under representational control a sense perception that at first seems monstrous and overwhelming. This process is unified by the term *Bildung*. The older Goethe need not even move from his Weimar seat to grasp the true structure of the Cologne Cathedral through the Boisserées' work; at the same time, the underlying cause of the impressions made by the Strasbourg Minster are also brought into line with the architectural understanding gained over time.

The first impression of the Strasbourg Minster is a youthful experience that is perhaps primarily a tourist experience. This kind of experience would be one in which the observer is impressed by the apparent immediacy of a well-programmed object. The touristic display of famous houses takes special advantage of this immediacy effect; the famous writer's house in particular relies additionally on the same logic of *Bildung* that Goethe establishes with respect to the cathedrals. Here I can only begin to suggest how Goethe's model of *Bildung* may still be operative in practices of narration and display in Weimar.

The *Goethehaus* in Weimar is scrupulously maintained. One can see there Goethe's desk, his pen, his coat. A decision needs to be made about what contributes to an understanding of Goethe and what does not. A line could be drawn at the threshold of the archive. Alternatively, of course, one need never go to Weimar or visit Goethe's house at all; one can simply reject it as kitsch or the "merely empirical."

On the other hand, an examination of the historical atmosphere in Weimar suggests that this type of display is itself bound up with the operations of *Bildung*. One 1989 publication of the Nationalen Forschungs- und Gedenkstätte der klassischen deutschen Literatur Weimar, Deutsche

Demokratische Republik, sees the *Goethehaus* itself as an opportunity for cultural inculcation. As the Strasbourg Minster did for Goethe, the house stands as historical *Überlieferung*: "Since the 1950s it has been a major concern to make possible for young people visits to the memorial sites and museums in order to deepen, both emotionally and rationally, their encounter with the classical heritage in school through immediate experience in Weimar."[10] The effectiveness of the tourist site assumes and depends on a symmetry between inside and outside, between subject as origin and house as message, that would enrich our understanding of the dead genius and the works he wrought, the materializations that he left behind or formed in his image. The understanding that binds together Goethe and his house relies on the model of organic unity or the so-called symbol. The illusion of the immediacy of vision—especially the vision of Goethe's private surroundings as they "really were"—allows the process of appropriation and internalization to continue. This is why no illustrations accompany this text, for their presence might suggest that a visual image would make clear what language can only gesture towards; that the visual would embody the spiritual and make it present in such a way as to disclose the interiority of its meaning. This moment of "aesthetic ideology" is part of the tradition—the *Überlieferung*—of classical Weimar, a heritage the Nazis appropriated and celebrated in cultural rallies in the town itself.

The role played by the grandfather's art collection in *Wilhelm Meister's Apprenticeship* allows a closer consideration of the connection among housing, collection, display, and *Bildung*. Wilhelm's relationship to the collection and its role in the novel trace a specific movement that can be identified with *Bildung*. In the opening chapter of *Wilhelm Meister* we encounter the famous description of his theatrical beginnings in a marionette theater. Wilhelm's memories take on much of their power from their connection to an exchange of houses. His childhood absorption in the marionette theater, we learn, originated as a remedy for the strangeness and emptiness of the "new house." Wilhelm tells his mother: "Don't blame the puppet theater. . . . Those were my first happy moments in the new and empty house."[11] The anxiety around this exchange of houses is reminiscent of Goethe's description in *Dichtung und Wahrheit* of his father's renovations of the family home in Frankfurt—a strange sounding project that took the foundation of the house out from under them and temporarily put the house on stilts (*HA* 9:15–16). In *Wilhelm Meister* the new house opens a gaping hole in the life of the family: "Didn't we have plenty of room in the old house," Wilhelm demands, "And was it really necessary to build a new one?" (3/ *HA* 7:11–12). For Wilhelm, trade and exchange and the rewards of commerce—*Handeln*—leave a void that cannot be balanced out by monetary recompense. The emptiness opened up by the new house gapes open again when Wilhelm's grandfather's art collection is sold. Wilhelm describes this event early in the novel in a conversation with "a stranger" he meets at an inn. The stranger recognizes Wilhelm as the grandson of the old *Meister* who possessed the great art collection. The value of the collection consists not simply in the value of each art object but also in their connection and syntax. The stranger remarks: "Your grandfather was not just a collector, he knew a great deal about art. . . . He had . . . an instructive array of bronzes. His coins were collected purposively with regard to art as well as to history" (37/ *HA* 7:68–69). The purposiveness of the collection reflects the good sense and intelligence of Wilhelm's grandfather. The spatial contiguity of the collection, underscored by the order of its display, assures its meaningfulness: "Everything was well arranged and displayed, even though the rooms in the old house were not designed symmetrically" (37/ *HA* 7:69). Display appropriates architectural space, forging it into a unified figure, and connects it to a subject as its owner. The collection interprets itself as a meaningful extension of the subject-owner. Its architectural ground, however, the house itself, extends beyond and exceeds the signifying ability of the collection and cannot be brought into symmetry with it. Collected objects punctuate the house and predicate its walls to its owner. The relation of collection and collector sets up a symmetrical symbolic correspondence between inside and outside; but the baroque house exceeds the framework of the classical symbol in its asymmetrical meanderings. *Bildung* gets underway as its objects are taken away. Loss and self-division mark the passing of time and the clearing of space. The loss of the collection reveals to Wilhelm for the first time the bare walls of finitude. "You can imagine," he tells the stranger,

> what a loss we children felt when all these things were taken down and packed. . . . Those were the first sad days of my life. I remember how empty the rooms seemed, as we watched one thing after the other disappear, things that we had enjoyed since childhood, things which had seemed to us as permanent as the house or the town itself. (37/ *HA* 7:69)

The appearance of the bare house signifies absence, lack, division, separation, death, and loss—the relativity and finitude of what seemed to hold forth forever in the frame of the picture.

The beloved art collection appears again in book 8, in which Lothario sends Wilhelm to his sister Natalie. With great trepidation about meeting the Countess or possibly the Amazon, Wilhelm arrives at the mysterious house at night. He is driven into the courtyard with no view of the approach; there is no description of the house from the outside, and he is led in by a servant. The darkness aids the transition over the threshold, the "moment of the greatest embarrassment," that ushers him in: "He went into the house, and found himself in the most solemn and, for him, sacred place he had ever seen" (314/ *HA* 7:512). Entering by a grand stairway, Wilhelm sees marble statues and busts; "some of them seemed familiar to him" (314). In ever-increasing amazement, Wilhelm realizes that he is seeing pieces of his grandfather's art collection. This restoration, though, retains a trace of the wound that makes it possible, for there could be no repetition or retrieval without a prior loss: "Youthful impressions never fade away, even in their smallest details. He recognized a muse which had belonged to his grandfather, not by its shape or quality, but because one arm had been restored along with various sections of the drapery" (314/ *HA* 7:512–13). The damage to the figure, visible in the marks of its broken pieces, holds memory together for Wilhelm. It is not clear whether the restoration had taken place in the past or the present, whether the missing arm and garment fragments had been replaced by the grandfather or the new owner. The line marking their joining is one and the same and thus collapses past and present. The mark of severing joins past and present and makes possible a certain kind of memory, a memory that would erect a unified figure, whole and restored. The art collection reappears in this wondrous place, a house with no baroque excesses. We read: "The next morning, while everything was still peaceful and quiet, he walked around looking at the house. The building had clean lines and was the finest and noblest he had even seen. 'Good art,' he said to himself, 'is like good society: it obliges us, in the most pleasing way, to recognize the measure according to which and with respect to which our deepest interiority is constructed [*gebildet*]'" (316/ *HA* 7:516). The house offers a standard, a hinge around which life turns, a measure standing as both origin and goal. This house is constructed according to an interior and in order to reveal an interior; it is an ideal symbolic house, planned and executed, rendered legible and recognizable even to the newcomer—except of course for the entrance, the strange threshold, the ticket booth, so to speak. The wondrous house connects past and present by editing the art collection with other pieces. In the same way Wilhelm's foreknowledge of his grandfather's collection is supplemented by knowledge he has gleaned from reading the manuscript of the beautiful soul. Wilhelm describes how his memories are joined by looking at the pieces:

> "I shall remember all my life the impression I had yesterday evening when I came in here, and there in front of me were those old treasures from my youth . . . linking my earliest memories to this present moment. Here I have rediscovered the family treasures, the joys of my grandfather, set between so many other noble works of art. . . ." The discovery that a notable part of these works of art had belonged to his grandfather, put him in a cheerful, sociable mood. The manuscript had made him acquainted with this house, and he now found himself reunited with his own inheritance [*Erbteil*]. (318/ *HA* 7:519)

Why, then, if all these pieces come together so fully, does Wilhelm feel so strange before them? Something is missing, something has been excluded. The editing or collation process that reunites the recognizable also deletes the obscure, the ornate, the excessive—what stands in the way. The "classicization" of excess necessarily edits out what cannot be contained and rewrites the walls to house an interior. We can't be sure that the original collection is quite intact, though it constitutes a *schätzbarer Teil*, a "considerable portion," of the new collection. The editing process that has cut and pasted the beautiful soul's manuscript with Wilhelm's own past crosses over the diegetic line of the narrative, combining his experiences with his reading. Reference and signification are interchangeable, the passage from thing to thing the same as the passage from word to thing. This passing over, this *Überlieferung*, divides what it hands down: Wilhelm's *Erbteil* is indeed a partial inheritance.

As Wilhelm wanders about the *Oheim's* house, it seems that he in fact has stumbled on Goethe's own house: "He found a library, a collection of natural history specimens, and another of stones and metals. He felt so strange before all these objects" (316–17/ *HA* 7:517). The *Wohnhaus am Frauenplan* in Weimar, too, is set up to display the owner's collections of rocks, medallions, prints, etchings, busts, plaster copies, bronze casts, coins, engravings, and manuscripts. The house reconstructs the room furnishings with varying degrees of historical precision; the collections occupy a special pride of place not so much in the house itself as in the narrative of its presentation. Only a small portion of Goethe's possessions and collections are actually displayed in the house, but what is displayed is there to suggest the same principles of recollection and unification that we have seen in *Wilhelm Meister*.

The visitor to the *Goethehaus*, like Wilhelm, is uninitiated. *Goethes Wohnhaus* (1996), a detailed publication of the Stiftung Weimarer Klassik, tells us: "The observer sees a variety of things in the rooms of the front part of the house: casts of works from antiquity, a late medieval painting, a portrait by Cranach, and then paintings and copper engravings going up to Goethe's own time. Goethe knew each of these works well and saw it in its historical context" (Maul and Oppel, 19). In short Goethe is the *Oheim*; he knows how to arrange and display his possessions to instruct and communicate knowledge. Goethe's building becomes our *Bildung*. His creation of himself creates his public; the housing of his present prescribes its future recollection.

Goethehaus and *Goethesammlung* are allowed to speak to us and teach us, following what is called Goethe's own model. Musealization allows us to be haunted by a model of correspondence and mirroring, of embodiment and spiritualization. The legibility of the collection pares away the excesses of the house to show us the wholeness of a subject who controls his universe and builds a house in which to keep it. The guide concludes, "In Goethe's work world [the back of the house] which, in its unadorned sparseness, is a symbol [*Sinnbild*] to show us that, behind that plenitude and its tasteful ordering and arrangement, there stood always the single man with his visionary and harmoniously synthesizing spirit" (24).

The term *Sinnbild* returns us to the problems of aesthetic ideology. The historical presentation of the Weimar residence strives to establish a classical mirroring between structure and substance, between inside and outside, spirit and body; it reduces excess and fills in gaps. In one sense Goethe himself has provided the model and the instructions for this kind of representational restoration. At the same time, however, our attention can be turned elsewhere, to the gaps and spaces that destabilize the homogenizing power of the image of spirit's wholeness. As the various strands in *Wilhelm Meister* begin to come together towards the end of book 8, Wilhelm becomes his own double as the totalizing image of a telos begins to replace the narrative extensions of his life story. This replacement itself—the step of *Bildung* into *Bildung*—produces spirit as a doubling of self, a ghost who wanders the house of its own life. And what better description could we find of a walk around Weimar than this reflection of Wilhelm's?

> In this condition, neither his mind nor body could be at rest, by night or by day. When everyone else was sleeping, he was pacing up and down in the house. The presence of those old familiar paintings partly attracted and partly repelled him. He could neither accept nor reject what surrounded him, everything reminded him of something else, he could see the whole ring of his life, but at the moment it lay in pieces before him which seemed as if they would not join together for all eternity. . . . He became so lost in these lugubrious reflections that he sometimes seemed to himself like a ghost, and even when he was feeling and touching objects outside himself, he could not get rid of his doubt as to whether he really were alive and standing there. (349–50/ *HA* 7:570–71)

The resulting anxiety tempts history to exclude excess and install unity and wholeness, just as Goethe himself tried to remodel and classicize the baroque house he moved into. The guide to the *Goethehaus* describes the complex reconstruction of the entrance and stairway, a place that occupied much of Goethe's attention, with the following detail: "Here, hidden from the visitor's view, there are remnants of the earlier baroque staircase" (26). These architectural remains point to a history for which the story of totality provides no accommodation. Weimar's cult of cultivation strives for a wholeness that blocks out what it cannot contain. But its wholeness is haunted by the location of Buchenwald just outside the town, a site at which the model of cultural tourism reveals its own inadequacy.

§2 Gothic Revival and *The Castle of Otranto*

Johann Wolfgang von Goethe's early essay "On German Architecture" clearly partakes in the interest in the medieval period and Gothic architecture emerging in Europe in the eighteenth century. Gothic revival in architecture flourished especially in England and Germany with the construction of garden towers, grottoes, hermitages, and other decorative medieval-like structures not built to fulfill any function. Both the eighteenth-century evaluation of Gothic architecture and the practices of Gothic revival tend to highlight details that exceed overall design. Gothic revival is also characterized by a peculiar transference of materials. Indeed, Giorgio Vasari says that the excessive vegetal details typical of Gothic architecture look like they are cut out of paper, a comment taken up by the early German art historian Joachim von Sandrart in 1675.[1] While Goethe's 1772 essay "On German Architecture" is widely recognized as a significant landmark in German Gothic revival, the proximity of Goethe and Gothic may extend beyond this text into his novels. The architecture of Gothic revival stands in the background of a large part of Goethe's career; it is also an important context for the Gothic novel, which was inaugurated by Horace Walpole's *The Castle of Otranto* in 1765.[2] The relation of Gothic and Gothic revival architecture to textual architectonics enacts the destabilization of reference that is characteristic of the Gothic. That is, Gothic revival both calls on a historical precedent and announces its autonomy in its obvious forgery. This peculiar withdrawal of architectural foundation places in a common setting Walpole's novel and Goethe's *Wahlverwandtschaften* (*Elective Affinities*), which might be considered Goethe's Gothic novel.[3]

The eighteenth-century turn to Gothic, a break with the dominant classicism, begins to be articulated as a wish for a return to the "native." In Germany and England, this means a turn away from the Roman. In an odd ambivalence the turn toward the Germanic—the Goths, the Vandals, etc., that is, the barbarians—is a turn towards the native, to precisely what is not barbaric.[4] The Gothic confuses the categories of native and foreign and the way they are correlated with civilization and barbarism. Barbarism, according to Aristotle's *Poetics*, articulates an unstable border between poetic invention and senseless repetition. Recall his definition: "An impressive diction, one that escapes the ordinary, results from the use of strange words, by which I mean foreign words, metaphors, expanded words, and whatever departs from normal usage. However, anything composed entirely in such language will either be a riddle or a barbarism—a riddle if composed in metaphors, a barbarism if in foreign words alone."[5] Barbarism is characterized by the repetition of the foreign word resistant to understanding, the incorporation of the untranslated alien. Excessive barbarism renders language opaque and incomprehensible, but the right amount of barbarism "will save the diction from being commonplace and drab, while the colloquial element will ensure its clarity" (69). The category of barbarism, regardless of its reference, institutes a distinction between a native inside available to understanding, and a foreign exterior connected to an excess ornamentation that cannot be understood.[6]

In contrast to the Greek and Roman determinations of native and foreign, Herder considers Roman "popery" to be barbaric and attributes to it the domination of the Germanic tribes by the abstract reasoning of late Latin culture. His evaluation of Roman barbarism again institutes an opposition between external, ornamental signification, on the one hand, and internal, living spirit on the other. The Romans impose abstract linguistic form on the living spirit of the Germanic people, driving them from the forests into cities.[7] The barbarism of Latin thus consists not only in the fact that it is foreign; it lodges in the desiccating structure of abstraction characteristic of late Latin culture and the dogmatism of popery: "The Latin religion taught thoughtless stubbornness in assertion, Latin literature suffocated the spirit and whittled down taste with speculation and nonsense, the monks' language introduced eternal barbarism [*ewige Barbarei*] into the language of the land" (11).

The political yoke of Rome has a scholarly branch as well. The domi-

nation of Latin in the institutions of learning gives rise to a kind of bad mimesis. Describing the rediscovery of the classics of the Medicis' Renaissance, Herder writes:

> Instead of awakening the ancients in order to form oneself after them and turn one's first tender impression towards them in order to allow their spirit to be breathed into oneself . . . instead, one left off at the outer husk, learned *what* the ancients thought instead of learning to think how they thought, learned the language in which they spoke instead of learning to speak like them. (15)

Barbarism, embodied in Latin and Romanism, comes to stand for this division between means and end that isolates language as a signifying instrument, a collection of repeatable statements and a set of learnable and repeatable rules. Earlier in the century, François Fénelon similarly compares Gothic ornament to rhetorical play divorced from meaningful function. Paul Frankl reports:

> Fénelon inveighs against antitheses and plays on words, demanding simplicity. . . . Antitheses are permissible if they are natural, but "to express one's

meaning circuitously in order to use a battery of words is childish. . . . Are you acquainted with the architecture of our old churches, which is called Gothic? . . . the roses, pinnacles, small ornaments, and so on, are in architecture the same thing as the antitheses and 'the other plays on words' in eloquence." (376)

The dead mechanism of imposed Latin is contrasted with the "living spirit" of Goths.[8] This familiar opposition will of course be further institutionalized through vulgar Romanticism and throughout the nineteenth century. Important here is that barbarism is no longer limited to the barbarians (Germans), but rather now is a characteristic of the Romans. The "foreignness" and unintelligibility it signified now come to be associated with the isolated abstraction of signification, of rules and forms separated from their use or operation. Herder's identification of the barbarism of the Romans virtually coincides with what Johann Georg Sulzer, around the same time, defines as the barbarism of Gothic. Sulzer characterizes Gothic as follows:

> Foremost, it seems to indicate a lack of skill, the lack of beauty and of good ratios in visible forms, and was generated out of the fact that the Goth who settled in Italy imitated the works of ancient architecture in an incompetent way. This would happen to any still half barbaric people who came to power and wealth too quickly, before it had time to think about the culture of taste. Thus Gothic taste is not peculiar to the Goths, but rather is common to all peoples . . . before taste has had a sufficient development. (433)

The Gothic points to the lack of a totalizing structure that would organize parts and whole, details and purpose. Sulzer writes: "It seems in general that Gothic taste arises out of the lack of reflection about that which one has to do. The artist who does not think precisely about what the work he executes is supposed to be, and how it is to be formed in order to be precisely that, easily becomes Gothic" (434). The definition of the barbaric remains the same: bad imitation, empty repetition, excessive decoration, lack of organic totality, dissociation between parts and whole. It is attributed now to the Germanic tribes, now to the Romans. It thus loses its substantial ground in medieval Gothic while continuing to draw upon it as a historical precedent.[9]

The revaluation and revival of medieval architecture began in England in the early seventeenth century as a minor trend alongside the dominant Palladian classicism. It was sanctioned by its simultaneous libertarian associations with the "Gothick constitution" and its institutionalization of the authority of the landed gentry.[10] The conscious turn towards architectural medievalism in England is especially connected with the invocation of the vim and vigor of the native English constitution limiting the power of the monarchy. The Gothic revival drew on earlier writers such as Tacitus and the sixth-century Jordanes, who represent the vitality of "gothic energy" in opposition to Roman decadence (39). The English Civil War and its outcome were also interpreted in terms of Gothic history; constitutionalism found its ground in "ancient Gothique law" (43). The vitality of the constitution was conceived as well in terms of Gothic building. An anonymous text published in the *Gentleman's Magazine* in 1739 reads:

> Methinks there was something respectable in those old hospitable Gothick halls, hung round with the Helmets, Breast-Plates, and Swords of our Ancestors; I entered them with a Constitutional Sort of Reverence and look'd upon those arms with Gratitude. . . . Our old Gothick Constitution had a noble strength and Simplicity in it, which was well enough represented by the bold Arches and the solid Pillars of the Edifices of those Days. (Brooks, 74, Frankl, 381)

The term "Gothic" first came to describe medieval architecture during the Renaissance. It names a set of architectural features that come to be understood as an architectural "style" only after it has passed. Importantly, as Brooks writes, medieval Gothic did not think of itself as a style but simply as the way one built (9). The designation of Gothic corresponds to the separation of function and ornament that allows a concept of the independence of style to emerge in Vasari. Gothic revival begins as an explicit borrowing of Gothic style.[11] As the style takes on political and ideological meanings, its elements are recognized as semiotic features rather than functional modes. This distinction allows for the condemnation of Gothic as excess ornamentation or barbarism. The sense of phonetic autonomy—the nonsense of barbarism—as a signal of the Gothic comes through in John Evelyn's abhorrence of the chapel at Westminster, which he describes in a text of 1707 as "crinkle crankle" (Frankl, 359). Crinkle crankle shares the features of the Gothic that it names: decorative repetition without concrete reference.

Not only the author of the first Gothic novel, Horace Walpole is also famous as the builder of Strawberry Hill, the first Gothic revival mansion, and as the founder of the first private press, which he housed in one of the outbuildings of his estate. Strawberry Hill, originally a "cottage," became famous as the first effort to transfer Gothic architectural elements to a house, and it is considered the first instance of domestic Gothic revival in England. Purchased by Walpole in 1747, Strawberry Hill flaunts the independence of architectural stylistic features—its crinkle crankle—by transferring small sets of elements to other materials. Sometimes criticized for this, the house was called a "toy," a confection[12]—the battlements copied from massive stone redone in plaster and wood; the tomb from Westminster Abbey copied for the fireplace in the parlor; the trellised windows of Chartres Cathedral transferred by Walpole and his friend Richard Bentley to the backs of chairs (Iddon, 25). Strawberry Hill is novel in copying specific Gothic buildings; before this, there was a kind of imitation of the Gothic in general but not exact reproduction of specific details.

At the same time the imitations are divorced from any sense of the whole from which they are taken. In the preface to his *A Description of the Villa*, Walpole points out the catalogue function of his description, which lists and displays architectural features in a way that renders them up to be deployed in other contexts: "A farther view [of the description] succeeded; that of exhibiting specimens of Gothic architecture, as collected from standards in cathedrals and chapel-tombs, and shewing how they may be applied to chimney-pieces, ceilings, windows, ballustrades, loggias, &c" (a). The mansion presents a peculiar mélange of authenticity and phoniness. Its materials and proportions do not resemble Gothic buildings, but rather reinforce the cottage origins and recall the processes of imitation and revival they show off. Historical reference is thus established and demolished in the same gesture. Strawberry Hill was an important inspiration for garden Gothic in Germany and was a direct model for the Gotisches Haus at Wörlitz built between 1773 and 1809.[13] Goethe and Karl August of Weimar visited the Gotisches Haus in 1778, shortly before Goethe began to redesign the park at Weimar (Robson-Scott, 32).

As Gothic revival loosens its connection to its historical prototype, it gives rise to an easily recognizable architectural rhetoric. In Walpole's Strawberry Hill, series of signs are recognizable, but are cut off from the function, telos, or meaning, as part of which they were originally designed. This liberated architectural rhetoric, clearly visible in the kind of design details mentioned above, creates the higgledy-piggledy conglomeration usually attributed to Strawberry Hill. The guidebook attributes this to Walpole's love of the irregular. He rejected the "methodization" of the classicizing architecture dominant in the Georgian period in England: "This 'methodization' had worked against Walpole's love of irregularity, surprise and mystery. One of his favourite words in relation to Strawberry Hill was 'sharrawaggi' or want of symmetry and a glance at the floor plan of Strawberry Hill will reveal how unsymmetrical it became" (6). It seems that Walpole used this word (coined in the seventeenth century but often attributed to Walpole) to simulate the very effect it names; it parallels Goethe's "amphigurish." Both words indicate the pleasure in the reified independence of signifying elements—their simultaneous tendency to mean and failure to mean, the monstrous persistence of details and pieces that cannot be assimilated into a whole. In *The Gothic Flame*, an early text of Gothic criticism, Devendra P. Varma points to the perverse aspect of these reified elements. "Walpole did not love Gothic for its virile or aspiring qualities, but for its suggestiveness to a truant fantasy. . . . As Lytton Strachey states: 'He liked Gothic architecture, not because he thought it beautiful but because he found it queer'" (46). The queerness of the Gothic consists in its simultaneous participation in and resistance to signification. It moves across—*quer*—the demarcation line between history and fantasy, referent and reified signifier.

One must cross the same line to draw the connection between Walpole's house and his novel *The Castle of Otranto*. Critics frequently assert that Strawberry Hill is the setting for Walpole's conception of *The Castle of Otranto*. In isolating the notion of "setting" and enumerating its details, the critical tradition itself begins to resemble the Gothic genre, laying out lists of Gothic architectural detail: the castle, the haunted palace, the gloomy passageways, the secret chambers, and so forth. The architectural setting of Gothic literature is an unmistakable element of its "machinery," a term used frequently to describe these markers of the Gothic. Accounts of the Gothic invariably include lists of these architectural elements, treated as thematic paraphernalia. The castle of Otranto, however, does not remain in the background of *The Castle of Otranto*. The novel engages directly with its architectural element to set into motion the unstable relation between the castle and the spirit.

As the first exemplum of a genre that would become one of the most hyper-conventional and repetitive ones in modern European literature,

Walpole's *Otranto* contains a thorough inventory of repeatable elements. "There is hardly a feature of Gothic romance," Varma writes, "that was not employed by Walpole in *The Castle of Otranto*. Walpole bequeathed to his successors a remarkable collection of useful 'properties,' and his 'machinery' and 'motifs' quickly accumulated as conventions of the Gothic school. . . . Countless Gothic novels have in their titles 'castle,' 'abbey,' 'priory,' 'convent' or 'church.' . . . The buildings seem to acquire a personality and an empery of their own, ever since the Gothic tale of Otranto" (57). Interesting in discussions of the Gothic is the stress on mechanics and architecture.[14] It is not coincidental that Michel Foucault should choose Ann Radcliffe as an example of the figure of the author, her work demonstrating the author's function of creating a sphere of "sameness" indicated and made available by the list:

> Ann Radcliffe's texts opened the way for a certain number of resemblances and analogies which have their model or principle in her work. The latter contains characteristic signs, figures, relationships, and structures that could be reused by others. In other words, to say that Ann Radcliffe founded the Gothic horror novel means that in the nineteenth-century Gothic novel one will find, as in Ann Radcliffe's works, the theme of the heroine caught in the trap of her own innocence, the hidden castle, the character of the black, cursed hero devoted to making the world expiate the evil done to him, and all the rest of it. (217–18)

Every genre or literary type consists of the repetition of recognizable sets of features. The exaggerated and mechanical repetition of architectural features in Gothic literature, described conventionally and consistently, installs the very structure of the genre.

On the one hand architectural structure is interpreted as a stable frame or setting for the variables of the Gothic genre, thus only as a material background. This interpretation of architecture as mere setting enables a logic of historical grounding that allows critics to place Walpole's novel in a historical setting. Just as the castle gives rise to and supports the plot of the novel, Walpole's mansion is thought to provide the setting for its conception. At the same time architecture provides the stability of the materiality of signifiers that, combined in various ways, actually produce the "gas" of subjectivity, of meaning, the "air" of characterization, plots, movement, and events. Architecture thus gives shape to the outside and the inside, the setting and the interior. The uncanny action

of the Gothic, often overlooked in accounts of its machinery or its reso-
lutions, takes place when signifiers are seen to produce and participate
in the signified. The Gothic building exudes a kind of atmosphere that
gives rise to the spirits, supernatural events, ghosts, and evil people it
contains. The Gothic castle contains by failing to contain itself. Again
quoting Varma, "The Castle has been called the true hero of the book,
the hub around which all action gravitates. . . . The haunted castle
forms the stage-setting; while its accessory properties powerfully seize the
imagination. If we eliminate it, the whole fabric of the romance would
be bereft of its foundation and its predominant atmosphere would fade
away" (57).[15]

In this reading *Otranto* presages Edgar Allan Poe's "Fall of the House
of Usher" in its utmost logic. I will resist the temptation to turn off here
into the passageway to Poe, whose story unravels the interior logic of the
Gothic, allowing the uncanny to infiltrate and unsolder it. The suggestion
about the role of architecture in the Gothic can be seen not only or not
simply as a historical question, but rather as a problem of signification.
The architectural problem of Gothic thus extends between historical relations and relations of signification: from Strawberry Hill to the Castle of
Otranto. To read these as mirror images of each other, however, would be
a classicizing gesture that would incorporate the exteriority of architecture
into the interiority of meaning. It is the difference between the empirical
and literature, between reference and signification, that prevents the total
absorption of the first into the second. Strawberry Hill and Otranto are
off balance.

By Walpole's own account, the idea for *The Castle of Otranto* came to him
in a dream. He writes to William Cole in a letter dated March 9, 1765:

> Dear Sir . . . I had time to write but a short note with *The Castle of
> Otranto*. . . . Your partiality to me and Strawberry have I hope inclined you
> to excuse the wildness of the story. You will even have found some traits to
> put you in mind of this place. . . . Shall I even confess to you what was the
> origin of this romance? I waked one morning the beginning of last June
> from a dream, of which all I could recover was, that I had thought myself
> in an ancient castle (a very natural dream for a head filled like mine with
> Gothic story) and that on the upper-most banister of a great staircase I saw
> a gigantic hand in armour. In the evening I sat down and began to write,
> without knowing the least what I intended to say or relate. The work grew
> on my hands, and I grew fond of it—add that I was very glad to think

of anything rather than politics—In short, I was so engrossed with my
tale, which I completed in less than two months, that one even . . . [I]f
I have amused you by retracing with any fidelity the manners of ancient
days, I am content, and give you leave to think me as idle as you please.
(*Letters*, 121–22)

Rather than focusing on the uncanniness of a severed hand writing on its
own, crossing over from dream to text, Varma, along with a whole tradition of criticism, takes this as evidence of the origination of the Castle
of Otranto in Strawberry Hill, thus invoking a historical ground for the
phantasmagorical production of the Gothic. While few critiques take
this dream scene seriously, still, most associate the image of the Castle of
Otranto with Strawberry Hill, no matter how loosely. Walpole's house has
modeled his fiction, but at the same time his house must be understood
as yet another of his works of fiction. The claim of historical grounding is
based on the repetition of architectural elements: "the staircase at Strawberry Hill which was 'the most particular and chief beauty of the castle,'
as he had mentioned earlier in 1753" (Varma, 46).

Likewise the claim of historical authenticity in the first preface to *The
Castle of Otranto* takes on architectural form. This preface is presented as
the work of a William Marshall, who offers the text as his translation of a
found sixteenth-century Italian manuscript printed in "black letter," that
is, Gothic script. As is often pointed out, this serves to give the text a historical grounding—a gesture that invokes the past and legitimizes the text
as a historical document. In the second preface, written some years later,
Walpole claims the text for his own.[16] The first preface begins,

> The following work was found in the library of an ancient catholic family
> in the north of England. It was printed at Naples, in the black letter, in the
> year 1529. How much sooner it was written does not appear. The principal
> incidents are such as were believed in the darkest ages of christianity; but the
> language and conduct have nothing that savours of barbarism. The style is the
> purest Italian. If the story was written near the time when it is supposed to
> have happened, it must have been between 1095, the aera of the first crusade,
> and 1243, the date of the last, or not long afterwards. (39)

Although the events of the story are relegated to the Gothic period, the
style is associated with the Renaissance: purest Italian with "nothing that
savours of barbarism." This dualism is described in the second preface as
the admixture of "two kinds of romance, the ancient and the modern. In

the former all was imagination and improbability: in the latter, nature is always intended to be, and sometimes has been, copied with success" (43). The two strains of the fantastic and the realistic might equally describe the system of signification characteristic of Strawberry Hill (and other Gothic revival structures), which entails both historical reference and its dissolution and replacement by isolated ornamental series. The details of architecture are indeed invoked to suggest a true historical foundation as a setting for what is invented.[17] In the second preface, Walpole writes:

> Though the machinery is invention, and the names of the actors imaginary, I cannot but believe that the groundwork of the story is founded on truth. The scene is undoubtedly laid in some real castle. The author seems frequently, without design, to describe particular parts. *The chamber*, he says, *on the right hand; the door on the left hand; the distance from the chapel to Conrad's apartment*: these and other passages are strong presumptions that the author had some certain building in his eye. (42)

The foundation founds historical foundation; the story is *laid* in its architectural setting as in reality. The comprehensibility of prose itself becomes the standard of realism: the chamber on the right, the door on the left. That is, the fact that these phrases can be understood at all creates the effect of realism, of language grounded in a reality outside itself.[18] Interestingly this is the very passage usually invoked to suggest that the conception of *The Castle of Otranto* is laid in Strawberry Hill; it goes almost without notice that the passage is meant to ground the story in a historical past and *not* in the imagination or surroundings of an author. Some of Walpole's contemporaries were irked by the uncertainty about whether to take this text seriously or ironically.[19] The confusion around this architectural system of reference enacts this ambivalence. The second preface, in which Walpole claims authorship of the novel, ends with a reversal of this architectural realism. Walpole goes into a lengthy criticism of Voltaire, in particular of his statement that the "mixture of buffoonery and solemnity is intolerable" (45). In both prefaces Walpole defends his use of comic relief and admixture of styles as following the venerable model of Shakespeare. It is, in fact, a crucially sore point; more of this will follow. He condemns Voltaire's privileging of simplicity, which, he says, would purge the fantastic side of the imagination—the extravagant, the silly, the ludicrous—from the seriousness of literature. Simplicity is a "merit which . . . would reduce poetry from the lofty effort of imagination, to a puerile and most contemptible labor." Out of context and somewhat incoherently, Walpole concludes with the following:

> I cannot help however mentioning a couplet, which to my English ears always sounded as the flattest and most trifling instance of circumstantial propriety; but which Voltaire . . . has singled out to defend in Racine:
>
> *De son appartement cette porte est prochaine,*
> *Et cette autre conduit dans celui de la reine.*
>
> In English,
>
> *To* Caesar's *closet through this door you come,*
> *and t'other leads to the queen's drawing room.* (48)

In the first preface Walpole praised exactly this kind of ground-plan realism, which insinuated a reliable historical origin. Here, however, the predominance of the architecture is ridiculed; instead it should be replaced by some kind of "moral": "Unhappy Shakespeare," the text continues, "hadst thou made Rosencranz inform his compeer Guildenstern of the ichnography of the palace of Copenhagen, instead of presenting us with a moral dialogue between the prince of Denmark and the grave-digger, the illuminated pit of Paris would have been instructed a *second time* to adore thy talents" (48).

Ichnography, the art of layouts and ground plans, marks out architectural elements as the real foundation of meanings and atmosphere. In its very ability to found or ground, however, the architectural recedes and gives way to the emerging interior, moral, or spirit. In the turn towards this model of propriety in his second preface, Walpole indirectly addresses the problems of his own novel, urging the replacement of the letter by the spirit of a meaning. Based on its architectural shape, *Otranto* privileges the letter, spreading beyond its necessary shape into the Gothic design of the black letters that sprawl in almost uncontrollable humor, rhetoric, digression, and opacities. These do not convey sense but affect the reader beyond the clear boundaries of signification.[20] We should remember here, too, that Walpole ran a press in his own home. The Gothic mansion is accompanied by its own excess in an outbuilding that produces Gothic letters.

Letters are, on the one hand, associated with an enlightenment purpose: to convey meaning, argument, and correct doctrine:

> Letters were then in their most flourishing state in Italy, and contributed to dispel the empire of superstition, at that time so forcibly attacked by the re-

formers. It is not unlikely that an artful priest might endeavour to turn their own arms on the innovators; and might avail himself of his abilities as an author to confirm the populace in their ancient errors and superstitions. If this was his view, he has certainly acted with signal address. Such a work as the following would enslave a hundred vulgar minds beyond half the books of controversy that have been written from the days of Luther to the present hour. (40)

The irrational operation of the letter on the reader—not of the argument—persuades through materially grounded action, not through the communication of a sense. Since this is admittedly the foregrounded manner of the novel, Walpole is sensitive in both prefaces to charges of digression, buffoonery, impurity, and impropriety. The supernatural is the first element identified as digressive or potentially "mere entertainment." Walpole tries to justify the style of his manuscript by invoking classical standards:

> If this *air* of the *miraculous* is excused, the reader will find nothing else unworthy of his perusal. Allow the possibility of the facts, and all the actors comport themselves as persons would do in their situation. There is no bombast, no similes, flowers, digressions, or unnecessary descriptions. Every thing tends directly to the catastrophe. Never is the reader's attention relaxed. The rules of the drama are almost observed throughout the conduct of the piece. The characters are well drawn, and still better maintained. Terror, the author's principle engine, prevents the story from ever languishing; and it is so often contrasted by pity, the mind is kept up in a constant vicissitude of interesting passions. (40)

Anyone who has read *The Castle of Otranto* would be hard pressed to ratify this description. In fact it is largely an exercise in digression and interruption. The whole story might be read as a digression from what Walpole asserts is the story's "moral": "that *the sins of the fathers are visited on their children to the third and fourth generation*" (41). This abbreviated interpretation is accurate if underdeveloped; Manfred's father Ricardo has usurped the rule of Otranto, and the whole novel tends towards its restoration to the rightful heir. This is announced at the beginning of the novel in the form of an obscure prophecy, "*that the castle and lordship of Otranto should pass from the present family, whenever the real owner should be grown too large to inhabit it*" (51).

The novel spans the distance between the synchronous sense of this prophecy and the time of its narrative fulfillment.[21] First, the biblical commonplace about the sins of the fathers is translated into the enigmatic terms of the novel. The prophecy is of course finally resolved; but if resolution were the only goal, the narrative itself would verge on superfluity. The synchronic and diachronic aspects of the story are thus in tension; the longer the delay, the less acutely the message will be delivered. Walpole tries to justify the narrative delay by submitting it to standards of classical drama, which would prescribe *just the right amount* of hesitation, but no more. This is why he defensively claims: "There is no bombast, no similes, flowers, digressions, or unnecessary descriptions. Every thing tends directly to the catastrophe. Never is the reader's attention relaxed."

The entire plot could be read as nothing but a series of interruptions, beginning with the interruption of the wedding plans of Conrad, son of the evil tyrant Manfred, and Isabella. (Manfred is eager to encourage offspring to keep the property in his line.) Barely one page into the novel, Conrad cannot be found, and the wedding ceremony is delayed. A servant is sent to find him and returns to Manfred in the following manner:

> The servant . . . came running back breathless, in a frantic manner, his eyes staring, and foaming at the mouth. He said nothing, but pointed to the court. The company were struck with terror and amazement. The princess Hippolita, without knowing what was the matter, but anxious for her son, swooned away. Manfred, less apprehensive than enraged at the procrastination of the nuptials, and at the folly of his domestic, asked imperiously, what was the matter? The fellow made no answer, but continued pointing towards the courtyard; and at last, after repeated questions put to him cried out, Oh, the helmet! The helmet! (52)

While the servant's report here may fall under the category of comic relief on the part of the underclass, it also partakes of the interruptive capacity of the materiality of the text. Articulation sinks into the gesticulations of the body: "frothing at the mouth" and "pointing," which tell but fail to tell, signify but convey no meaning. A paragraph later others join in these cries in answer to Manfred's questions: "Oh, my lord! The prince! The prince! The helmet! The helmet!" (52). The reader, along with Manfred, is given only this stuttering speech along with bodily gesticulations. The narrative totters as Hippolita "swoons away"; the narrative itself almost loses consciousness altogether, stumbling into the incomprehensible barbarisms of stuttering sounds and bodily gestures. After the protracted performance of the servants, we are finally told that Conrad has been "dashed to pieces, and almost buried under an enormous helmet, an hundred times more large than any casque ever made for human being, and shaded with a proportional quantity of black feathers" (52).

The landscape or setting of the castle begins to be punctuated by such portentous apparitions. Manfred's silence, in contrast to the garbled mutterings of the populace, connects the fallen helmet to an other, an allegorical level. First the connection is made only negatively through suspension or interruption:

> his silence lasted longer than even grief could occasion. He fixed his eyes on what he wished in vain to believe a vision; and seemed less attentive to his loss, than buried in meditation on the stupendous object that had occasioned it. He touched, he examined the fatal casque; nor could even the bleeding mangled remains of the young prince divert the eyes of Manfred from the portent before him. (53)

Renamed a portent, the casque now becomes a potentially, but not yet, meaningful sign, recuperating the senseless yammerings of the stuttering servants. Manfred's actions from this point on oscillate between the literal level of the narrative—the bare events that take place in the castle—and a figurative or allegorical level which will, eventually, gather the mysterious bits together to reveal another meaning. Soon Manfred tries to cross the prophecy on the level of plot; he tries to divorce his wife Hippolita and marry his son's fiancée Isabella—a union treated as incest. Manfred is halted in a rape attempt by a quivering or trembling of the letter that interrupts the literal level of the plot and begins to incline it towards another story: "Manfred rose to pursue her; when the moon, which was now up, and gleamed in at the opposite casement, presented to his sight the plumes of the fatal helmet, which rose to the height of the windows, waving backwards and forwards in a tempestuous manner, and accompanied with a hollow and rustling sound" (59). While the repetition of the rustling and quivering plumes will come to mark places at which the literal level of the plot points to another level, in the diachrony of the narrative, its meaning remains semi-mute and inarticulate: the hollow rustling of a possibly empty signifier. To supplement the waving plumes, a supernatural event appears to Manfred's eyes alone: "At that instant the portrait of his grandfather, which hung over the bench where they had been sitting, uttered a deep sigh and heaved its breast." The portrait gets down off its panel and begins to move, motioning to Manfred to follow; in the meantime Isabella runs off.

> Do I dream: cried Manfred returning, or are the devils themselves in league against me? Speak, infernal spectre! Or, if thou art my grand-sire, why dost thou too conspire against thy wretched descendent, who too dearly pays for—Ere he could finish the sentence the vision sighed again, and made a sign to Manfred to follow him. Lead on! cried Manfred; I will follow thee to the gulph of perdition. The spectre marched sedately, but dejected, to the end of the gallery, and turned into a chamber on the right hand. Manfred accompanied him at a little distance full of anxiety and horror, but resolved. As he would have entered the chamber, the door was clapped-to with violence by an invisible hand. The prince, collecting courage from this delay, would have forcibly burst open the door with his foot, but found that it resisted his utmost efforts. (60)

Just as the plumes wave to both signify and not signify, the specter appears in order to lead both Manfred and the reader towards the solution of the mystery. Manfred follows him down the gallery and turns into a chamber on the right hand. Reading is led by the artificial realism of housing position that houses fictional characters and their motions. We are taken in and follow. Yet the same housing intervenes to prevent understanding; the "invisible hand" of writing acts in collusion with housing to slam the door on the progress of the narrative and counteracts the pursuit of understanding.[22] The shutting of the door *is* suspense. Architecture leads towards sense but suspends it, lays it out and delays it.

The pairing of interrupted speech or stammering and the intrusion of clues into the narrative is striking in the scene where the servants, Jaquez and Diego, discover the giant foot in the gallery. It takes more than a page for the distracted servants to tell Manfred what they have found:

> But what? Cried the prince: has she escaped?—Jaquez and I, my lord—Yes, I and Diego, interrupted the second, who came up in still greater consternation—Speak one of you at a time, said Manfred . . . Oh, my lord! Said Jaquez, Diego has seen such a sight! Your highness would not believe your eyes.— . . .

Give me a direct answer, or by heaven—Why, my lord, if it please your high-ness to hear me, said the poor fellow; Diego and I—Yes, I and Jaquez, cried his comrade. . . . (67)

After another good page of stammering, they report:

Diego had no sooner opened the door, than he cried out and ran back—I ran back too, and said, Is it the ghost? The ghost! No, no, said Diego, and his hair stood on end—it is a giant, I believe; he is all clad in armour, for I saw his foot and part of his leg, and they are as large as the helmet below in the court. As he said these words, my lord, we heard a violent motion and the rattling of armour, as if the giant was rising; for Diego has told me since, that he believes the giant was lying down, for the foot and leg were stretched at length on the floor. Before we could get to the end of the gallery, we heard the door of the great chamber clap behind us. (69)

Increasingly, the dismembered parts quiver into life and become more and more suggestive of a meaning that will resolve the enigmatic proph-esy; Manfred "recollected the apparition of the portrait, and the sudden closing of the door at the end of the gallery"—and begins to take the story seriously.

These scenes should be the most mysterious, terrifying, or awe-in-spiring ones in the novel because they are the moments of key suspense. Yet what is stated is simply ludicrous—giant, specter, walking portraits, medieval knights—and these stated items become the staple elements of Gothic writing. Instead, perhaps it is the quivering motion of these body parts—the dismembered body, the inarticulate and barbaric letters of what has not yet been gathered into a coherent statement or word—that gives rise to a sense of the uncanny here. The uncanny is associated here with a certain kind of impropriety, namely that associated with a rever-sal of the traditional Judeo-Christian hierarchy of spirit and letter. The autonomy of the letter in the ludicrous stammering of the servants—the ability of language to break away from meaning and interrupt and delay it—is connected to the primary position of the castle in this text, an un-derlying material that only rarely or indirectly comes to utterance.

When Manfred accidentally kills his daughter Mathilda, thinking her to be Isabella, he can avoid his guilt no longer. Once she dies the tem-porality of the plot-narrative comes to an end. All is revealed and the mysteries are solved, but this can only happen in the wake of a revolution or catastrophe that reverses the relationship between letter and spirit, exterior castle and interior subject:

> A clap of thunder at that instant shook the castle to its foundations: the earth rocked, and the clank of more than mortal armour was heard behind. Frederic and Jerome thought the last day was at hand. The latter, forcing Theodor along with them, rushed into the court. The moment Theodore appeared, the walls of the castle behind Manfred were thrown down with a mighty force, and the form of Alfonso, dilated to an immense magnitude, appeared in the centre of the ruins. Behold in Theodore, the true heir of Alfonso, said the vision: and having pronounced those words, accompanied by a clap of thunder, it ascended solemnly towards heaven, where the clouds parting asunder, the form of saint Nicholas was seen; and receiving Alfonso's shade, they were soon wrapt from mortal eyes in a blaze of glory. (145)

Until this point the castle itself has held apart the pieces of the vision; as the pieces of the armoured body come together, it bursts the shackles of the materiality of the building and comes forth in the form of a personified image. We might call this moment Gothic revival in its most pointed sense: the spirit is revived through its Gothic setting, revived and restored to its place of primacy. The Gothic is the destruction of the Gothic, in both senses of "of"; the Gothic castle is destroyed in order for the spirit of Gothic to emerge. The restoration of the proper heritage corrects an error caused by writing; for Ricardo, Manfred's father, murdered Alfonso, the rightful lord, and forged a will declaring himself heir. Writing is replaced by the natural relationship of primogeniture.

The Gothic novel, as it has been identified and discussed in the critical tradition, is both "transgressive" and restorative.[23] The Gothic is restorative in installing its thematic and allowing a restoration of traditional order in the end. Most Gothic novels end with a thematic resolution, and this may be called their success. But failure inheres in the very setting of the Gothic, in that which obstructs resolution.[24] The uncanny lasts as long as the transgressions quiver in the narrative: where the relation between letter and spirit, materiality of language and meaning, is destabilized, set in motion, at the level of the narrative itself. Its decorative and excessive nature—its "sharrawaggi"—however, remain inassimilable shards, architectural fragments. The castle's fragments, which remain beyond the parameters of the resolved enigma, are ruins, in Benjamin's sense, not pieces destined to be gathered into a sense, but bits of stranded matter. The persistence of these elements or their predominance I associate with the failure of Gothic revival.

Readers of *The Castle of Otranto* have turned to Walpole's Gothic revival mansion Strawberry Hill as the empirical embodiment of the Castle of Otranto. Strawberry Hill, however, the anomalous conglomeration of imitated Gothic elements plastered anachronistically onto an incongruous frame, is the excess of *The Castle of Otranto*—drawn in by explanation, partly, as a ground or setting, yet inexhaustible, extravagant, non-interpretable, not reducible to the fable of Walpole's novel: also the site at which the letters of the text are spawned, in Walpole's private pressroom, the former stable only later attached to the main part of the house. The Gothic and its revival span the two castles, connecting but not uniting them. The two houses are not related in a causal relationship; rather, they are in a congruent series connected in the way the Gothic elements of Strawberry Hill are connected: gathered together textually, juxtaposed, con-structured, but not subordinated to a single model, not coeval products of a single cause.

§3 Adumbrations of the Gothic

The Castle of Otranto sets up a struggle between the mechanics of its setting—the architecture of the castle—and the restoration of sense that destroys the castle from which it emerges. The narrative resistance to resolution can be allied with the resilience of the letter, while the restorative tendency sets up a unified spirit in the place of its architectural surroundings. I have associated these two tendencies of the struggle between the letter and the spirit with the uncanny and the Gothic, respectively. The Gothic signals the effort to contain the uncanny or, we might say more generally, to contain what cannot be contained. This excess is actually a kind of self-excess that equally belongs to the Gothic, although it points to a logic so destructive of propriety that it can not really be said to "belong" properly to anything. I would like to examine this dynamic interplay a bit further in terms of the traditional dichotomy of the letter and spirit and how it structures the doings and undoings of the Gothic and the uncanny.[1] This dynamic undoing exposes itself architecturally in Edgar Allan Poe's stories "The Fall of the House of Usher" and "The Oval Portrait." A brief glimpse at Jane Austen's *Northanger Abbey* will further suggest the self-excess of reading Gothic.

The Gothic is of course often considered a transgressive genre foregrounding the supernatural and the irrational, dealing with the "dark side" of the mind, prohibited desires, incest, and even crime. The word "uncanny" frequently appears in conjunction with the "terror" and "spectral qualities" of the Gothic. While there are many themes common to the uncanny and the Gothic, the definition of the uncanny that Sigmund Freud borrows from Schelling is a more dynamic one that can be interpreted more broadly. In allowing ingress into what is generally closed off, the Gothic partakes of Freud's definition of the uncanny: "That is uncanny which should have remained a secret or hidden and has come forth."[2] The uncanny indicates the incursion on the present of something that "ought" to be absent: whether the repressed, the forbidden, the indecorous, or the improper. The uncanny destabilizes the structure of identity as presence precisely by insinuating what is absent, invisible, or other.[3]

In a tradition structured by logocentrism, as defined by Derrida primarily in *Of Grammatology*, the fullness of meaning, of the signified, is privileged as presence and interiority; correspondingly voice is privileged as the direct signifier of this signified. Writing, in contrast, is degraded and marginalized as the signifier of the signifier or the exteriority of the voice, and must be held down in this hierarchical relationship. Describing the logocentric structure, Derrida writes:

> In every case, the voice is closest to the signified, whether it is determined strictly as sense (thought or lived) or more loosely as thing. All signifiers, and first and foremost the written signifier, are derivative with regard to what would wed the voice indissolubly to the mind or to the thought of the signified sense, indeed to the thing itself. . . . The written signifier is always technical and representative. It has no constitutive meaning. This derivation is the very origin of the notion of the "signifier." . . . The epoch of the logos thus debases writing considered as mediation of mediation and as a fall into the exteriority of meaning. (11–13)

According to logocentric "propriety," the letter *is merely adjunct and not productive*. Letters should be a merely external vehicle to the interiority of meaning understood as spirit. This logic itself produces the "mere exteriority" of writing, which thus takes on an autonomy that cannot be controlled by the interiority of the logos. The very effort to secure the interior creates an external threat to it. The spectacle of the exterior's ability to function autonomously is transgressive; the letter must be killed over and over. If letters are seen to cooperate in the production of sense, they trespass into the region of voice. The participation of letters and signs in the production of sense—a sense always delayed, not yet arrived—is itself taboo, its coming forth uncanny. The uncanniness Freud locates in the random repetition of numbers—the example of the number "62" in the essay on the uncanny (250)—displays precisely this tension. The mere ciphers are random, but as they are joined together in the subject's experience, they seem to take on a meaning, though one that is unrevealed. This hovering of the letter between bare exteriority and potential meaning is an important linguistic way to understand the action of the uncanny. Poe's "Man of the Crowd" could be understood in a similar vein. The man is himself a moving element that the narrator recasts as a sign; his repeated movements suggest some kind of hidden meaning. Yet the only meaning revealed is that there is no meaning; the man of the crowd is precisely the man with no interior, the man who *never goes home*—therefore is literally *unheimlich* or unhomely. The story privileges the walking body, the signifying process, over any interior or meaning which might characterize it as a whole or replace it as an end. In walking, the excesses of time and space, the materiality of writing, and the process of signification have priority over any signified sense, any subjective interior, or any invisible cause or ground.[4]

The vocabulary of the spirit and the letter that helps describe the "proper" ordering of inside and outside derives from biblical references to circumcision. In Deuteronomy 10:16, the Israelites are commanded: "Circumcise, then, the foreskin of your heart." This mark spans the distance from exterior to interior, from penis to heart; the literal incision is immediately connected to its internalized sense as a feature of the heart. In this model the external mark is a reliable sign, an index, of a corresponding interior. The outside guarantees the inside; the inside follows the outside. But this same distance—the spacing of writing itself—opens the possibility of a deviation between mark and sense, between letter and meaning. The disparity between sign and meaning becomes an issue in the New Testament. The writing on the heart is invisible, internal, and thus does *not* originate in the external mark. Paul points to the disparity between possessing the external mark of circumcision and the actual behavior according to the law: "When Gentiles, who do not possess the law, do instinctively what the law requires, these, though not having the law, are a law to themselves. They show that what the law requires is written on their hearts, to which their own conscience also bears witness" (Romans 2:14). With the privileging of the meaning of the law over its mark, the true sense is understood as something internal and metaphorical. This interior region is set apart from the external and in fact can cause it to negate itself: "Circumcision indeed is of value if you obey the law; but if you break the law, your circumcision has become uncircumcision. . . . For a person is not a Jew who is one outwardly, nor is true circumcision something external and physical. Rather, a person is a Jew who is one inwardly, and real circumcision is a matter of the heart—it is spiritual and not literal" (Romans 2:25–29). Finally, the spirit, aligned with interiority, truth, and metaphor, is on the side of life contrasted with the deadly nature of the materiality of writing: "you show that you are a letter of Christ . . . written not with ink but with the Spirit of the living God, not on tablets of stone, but on tablets of human hearts. Such is the confidence that we have through Christ toward God . . . who has made us competent to be ministers of a new covenant, not of letter but of spirit; for the letter kills, but the Spirit gives life" (2 Corinthians 3–4).

The letter/spirit dichotomy first creates the distinction between and then organizes the relationship between a series of pairs: writing and meaning, death and life, exterior and interior, literal and figurative or metaphoric, past and present (that is, Old and New Testament). Paul establishes the exteriority of writing as an institution: a conventional repetitive form not connected to any living interiority or truth. The very distinction thus recreates the anxiety it is meant to control and prescribes the impropriety it is meant to marginalize. The action of the letter and any contribution it makes towards meaning tends towards a reversal of the letter/spirit model. The autonomous activity of writing, or the process of signification embedded in material inscriptions, *ought to remain hidden*, that is, repressed; it ought not to show itself as part of the process of meaning, but should remain marginal as a mere vehicle or medium. Its coming forth, or the undoing or overturning of the letter/spirit hierarchy, brings about the impropriety of the uncanny: the transgression of the boundary between inside and outside, spirit and letter, meaning and writing.[5]

The commingling of letter and spirit takes the shape not simply of ghosts and haunted palaces and the falling of reason. It is also a problem of signification. This is why the stammerings of the servants in *The Castle of Otranto* are so important and why these scenes of comic relief are so closely associated with key points of tension in the narrative. The fluttering of letters—the tendency of disparate body parts to move together, the quivering of plumes—indicate points where the distracted and spaced out elements of writing come together to give shape to an allegorical "sense" of the story—where letters converge to order themselves in relation to spirit. While I would characterize the manner of signification as uncanny, its result is finally Gothic in that it translates from letter into spirit and restores the proper hierarchy between them, just as it restores the order in succession to the (now demolished) castle. Oddly there is little mention of the fact that the restored rulers now have no castle to live in at all except for the castle in the sky: a supersensible or spiritual castle.

It is in this point, too, that *The Castle of Otranto* differs from Strawberry Hill. For the series of elements in *The Castle* are finally replaced by a synchronous mythos or resolution. The combined elements of Strawberry Hill, however, do not form a classically ordered whole, but rather maintain a disordered, higgledy-piggledy structure duplicated by the random nature of Walpole's collections; Walpole's house is not a museum, but a curiosity cabinet. He himself calls it "a little plaything-house that I got out of Mrs. Chenevix's shop [a toy shop], and is the prettiest bauble you ever saw," a "confection, a non-serious trifle, a set of decorations, criss-crossing series of historical designs, all imprints and imprinted with the gloomth of abbeys and cathedrals" (*Description*, 10). The empirical house is a remnant that cannot be recruited as an explanatory ground for the novel.

Poe's tale "The Fall of the House of Usher" helps bring out the problem of Gothic emerging in Walpole's novel. The story can be read as an allegory of the Gothic. In this story the image of the house and its décor certainly provide direct reference to the Gothic tradition: the "time-honored Usher race," the pointed Gothic windows, the "sombre tapestries of the walls, the ebon blackness of the floors, and the phantasmagoric armorial trophies which rattled," the "vaulted and fretted ceiling" (233–34). Were the strange effects of the tale limited to these "trappings," the tale could remain safely within the realm of the Gothic. Its linguistics operations, however, which empower the signifier and allow it to topple any recuperation by sense, draw it into the realm of the uncanny. While the house itself gives way in the end, it destroys and does not restore; the lineage comes to an end and literally merges with the house as its sinks into the tarn in a gaseous haze.

The tale shares with *Otranto* the reversal of letter and spirit; it fully displays the grounding of the mind in its material setting. This is most obviously manifested in the thematization of the house's ability to affect the mind, first imagined by the narrator, then firmly believed by Roderick, the master of the house. This belief—in the animation of matter or, we might say, in prosopopeia—is itself a mad extravagance, a delirium: "in his disordered fancy," the narrator writes of Roderick,

> the idea had assumed a more daring character, and trespassed, under certain
> conditions, upon the kingdom of inorganization. I lack words to express the

full extent, or the earnest *abandon* of his persuasion. The belief, however, was connected . . . with the gray stones of the home of his forefathers. The conditions of the sentience had been here, he imagined, fulfilled in the method of collocation of these stones—in the order of their arrangement, as well as in that of the many *fungi* which overspread them, and of the decayed trees which stood around—above all, in the long undisturbed endurance of this arrangement, and in its reduplication in the still waters of the tarn. Its evidence—the evidence of the sentience—was to be seen, he said (and here I started as he spoke), in the gradual yet certain condensation of an atmosphere of their own about the waters and the walls. The result was discoverable, he added, in that silent yet importunate and terrible influence which for centuries had moulded the destinies of his family, and which made *him* what I now saw him—what he was. (239)

Madness is measured by the complete congruity of parts, which allows them to combine, transgress their physical boundaries, and impress the viewer or reader. The House of Usher's ability to impress upon its observers parallels the persuasive effect of *The Castle of Otranto* on its vulgar public. The narrator and reader are likewise affected by the repeated impressions of assembled building parts—of both house and text: "I know not how it was,—" the narrator tells us at the beginning of the story, "but, with the first glimpse of the building, a sense of insufferable gloom pervaded my spirit" (231). The heavy use of dashes in this passage enacts the imprinting of the reader by non-signifying graphic elements. The dashes, interruptions, and repetitions operate like the autonomous signifiers of the servants' speech and the dismembered body parts in *The Castle of Otranto*: "I looked upon the scene before me—upon the mere house, and the simple landscape features of the domain—upon the bleak walls—upon the vacant eye-like windows—upon a few rank sedges—and upon a few white trunks of decayed trees—with an utter depression of soul which I can compare to no earthly sensation" (231). The letters and the bare architectural elements—the "mere house"—cooperate here to involve the narrator and the reader into the "setting." Like the helmet at the beginning of *Otranto*, the experience of the house is "a mystery all insoluble," but in contrast to *Otranto*, no further examination will solve it. Like the stuttering fragments of speech and the particulars of architecture in the castle, the house is set up to present both an image of a possible totality—a resolution to the mystery—*and* the irrecoverable material excess, the rubble and debris, of narrative that leads nowhere: of the slamming door. Despite its "excessive antiquity," the house seems to be a tenable whole, held together by the

> minute fungi . . . . No portion of the masonry had fallen; and there appeared to be a wild inconsistency between its still perfect adaptation of parts, and the crumbling condition of the individual stones. In this there was much that reminded me of the specious totality of old wood-work which has rotted for long years in some neglected vault, with no disturbance from the breath of the external air. Beyond this indication of extensive decay, however, the fabric gave little token of instability. Perhaps the eye of a scrutinizing observer might have discovered a barely perceptible fissure, which, extending from the roof of the building in front, made its way down the wall in a zigzag direction, until it became lost in the sullen waters of the tarn. (233)

The house holds the possibility of both totalization and fragmentation; it is both the means and the obstacle to transcendence. The doubling and ambivalence of the uncanny here adheres to the extension of narrative rather than to its synchronous resolution.

The conclusion of "The Fall of the House of Usher" likewise has a double structure. The theme of premature burial—the absorption of the living by the dead, of the sense by the signifier—accompanies a kind of allegory of reading acting out the capacity of writing to *bring about* the effect it describes, just as the protracted use of dashes and repeated words makes the reader halt and stumble along with the narrator. A wild storm rages outside; to calm the ailing Usher the narrator begins to read out loud from a romance called "The Mad Tryst." This text, with its allusions to chivalry, could itself be considered a Gothic novel, which was typically called "romance" until Montague Summers's work on the Gothic in 1923. As passages are read aloud, the narrator hears corresponding sounds:

> At the termination of this sentence I started and, for a moment, paused; for it appeared to me (although I at once concluded that my excited fancy had deceived me)—it appeared to me that, from some very remote portion of the mansion, there came, indistinctly to my ears, what might have been, in its exact similarity of character, the echo (but a stifled and dull one certainly) of the very cracking and ripping sound which Sir Launcelot had so particularly described. (243)

At the next instance the sound the narrator hears answers precisely to the image preexisting in his mind; his reading is exteriorized: what he hears is "the exact counterpart of what my fancy had already conjured up for the dragon's unnatural shriek as described by the romancer" (244). Finally Usher describes the premature burial and prophesies:

> *"I tell you that she now stands without the door!"* As if in the superhuman energy of his utterance there had been found the potency of a spell, the huge antique panels to which the speaker pointed threw slowly back, upon the instant, their ponderous and ebony jaws. It was the work of the rushing gust— but then without those doors there *did* stand the lofty and enshrouded figure of the lady Madeline of Usher. (245)

The doubling between text and reality, the mirroring between one narrative level and another, creates an uncanny effect that exceeds the repetitions of the romance being read—of the Gothic novel itself. Gothic is exceeded by its own uncanny dynamic when language becomes a spell, spelled out in letters independent of referents.[6]

The doubling of the narrative levels does and does not duplicate the doubling between house and mind, setting and atmosphere. A fissure is opened between Gothic machinery and uncanny workings. Tectonic shifting rips open the image of a House of Fiction, of a firm foundation, of a grounded structure, of a container that holds and mirrors its interior. Poe's story presents architecture not as a foundation for housing, but as the withdrawing of foundation. The independence of architecture violates the rules of representation and of narrative security; we can read this in Roderick's poem, "The Haunted Palace," in which the building is the "setting" not for the security of a subject that it would contain, but for the "tottering" of reason: "And travellers now within that valley, / Through the red-litten windows see / Vast forms that move fantastically / To a discordant melody; / While, like a rapid ghastly river, / Through the pale door; / A hideous throng rush out forever, / And laugh—but smile no more" (239). Thoughts rush out like the throng, never to be recollected or put to use. Roderick's painting is perhaps the most poignant instance of the anarchitectural of architecture, what the narrator calls "the naked idea":

> One of the phantasmagoric conceptions of my friend, partaking not so rigidly of the spirit of abstraction, may be shadowed forth, although feebly, in words. A small picture presented the interior of an immensely long and rectangular vault or tunnel, with low walks, smooth, white, and without interruption of device. Certain accessory points of the design served well to convey the idea that this excavation lay at an exceeding depth below the surface of the earth. No outlet was observed in any portion of its vast extent, and no

torch or other artificial source of light was discernible; yet a flood of intense rays rolled throughout, and bathed the whole in a ghastly and inappropriate splendor. (237)

This vault is cockeyed, for it shows an interior with no exterior, a light with no source, a room with no foundation. "Gothic is merely architecture," Walpole writes; yet what could be further from his Strawberry Hill than this surreal non-space, the premature burial, the last confusion between life and death. Poe's Gothic revival re-kills.

The painting, or the vault—"the naked idea"—is a re-presentation, but not *of anything*. The narrator describes:

> From the paintings over which his elaborate fancy brooded, and which grew, touch by touch, into vaguenesses at which I shuddered the more thrillingly, because I shuddered not knowing why—from these paintings . . . I would in vain endeavor to educe more than a small portion which should lie within the compass of merely written words. (236–37)

The painting is uncanny because it shows forth the presence of representation—not of what is represented. It thus foregrounds the activity of matter that affects—through shuddering—rather than a communicable meaning that could be paraphrased in words. The same quality is exhibited in "The Oval Portrait." The feverish narrator feels himself "suddenly and vehemently moved" by a portrait of a young girl in a corner of his chamber. The existence of the frame and the vignetting convince him that his awe is not due to the belief that the image is actually alive. "At length, satisfied with the true secret of its effect, I fell back within the bed. I had found the spell of the picture in an absolute lifelikeliness of expression, which, at first startling, finally confounded, subdued, and appalled me" (291). The spectacle of verisimilitude, or the presence of representation itself, not of what is represented, causes an uncanny confusion between presence and absence, or life and death, here called "lifelikeliness." The narrative about the portrait describes its vampiric history: how the young bride wanes away in the turret while her painter husband, as it were, draws the blood from the bride to the canvas: "And he would not see that the tints which he spread upon the canvas were drawn from the cheeks of her who sat beside him." At the moment of completing the painting the painter cries: "'This is indeed *Life* itself!' turned suddenly to regard his beloved:—*She was dead!*" (292). The figure or imitation of *Life* comes into being as its ground in reality disappears. The portrait, like Roderick's painting of the vault, tells the story of the ungrounding of representation. The display of representation's presence is itself the spectrality of representation associated with the uncanny.

The confusion of representation and what is represented is dramatized in this story as the confusion between life and death, image and original. This confounding is signaled in the problem of the boundary between foregrounded image and background or setting. The narrator describes the painting: "The arms, the bosom, and even the ends of the radiant hair melted imperceptibly into the vague yet deep shadow which formed the background of the whole" (291). This description raises one of the main questions of Gothic: the relation between its architectural setting and the story that takes place in its shadow. The presence of the architectural causes a confusion between the animate and the inanimate, the real and the fictional. Poe's "The Oval Portrait" in fact begins: "The château into which my valet had ventured to make forcible entrance . . . was one of those piles of commingled gloom and grandeur which have so long frowned among the Apennines, not less in fact than in the fancy of Mrs. Radcliffe" (290).

Literary convention and animated figure are commingled yet not synthesized here. The setting, in affecting the characters, takes on the human trait of "frowning," while its operation is clearly marked as a literary "device" or piece of machinery. The setting is set up to exceed itself, to create an atmosphere and impress both characters and readers:

> We established ourselves in one of the smallest and least sumptuously furnished apartments. It lay in a remote turret of the building. Its decorations were rich, yet tattered and antique. Its walls were hung with tapestry and bedecked with manifold and multiform armorial trophies, together with an unusually great number of very spirited modern paintings in frames of rich golden arabesque. In these paintings, which depended from the walls not only in their main surfaces, but in the very many nooks which the bizarre architecture of the château rendered necessary—in these paintings my incipient delirium, perhaps, had caused me to take deep interest. (290)

The paintings are both set on and set off from the walls, depending on them both literally and figuratively. As modern, they are differentiated and brought to life as the present-day, in contrast to the ancient surroundings, yet the striking "lifelikeliness" comes to light only in the context of the "bizarre architecture" and the strange spaces it creates for them. The architectural setting is itself unsettled, becomes atmosphere, affects the narrator and reader, and insinuates itself into the very portrait. Both reading and painting take place in a remote turret.

As in "The Fall of the House of Usher," the workings of the Gothic machinery bring about an excess, an event that exceeds the handed-down conventions of Gothic setting. The narrator goes through a similar process of absorption and differentiation as the narrator in "Usher" who, like this one, survives the demise he describes. The narrator's view alternates between setting and text: "Long, long I read—and devoutly, devoutly I gazed." Similarly he tears his view away from what he sees in order to verify it, to gain narrative distance that separates him from the setting:

> I glanced at the painting hurriedly, and then closed my eyes. Why I did this was not at first apparent even to my own perception. But while my lids remained thus shut, I ran over in mind my reason for so shutting them. It was an impulsive movement to gain time for thought—to make sure that my vision had not deceived me—to calm and subdue my fancy for a more sober and more certain gaze. (290–91)

The mind attempts to tear itself away from the "letter," the literality of the image on the wall; but the interruption only reinforces the original perception. Likewise, the text the narrator reads does not provide enlightenment about the "lifelikeliness" of the portrait but instead reintroduces the Gothic theme of transference between life and death, of the tyrant husband torturing an innocent young wife locked up in a turret. The doubling between the setting—the viewing of the portrait—and the Gothic scenario of the story read is the one feature that exceeds the Gothic, just as reading in "The Fall of the House of Usher" splits apart the unity of affect of the Gothic mansion.

Jane Austen's *Northanger Abbey* presents another case of Gothic exceeding itself through reading, but in this novel the result is parodic rather than uncanny. The building itself demonstrates a mixture of styles that parallels the temporality of the Gothic past and its revival through reading in the present:

> With the walls of the kitchen ended all the antiquity of the Abbey; the fourth side of the quadrangle having, on account of its decaying state, been removed by the General's father, and the present erected in its place. All that was vener-

able ceased here. The new building was not only new, but declared itself to be so; intended only for offices, and enclosed behind by stable-yards, no uniformity of architecture had been thought necessary. (196)

Similarly, Catherine, the "heroine," is lodged in an ancient room fitted up with modern furniture and comforts. An avid reader of Mrs. Radcliffe, and particularly of *The Mysteries of Udolpho*, Catherine is prone to read reality through the lens of the Gothic novel. For example, she remarks about a bit of scenery in Bath: "'I never look at it,' said Catherine, 'without thinking of the south of France.' 'You have been abroad then?' said Henry, a little surprised. 'Oh! No, I only mean what I have read about. It always puts me in mind of the country that Emily and her father travelled through, in the 'Mysteries of Udolpho'" (110). In preparing for their arrival at the abbey, Henry teases Catherine by projecting Radcliffean details onto the building: "He smiled and said, 'You have formed a very favourable idea of the abbey.' 'To be sure I have. Is not it a fine old place, just like what one reads about?' 'And are you prepared to encounter all the horrors that a building such as 'what one reads about' may produce?—Have you a stout heart?—Nerves fit for sliding panels and tapestry?'" (165). Henry proceeds to give an impromptu "reading" of a Gothic novel, projecting Catherine into the position of Gothic heroine. He narrates her introduction into the "gloomy chamber—too lofty and extensive for you, with only the feeble rays of a single lamp to take in its size—its walls hung with tapestry exhibiting figures as large as life, and the bed, of dark green stuff or purple velvet, presenting even a funeral appearance. Will not your heart sink within you?'" he asks (166). Finally, Henry presages that she will come upon first a mysterious chest, and then, through an odd change in perspective, an unexpected black and gold cabinet:

> In repassing through the small vaulted room, however, your eyes will be attracted towards a large, old-fashioned cabinet of ebony and gold, which, though narrowly examining the furniture before, you had passed unnoticed. Impelled by an irresistible presentiment, you will eagerly advance to it, unlock its folding doors, and search into every drawer . . . at last . . . an inner compartment will open—a roll of paper appears:—you seize it—it contains many sheets of manuscript—you hasten with the precious treasure into your own chamber, but scarcely have you been able to decipher "Oh! thou—whomsoever thou mayst be, into whose hand these memoirs of the wretched Matilda may fall"—when your lamp suddenly expires in the socket,

and leaves you in total darkness. "Oh! No, no—do not say so. Well, go on." But Henry was too much amused by the interest he had raised, to be able to carry it farther. (168)

This pseudoreading of a Gothic novel is then duplicated when Catherine reaches her room and culminates in the discovery of a curious black and gold japanned cabinet. Catherine repeats the novelistic effort to open the locked drawers, searching the cabinet through and through, and finally comes across the pages she seeks. While the repetition of this coincidence is suggestive, the Gothic effect is deflated when it turns out that the papers are merely laundry bills. Catherine's most egregious projection is her initial belief that General Tilney, Henry's father, has murdered his wife or is keeping her captive in a dungeon. When Henry becomes aware of her ideas, he shakes her out of the repetition of the Gothic into the present, admonishing her: "My dear Miss Morland, consider the dreadful nature of the suspicions you have entertained. What have you been judging from? Remember the country and the age in which we live. Remember that we are English, that we are Christians" (212).

The structure of repetition binding two narrative levels—that of the Gothic novel and that of *Northanger Abbey*—is marked by a difference that renders Austen's novel a parody rather than an example of a Gothic novel. The inclusion and excess of the Gothic is embodied in the Abbey itself, part Gothic and part "modern." The promised repetition that is fulfilled in Poe is left empty in Austen; both repeat and exceed the mechanics of Gothic through the thematization of reading and the events it tries to produce.

§4 Building Affinities:
Goethe's *Wahlverwandtschaften*

Like Walpole's *The Castle of Otranto*, Goethe's *Wahlverwandtschaften*
(*Elective Affinities*) operates through a complex interplay between grounding and ungrounding. Some of the strangeness of the novel has to do with
the installation and reversal of its architectural order. Building projects
and the famous parable of elective affinities (*Gleichnisrede*) seem to lay the
ground for expectations that are ultimately disappointed. The novel concludes with a kind of simulacrum of Gothic revival as Edward ("Eduard"
in the original) and Ottilie are laid to rest in the Gothic chapel. While
this ending is suggestive of the revival of the spirit at the end of *The Castle
of Otranto*, the apparent enclosure of the Gothic vault does not synthesize
the narrative projects and architectural fragmentation extended throughout the novel. The final lurid resurrection scene, reminiscent of Mignon's
funeral in Goethe's *Wilhelm Meisters Lerhjahre*, smacks of Gothic, but
the moment of restoration, usually disregarded in the critical literature,
ironizes resolution. While the architectural and building thematics set up
teleological expectations parallel to the quasi-allegorical structure of the
Gothic novel, *Elective Affinities* destabilizes the Gothic elements that are
its subtle underpinnings.[1]

The novel begins set squarely on Edward's property, the focus of his
and his wife Charlotte's building projects and plans for the future. These
building projects are both material and spiritual: "The plans [*die Anlage*]
for our life," says Edward, "with which we have up to now been so in-
tensely involved are well thought-out; but are we never to add to them,
never to expand upon them? Are my gardening and your landscaping to
be for hermits only?" (96/ *HA* 6:247). Edward's remark suggests that his

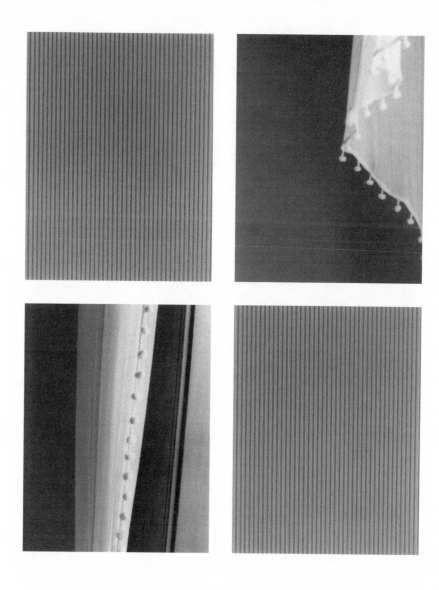

land and their building projects serve as a ground for further development, of life and of the novel. Edward's argument is made in the course of the first struggle of the novel, consisting of the effort to expand the dyad of Edward and Charlotte to the quadrangle including Ottilie and the Captain. One might say that the formation of this quadrangle puts the apparent foundation of the novel into place.

The initial focus on installation (*Anlagen*) invokes the expectation of building and development. The Captain's activities seem to further this expectation and allow the architectural to get fully underway. One of his first projects is the surveying of Edward's property. This survey has a double effect. On the one hand, through graphic representation the property takes on a greater unity that allows it to be more properly appropriated by its owner, Edward: "Soon the whole was covered with water paints, and Edward saw his estate taking shape on paper like a new creation. He felt that he was seeing it now for the first time; and for the first time it really seemed to belong to him" (106/ *HA* 6:261). Secondly, the unifying mapping that ties together the land as ground allows plans to be conceived more uniformly: "This gave occasion for them to discuss the whole area, noting that planting could be undertaken much better when one could see the total picture than when one was obliged to tinker with nature on the basis of random impressions" (106/ *HA* 6:261).

The Captain's unifying interventions reveal that Charlotte's undertakings have been piecemeal and irrational. He describes it: "such people . . . can't imagine what the end effect will be; it works out, they change—change perhaps what should be left alone and leave what should be changed, and in the end it is just a jumble that delights and stimulates but cannot satisfy" (106/ *HA* 6:261). Charlotte's building, it turns out, is not the systematic foundation-laying we first expected; instead, it is a kind of random movement backward and forward addressed at the material results of building, not at the fundamental ground plan, goals, or unified overview. Thus she poses a counter- or regressive force that goes against the movement of architectural progression in the novel.

The addition of Ottilie to the group is also not quite "right." The daughter of a deceased close friend of Charlotte's, Ottilie is a contemporary of Luciane, Charlotte's daughter from a previous marriage. Ottilie is thus a substitute for Charlotte's own daughter, for whom the mother expresses no longing or interest throughout the novel; thus the bond between Edward and Ottilie is suggestive of incest. Charlotte has long desired to bring Ottilie into the household as someone whom she could *heraufbilden*, build up, into a beautiful creature, yet she has held back this wish as it did not fit into the original plan. Charlotte is equally resistant to bringing in the Captain, fearing that the original situation would be ruined by the addition of foreign elements: "'Then let me confess to you honestly,'" she tells Edward, "'that this plan is at odds with my intuition. I have an inner feeling that doesn't augur well'" (97/*HA* 6:247–48). Rather than an architecturally controlled expansion from the pair to the quadrangle, there occurs instead the famous chiasmus and re-pairing.

The installation of the quadrangle "builds" the company and gives rise to various building projects: the survey, the construction of the pavilion, and the dams built to unify the lakes, as well as the building up of Ottilie's character and social persona. Charlotte and Edward, however, exert opposing forces on the structure of the quad. Charlotte aims always at renunciation and restriction in order to keep the angles properly straight and the company properly upright. She is willing to forsake Ottilie for the sake of the original plan: "'But seeing that it does not fit into our plans and since one should not push and pull at one's life so much, constantly bringing something new into it'" (99–100/*HA* 6:251). Charlotte likes to hold the straight course. She is talked out of her previous piecemeal landscaping through a reading plan designed by Edward and the Captain. The following passage illustrates the orderly progression from ground plan to construct; it also shows the progression from the model of construction to a particular instance of it. The passage is interesting in light of Goethe's reflections on the Cologne Cathedral; we recall that he mastered and ultimately approved of it through the orderly perusal of engravings indicating the various levels of plan and construction. Edward and the Captain agree to sway Charlotte's mind about the landscaping plans by showing her a set of engravings:

> The books were consulted accordingly. They showed in each instance a map of the area and a view of the landscape in its natural state, then on separate flaps the change artfully made to utilize and enhance its original good properties. From this the transition to their own estate, their own surroundings, and what could be made of them, was an easy one. (124–25/*HA* 6:288)

Charlotte's logic enacts a kind of pseudogrounding. As in this passage we see it move strongly from one image to another. Yet the grounding is only relative, moving between representations and finally from image to ground—Edward's ground—rather than vice versa. She exhibits the straight way from point to point but does not question the original ground on which the series is constructed.

While Charlotte gradually comes away from her original ideas about the park, they decide to build a new *Lustgebäude*, pleasure pavilion, well placed in relation to the *Schloß* and with respect to the view of the park and land. As the Captain points out, the new plan exhibits an economy; the stones that will be removed to form the path to the new house will equal precisely what is needed to build the wall along the stream that he has had in mind. Charlotte takes over control of the bank, dividing up the work into weeks and months to correspond to the available funds. Even in the worst of times, after Edward leaves, Charlotte is enlivened by the pleasure of building. This comes out when the new house is finished and Charlotte becomes involved in the interior decoration: again a building and making that presupposes and does not directly confront its structural ground. We hear about the new house:

> How wonderful it would be to stay here, and what a sudden urge to build and create welled up in Charlotte again now that all the rough work had been finished! All they needed was a cabinet maker, a paperer, a painter who knew how to use stencils and do delicate gilding, and the house would be fixed up in short order. . . .
> So the women and the baby lived up on the hill, and from this location, as if from a new focus, unexpected walks opened up for them. (221/ *HA* 6:428–29)

Charlotte tends to duplicate the centered structure even as it is disseminated by multiplication.

Charlotte exhibits a kind of tightening and restriction that grates against Edward's impulsiveness and tendency towards extravagance. Just as he first drove the wedge that split open the marital dyad, his plans become excessive and his behavior tends to exceed "measure."[2] He is impulsive, impatient, irritable, energetic. He moves centrifugally. Even while reading, his irritation is incited when Charlotte looks over his shoulder at the text: "His old impatience flared up, and he reprimanded her in a rather unfriendly tone. . . . 'When someone reads over my shoulder I always feel as if I were split in two'" (112/ *HA* 6:269). Splitting in two, Edward tends to move outward and multiply, while Charlotte seeks to draw forces inward and solidify. Edward's irritation takes place at the convergence between the diegetic frames of the main narrative and the text he is reading aloud. His reading is distracted by the attention drawn to the difference between the printed text and the spoken reading. It disrupts his illusion of speaking the signified directly, of a unity between signifier and signified, by pointing to the presence of writing, of the signifier per se. The "two pieces" into which Edward is torn are two strings of signifiers and disrupt his sense of himself as an interior.

Edward and Charlotte articulate different rhythms: "Charlotte, whose tact distinguished itself in circles large and small by her ability to cover for any disagreeable, violent or even just too boisterous remark, interrupt a conversation dragging on too long or stimulate a flagging one" (112/*HA* 6:269–70). While Edward lashes out impetuously, Charlotte can bring conversation to a standstill. Edward's disorderly eccentricity and Charlotte's regulative styles are contrasted in their duet playing: "for while Charlotte, with deliberate skill, was able to slow down at one spot and speed up at another to keep pace with her husband's erratic playing, Ottilie . . . seemed to have learned it in the same manner as Edward was accustomed to play" (131/*HA* 6:297). Similarly, Edward is contented later to have only Ottilie read over his shoulder, feeling as he does that they are but a single reader. When he later allows Ottilie to look over his shoulder with pleasure, it is because they fuse into one interior and support the sense of a signified self: "Then they were not two people, but one person" (254/*HA* 6:478). Even when Charlotte brings her rhythm into sync with Edward, their difference is maintained: Edward out of step, Charlotte regulatory and conservative. In another disruption, Edward impetuously draws a square to mark the spot of the new pavilion on the Captain's map. "The Captain was taken aback; he didn't like to have his careful, cleanly drawn map disfigured in this way" (129/*HA* 6:295). While the proposed placement of the pavilion is rationalized and accepted, this intrusion on the orderly map is a kind of violent interference that bothers the Captain.

As Edward falls in love with Ottilie, he becomes progressively unmeasured; to the same extent Charlotte strives to draw the pair back into their earlier coordinates. He becomes unhinged: "Edward for his part was in a very different state. . . . The warm night tempted him out of doors; he roamed about, the most restless and yet the happiest of mortals. He walked through the gardens; they were too confined for him; he hastened out into the fields, and they were too free" (151/*HA* 6:327). While drawn outward, he experiences spatial disorientation and a general "unfitness," a lack of harmony with his surroundings. This dislodges his very sense of identity:

> In Edward's thoughts, in Edward's actions there is no longer any moderation. The knowledge of loving and being loved urges him on to infinite extravagance. How changed is the aspect of every room, everything around him! He no longer knows his own house . . . all that was repressed in him bursts forth and his whole being streams toward Ottilie. (152/*HA* 6:328, translation modified)

Although he is technically the master of the property and the builder of the new pavilion, his inability to remain centered—to stick within the parameters of architectural work—splits and estranges his identity. The landed property does not mirror him back to himself as its rightful owner and head. Instead his energy is flung outward, splitting off into new entities and projects that eventually lead him fully away from the property into the open field of battle after joining the army.

Charlotte continues to work for restoration. She and the Captain discuss the situation, and she resolves to remove both the Captain and Ottilie in hopes of retrieving the relative peacefulness of the beginning of the novel. But the narrative ironizes Charlotte's apparently rational clinging to architectural order: "She worked this out so cleverly in her thoughts that it only confirmed her delusion that they could go back to their earlier, more restricted way of life, and that explosive passions could once more be brought under control" (153/*HA* 6:329).

Behind Charlotte's apparently architectural will, there lies a hidden or denied disorder and ungrounding. Before becoming engaged to Edward, Charlotte had in fact figured Ottilie as a possible match for him; Edward remembers that this could be the original situation that ought to be restored. As we saw, Charlotte's landscaping projects, though they appear to install order, actually proceed piecemeal and are based on no overall plan. Her redesigning of the churchyard, too, seems to install the security of the quadrangle as she moves the headstones to the wall outlining the graveyard. At the same time she dislodges the relation between sign and body that many consider crucial to the commemorative function of the graveyard.

In the same way, the famous parable of the novel's title presents an ungrounded figure that has no beginning. On the one hand, *Walhverwandtschaften*, elective affinities, suggest human relations. Both Edward and the

Captain agree that this is a misunderstanding, that originally or scientifically, the term merely describes relations between inanimate elements and minerals. Yet the "scientific" explanation of the action between elements takes places only through human comparisons. For example, Edward explains: "'In some cases they come together readily like old friends and acquaintances, meeting and uniting, without any change in their own nature'" (114/ *HA* 6:272). The Captain adds: "'In this instance both a separation and a combination have taken place, and it almost seems justified to speak of "elective affinities," since it actually appears as if the substances choose one combination in preference to the other'" (115/ *HA* 6:274). Finally the chemical meaning of *Wahlverwandtschaften*, based on human attributes, is carried over to describe human relationships. Though mediated through letters indicating a mathematical formula, likeness describes likeness, and we find no satisfying original here except the lack of an original reference for *Wahlverwandtschaften*. In the effort to ground the term in the solid materials of geology, the text erodes the figure's ground.[3]

At the same time, because of the resonance with the title, this episode invokes the expectation that it will be a key or keystone to the overall understanding of the novel, that somehow it will unravel and reveal the meaning of the text. Yet its primary function is to show the fictional status of any such keystone or ground: the "as if" of simile or comparison. Like Charlotte's planning, the figure of the *Wahlverwandtschaften* renders a semblance of architectural order, one that hides its lack of a solid ground. And Charlotte has her finger on this too in the discussion of elective affinities: "'We women are not so particular,' Charlotte said, 'and to be honest, I really just want to understand the meaning of the word: for nothing makes one look more foolish in company than using an unusual or technical expression wrongly'" (113/ *HA* 6:270–71). Linguistic correctness, then, is fundamentally ungrounded, though it operates in terms of an artificially initiated "propriety" or uprightness.

In the end, the parable of elective affinities leaves us uncertain about whether there is freedom of choice or whether the alterations of preference follow natural necessity. Every ground ungrounds itself by splitting into at least two grounds, just as Edward's castle is split and doubled with the construction of the pavilion. This splitting/doubling is part of the movement that dissolves the home or house as solid ground and container for its owner. The grounding effect of the *Wahlverwandtschaften* scene is duplicated in the episode of the laying of the foundation stone at the second house. The laying of the foundation lays bare the split between master and executor, architect and mason, design and building. The mason who leads the ceremony points to three important factors in the construction of a building: that it be well situated, the job of the master or proprietor (Edward); that it be well built, the function of the many laborers; and that it be well grounded. This last is his own job: "'But the second thing, the foundation, is the mason's task and—let us state this boldly—the chief business of the whole undertaking. It is a serious matter, and our invitation to you is a serious one. . . . Here in this narrow, hollowed-out space you do us the honor of appearing as witnesses to our secret task'" (133/ *HA* 6:300).

The foundation stone installs and squares the building. It duplicates and replaces the holistic conception of the designer and puts it into place: "'We could easily just lower this stone, whose corner marks the right-hand corner of the building, whose rectangular form represents, in miniature, the building's rectangular shape, and whose horizontal and vertical planes stand for the true level of all its walls'" (133/*HA* 6:300). Thus it is the *Grundstein* (foundation stone), and not the architect, that makes the house a house.[4] The *geheimnisvolles Geschäft*, the secretive work, installs the *Heim* (home) by concealing its key or basis. The *Grundstein*, which provides a unified map of the whole structure, sunders the empirical from the ideational; this is perhaps its most covert activity. It installs the ontic that then stands upright on its own. The difference between the original design plan and the laying of the stone wedges a schism into the unifying function of grounding. In grounding there are at least two grounds. This is the *Geheimnis*, or secret, of the foundational activity: the capacity of the home to become foreign, the occlusion of its foundation, the possibility of its future vacancy.

The concealing of the *Grundstein* presents grounding as ungrounding, just as it foresees its own future demise. The foundation stone is made into a memorial into which the gathered public puts various items to commemorate the singularity of the present moment. The journeyman explains:

> We are laying this stone for all time, to ensure that the present and future owners will have the longest possible enjoyment of this house. But insofar as we are also burying a treasure, as it were, we reflect, during this most fundamental of tasks, on the transience of all things human; we contemplate the

possibility that this firmly sealed cover may be opened again, which could
not happen unless everything else that we have not yet even finished building
were to be destroyed. (134/ *HA* 6:302)

The building is its own future ruins, the ground its own future ungrounding. Because of the ambivalent status of the *Grundstein*, this scene also cannot function as a ground for interpreting the novel as a whole, though it seems to offer itself as an interpretive key.

The *Wahlverwandtschaften* episode and the foundation stone scene provide two grounds, as if two riddles or prophetic enigmas, that both promise and repeal the fulfillment of interpretation. Because they are two, the grounds are undone. We might say that the quadrant of a/b = c/d begins to rotate into the 360 degrees of the thirty-six chapters of the novel, divided into two parts. This action may be connected with what Walter Benjamin calls the *Technik*, or technique, of Goethe's novel. First, it describes an operation of the novel without dissolving it into an interpretation of its meaning and thus it preserves the "open secret" of the novel.[5] Benjamin writes: "Because for the author the representation of the material contents is the enigma whose solution is to be sought in the technique. Thus, through technique, Goethe could assure himself of stressing the mythic powers in his work. . . . The author sought, however, to keep this technique as his artistic secret" (313/ *GS* 1.1:146). A bit earlier in the essay Benjamin associates the mythic element of the novel with housing: "The incorporation of the totality of material things into life is indeed a criterion of the mythic world. Among them, the first has always been the house. Thus, to the extent that the house approaches completion, fate closes in. The laying of the foundation stone, the celebration of the raising of the roof beams, and moving in mark just so many stages of decline" (308/1.1:139). Goethe as mythic creator is also associated with the master builder: "As Olympian, he laid the foundation of the work and with scant words rounded out its dome" (314/1.1:147).[6]

As the square begins to turn, elements are loosened and give rise to independent mimetic series. For example, the Captain is eventually to some degree replaced by the architect, and then to some extent by the assistant from the pension. Edward leaves and is duplicated by the traveling Englishman, who tells Edward's story as if from the other side. Discussions ensue about the resemblance between apes and humans, about the applicability of medieval insignia to a small Gothic chapel, about the nature of collecting. Paintings are imitated in the *tableaux vivants*; Ottilie is imitated in the wall painting of the Gothic church; Ottilie and the Captain are imitated in the baby Otto; the baby's death imitates the quasi death of a local youth during the collapse of the dam early in the novel; Ottilie imitates the Madonna in a later tableau. Initially the novel seems to be constructed around the two scenes of foundation and the quadrangle of characters; yet for little reason, this structure begins to expand seemingly arbitrarily. While a reading may seek to connect various strands of the narrative, largely through similarity, in the end they cannot be woven together into a single pattern or overall interpretation.[7]

As the action of the novel moves away from the building projects in the first half, which promised to promise an eventual fulfillment, various episodes deal with representational phenomena that lead back to a previous image rather than laying a foundation for a new structure. Missing her own pet monkey, Luciane takes delight in a book of pictures of monkeys and especially enjoys finding resemblances between the pictures and people they know. The monkey book and the *tableux vivants* are perhaps the most flagrant instances of this mimetic regression, according to which the inanimate imitates the animate or the human the animal rather than vice versa. Luciane especially embodies the love of aping. The architect's project to renovate the small Gothic church on the grounds, especially a side chapel, connects this mimetic regression to the contemporary interest in Gothic architecture and the problems of Gothic revival. To complete this project the architect borrows some workers from the construction of the pavilion; the side chapel sidetracks the constructive action of the novel's opening.

The architect focuses especially on the restoration of the side chapel, which he keeps secret from the ladies. At the same time, he entertains them with views of his collection of engravings, rubbings, and sketches of old grave monuments, weaponry, and various objects gathered from Nordic grave mounds. These are specifically Germanic things: coins, seals, rings. While drawing on the Gothic energy of these paraphernalia, the architect houses them in the most classical of cabinets:

> He kept everything very neatly in portable drawers and compartments on carved, cloth-covered boards, with the result that these ancient, solemn objects took on a somewhat prettified air, and could be looked at with the same enjoyment as the display cases of a fashion dealer. (179/*HA* 6:367)

The narrative insinuates the superficial world of fashion enforced in the framing devices the architect chooses for these otherwise "ernest" Germanic things; there is almost something ludicrous and certainly suggestive of the kitsch in the reaction this collection brings about:

> All these things turned the friends' thoughts to ancient times, and when he finally illustrated his conversations with the earliest prints, woodcuts and copper engravings, and the church simultaneously moved closer to the past day by day as it was painted and decorated, they almost had to ask themselves if they were really living in modern times, and if it were not a dream that customs, habits, fashions and convictions were now quite different. (179/ *HA* 6:367)

We are now fully on the ground of Gothic revival: the selective extraction and reproduction or display of Gothic images or objects in a modern setting. Revival allows the past and its representations temporarily to take on a life of their own. Likewise, persuasive imitations lend autonomy to the presence of representation itself. The grand success of the *tableux vivants* gives rise to a sense of the uncanny in confusing reality with appearance: "The characters were so well cast, the colors so well chosen, the lighting so artistic that one seemed indeed to be in another world, except that the presence of real figures instead of painted ones created a kind of unsettling sensation" (197/ *HA* 6:393). This could describe the experience of the Gothic chapel just as well; Ottilie's very life, as in "The Oval

Portrait," is transferred to the vaulted ceilings the architect repaints. The successful lighting is described in similar terms:

> From its single high window came solemn, multi-colored light; for the window had been exquisitely put together from panes of stained glass. The whole chapel thus took on an unfamiliar aspect and created a special atmosphere. The beauty of the vault and walls was enhanced by a decorative floor. . . . Ottilie was delighted to see the familiar parts that now appeared as an unfamiliar whole. She stopped, walked back and forth, looked and looked again; finally she sat down on one of the seats, and it seemed to her, as she gazed up and all around, as if she were alive and not alive, conscious and unconscious; as if all this might vanish from her sight and she from herself. (183–84/ *HA* 6:373–74)

Gothic revival foregrounds the reality of the fake. As in Walpole's Strawberry Hill, "genuinely" imitated sets of details are transposed into obviously "false places."

Luciane, who loves to change clothes several times a day, dress up as characters, and march around dramatically to entertain the others, is queen of the mimetic in the novel. She wears masks and disguises herself as a peasant, fisherwoman, or fairy. But Ottilie, too, plays her part when she imitates the mother of God. The semblance reawakens a trite motif:

> When the curtain went up, Charlotte was genuinely surprised. The scene before her had been represented so often that a new impression could hardly be expected. But the reality which had here been turned into a picture had its own charms and delights. . . . There were angels there, too, their own radiance dimmed by the divine light, their ethereal bodies made duller and more opaque by comparison with the divine body in human form. (203–4/ *HA* 6:403)

Through theatrical chiaroscuro, effects of animation are achieved in the Gothic manner, called *frommen Kunstmummerei* (pious mummery) by the narrator. The mumbling stumbling of these words recalls the crinkle crankle barbarism of Gothic. When Ottilie dies she is laid to rest in the Gothic chapel. When the architect goes to view Ottilie's body in the chapel, his own work on the walls comes back to him as if animated by Ottilie's vanished spirit: "The architect entered the chapel. Its walls with their pious decorations appeared to him more ancient and fraught with meaning than he could ever have believed" (260/ *HA* 6:487). Interestingly, the architect experiences the scene as a duplicate of Van Dyck's painting *Belisar*, one of the *tableaux vivants*. The Gothic dome of the chapel becomes his own oval portrait.

Semblance, unsatisfactory as it seems, wins the day at the end of *Die Wahlverwandtschaften*. Things are the same but not the same, like Edward's cup rescued during the laying of the *Grundstein*. Just as the foundation turns out to be no foundation at all, Edward's fateful symbol turns out to be a substitute: "One day, as Edward raised his beloved glass to his lips, he set it down again in horror; it was the same and not the same; he could not see a small mark he knew" (261–62/ *HA* 6:489). His servant explains that the glass was broken and replaced without Edward's knowledge; thus its connection to the foundational scene has been severed and replaced by an arbitrary association grounded only in similitude. Edward, like the glass and like Ottilie before him, is himself and not himself; no longer master of his property nor properly husband of his wife, he admits: "'Oh, how unhappy I am . . . all my achievements have been a falsehood, an imitation!'" (262/ *HA* 6:489). The sense of irreality and the dissolution of identity adhere to the apparent restoration of order at the end of the novel:

> Thus in our friends' daily life everything moved almost in its accustomed way. Ottilie still showed her attentiveness through many a quiet little action, and the others behaved as usual. In this way the domestic circle was like a replica of their previous way of life, and they could be forgiven their delusion that all had remained the same. (254/ *HA* 6:479)

Restoration is madness, superimposing an outward-moving circle on the original quadrangle. The excessive praise of Ottilie's virtues, her saintly qualities, and the glowing scenario around her death give voice to this madness and allow a temporary regression into the Gothic. Unexpectedly, many aspects of the Gothic novel can be identified in *Die Wahlverwandtschaften*: the concern about the discontinuity of the lineage, an unmeasured passion tinged with incest, the predominance of setting and the inclusion of Gothic architectural detail. The Gothic vault and the phantasm of restoration—of resurrection—have the final word of the novel: "So the lovers rest side by side. Peace hovers above their resting place, smiling angels in their likeness look down at them from the vault, and what a charming moment it will be when in time to come the two awake together" (262/ *HA* 6:490). The painted angels come to life as the dead will rise again. The uncanny quiverings of identity throughout the novel—of being and not being, of being and seeming—are forgotten in the closure of this Gothic conclusion. Yet the restoration in the novel is not the fulfillment of a promise or a prophesy nor the real return to a proper lineage; rather, it is almost a parody of the supernatural restoration at the end of *The Castle of Otranto*. One might say that Edward, hell-bent on the excessive and eccentric path that drives him out of his home and renders his life uncanny, in a way repeats and fulfills the prophesy of *Otranto*: *"That the castle and lordship of Otranto should pass from the present family, whenever the real owner should be grown too large to inhabit it"* (51).

The madness of the Gothic explanation is, in part, deflated by the appearance of the Englishman, who steps in as Edward's William Wilson. The English lord, who has no proper name, experiences the landscape primarily through its repetition in his portable camera obscura. In search of the picturesque he gathers snapshots.[8] Most importantly, his lifestyle presents the opposite of that of the master of the castle. In reply to the question of where he most likes to live, the Englishman replies: "'I've become used to being at home everywhere, and in the last analysis I find nothing more convenient than that others should build, garden, and do the domestic work for me'" (222/*HA* 6:431). He has lost interest in his own property primarily because his own son has abandoned it. Like Edward he has moved eccentrically and replaced the comforts of home with the spoils of empire by going off to India. The Englishman articulates the principle of the uncanny that dislodges the intimate mirroring between subject and home, between exterior and interior: "'Even when we are very well off we are only ever half at home. . . . We set up house, only to move out again, and even if we don't intend to, we are forced into it by relationships, passions, accidents, obligations or whatever'" (222–23/*HA* 6:431).

The Englishman spells out the dissonance between the ideal architectural model, thanks to which the house is grounded in the subject and the subject in the house, and the intrusion of the empirical: the accidental, the extraneous, the unforeseeable—in short, all those aspects of finitude that can never be included in the original plan or given a ground in any metaphysical foundation. Ottilie is particularly disturbed by the Englishman's views:

> Ottilie . . . was thrown into a most terrible state by these confidences. A delicate veil tore rudely before her eyes, and it seemed to her as if everything that had been done for the house and the estate, the gardens, the park and

the whole surrounding landscape had actually been done in vain, since he who owned it all could not enjoy it, and was, like their present guest, forced by his nearest and dearest to roam the world in the most dangerous way. (223/ *HA* 6:432)

The Englishman articulates the homelessness of identity echoing mildly in the Anglo-German affinities of the Gothic revival.

§5 Housing Freud

> "Philosophy," says Hegel, "is utterly useless and fruitless, and for this very reason, is the sublimest of all pursuits, the most deserving of our attention, and the most worthy of our zeal"—a somewhat Coleridgey assertion, with a rivulet of deep meaning in a meadow of words.
> It would be wasting time to disentangle the paradox. . . . There is reason, it is said, in the roasting of eggs, and there is philosophy even in furniture.
>
> Edgar Allan Poe, "The Philosophy of Furniture"

The philosophy of furniture combines two terms that are not commonly considered together. Poe's juxtapositioning of Hegel and interior decoration is humorous and jarring in setting up a communication between the terms of the essential and the accidental, the true and the relative, the logical and the decorative. The movement of scholarly research through archival spaces raises a question about the distinction between the necessary and the contingent, the scientific and the random. The opening of the Sigmund Freud Museum in his apartment in Vienna in 1971 and the Freud Museum in London in 1986 have inspired interest in the interplay between the setting and theory of Freud's psychoanalysis. Freud's installation, from the couch to the collections, has been studied and scrutinized by both experts and tourists. Again and again the founding and foundation of psychoanalysis are situated in Freud's furnishings in a way that both assumes and reinforces the homology between self and house. At the same time efforts to contain insight in the four walls of the analytic chamber constantly run up against limits and obstructions that undo the security of the home and the interiorization of understanding.

H.D.'s Tribute to Freud's House

Tribute to Freud by American poet H.D. (Hilda Doolittle) is one of the few texts that discusses the physical setting of Freud's apartment in Vienna as part of an understanding of the analytic experience.[1] *Tribute to Freud* is a generic hybrid. The text is a commentary on H.D.'s analytic sessions with Freud, which took place during 1933–34. The text darts in

and out of the narrating present—recounting from a distance the analytic text, dipping into the space of Berggasse and the Regina Hotel—just as the narrated analytic sessions delve in and out of dreams, recollections from childhood, and ancient cultural memories, images, and inscriptions. By its own account, *Tribute* is neither a factual or scientific exposition of psychoanalysis nor, strictly speaking, an autobiography. Instead it distills a certain experience set to words meant to tell us something not just about this woman herself but about the psyche and about poetry. H.D. writes, describing her sessions: "We travel far in thought, in imagination or in the realm of memory. Events happened as they happened, not all of them, of course, but here and there a memory or a fragment of a dream-picture is actual, is real, is like a work of art or is a work of art" (35). Analysis repeats, re-presents, or allows events to take place as themselves; there is no hierarchy of original and copy, real and imaginary. The leveling of representation that allows these events to happen is called a work of art, or is like a work of art. Memory and experience are preserved and communicated in their multifaceted texture, not homogenized or reduced to a simple narrative. The scission is duplicated in the dual structure of the text. The first part, "Writing on the Wall," was composed from memory; the second, "Advent," was composed directly from H.D.'s notes taken during the time of her sessions in Vienna. These had been left in Switzerland and were only recovered later. This addition adds an aleatory element to the text's composition, unsettling very slightly the edited paragraphs and ever-accumulating imagery of the first part of the text. Indeed, the writing itself is an effort to hold on to something that could be lost: "I tried to outline several experiences I had had on my first trip to Greece. I have tried to write of these experiences. In fact, it is the fear of losing them, forgetting them, or just giving them up as neurotic fantasies, residue of the war, confinement and the epidemic, that drives me on to begin again and again a fresh outline. . . . It is obviously Penelope's web that I am weaving" (153).

Despite the way in which H.D.'s text sets itself up as a feminine "other," a discourse of the student rather than the master, the frame of the web holds fast what it relates. The fall into the unconscious, the loss of self in the other, the dissemination of self in the infinity of a fragmented and unrecollected history, is held in check by the text's poetic density. Gradually images and memories are made sense of—not absolutely, with no remnant, but still, given a certain understanding, a certain interpretation. A potentially chaotic experience of self-loss and disarticulation is drawn into a kind of quadrilateral—the frame of Penelope's weaving, the frame of the room. The text in fact begins with a precise description of a room and a precise location and time: "It was Vienna 1933–34. I had a room in the Hotel Regina. . . . I went down Berggasse, turned in the familiar entrance; Berggasse 19, Wien IX, it was. There were wide stone steps and a balustrade. Sometimes I met someone else coming down" (3).

H.D.'s text is structured by an interesting ambivalence. On the one hand it reaches outward to describe and include the nonsystematic and material details of her analytic experience—features and details not prescribed by any psychoanalytic understanding, nagging at the body, recalling the limit to the logos: "The stone staircase was curved" (3). Her text has a kind of expansiveness that touches on the coming of fascism, her childhood, Ezra Pound and D. H. Lawrence, the myth of Moses, the symbol of the serpent and thistle, hallucinations, and Freud's maid Paula. While this expansiveness lends richness to both the text and the cultural context it presents, the limitless associativeness of the atmosphere becomes threatening; in fact, it is suggestive of the historical situation: "I did not specifically realize just what it was I wanted," H.D. writes, "but I knew that I, like most of the people I knew, in England, America and on the Continent of Europe, was drifting. We were drifting. Where: I did not know but at least I accepted the fact that we were drifting" (13).

Freud's house seemed to promise some kind of shelter, a quadrilateral utopia in which time and space are suspended:

> Length, breadth, thickness, the shape, the scent, the feel of things. The actuality of the present, its bearing on the past, their bearing on the future. Past, present, future, these three—but there is another time-element, popularly called the fourth dimensional. The room has four sides. There are four seasons to a year. This fourth dimension, though it appears variously disguised and under different subtitles, described and elaborately tabulated in the Professor's volumes—and still more elaborately detailed in the compilations of his followers, disciples, and pseudo-disciples and imitators—is yet very simple. It is as simple and inevitable in the building of time-sequence as the fourth wall to a room. If we alter our source around this very room where I have been talking with the Professor, and start with the wall to my left, against which the couch is placed, and go counter-clockwise, we may number the Professor's wall with the exit door 2, the wall with the entrance door (the case of pottery

images and flat Greek bowls) 3, and the wall opposite the couch 4. This wall actually is largely unwalled, as the space there is left vacant by the wide-open double doors. (23)

Despite the recollection of hallucinations in Corfu (the "writing on the wall"), decipherable to the point of inverted S's understood as question marks, and intimations of catastrophe, H.D.'s text is architecturally controlled, its dimensions in place despite the "unwalled wall" gaping in front of her—the swastikas on the pavement that she cannot bring herself to mention to Freud. Likewise, fragmentation does not take its uncontrolled toll here; the shards of Freud's antiquities, H.D.'s memories, can be reassembled, brought to life in the magic square of the room, on the safety of the couch:

> Tendencies of thought and imagination, however, were not cut away, were not pruned even. My imagination wandered at will; my dreams were revealing, and many of them drew on classical or Biblical symbolism. Thoughts were things, to be collected, collated, analyzed, shelved, or resolved. Fragmentary ideas, apparently unrelated, were often found to be part of a special layer or stratum of thought and memory, therefore to belong together; these were sometimes skillfully pieced together like the exquisite Greek tear-jars and iridescent glass bowls and bases that gleamed in the dusk from the shelves of the cabinet that faced me where I stretched, propped up on the couch in the room in Berggasse 19, Wien IX. The dead were living in so far as they lived in memory or were recalled in dream. (14)

The precision of the address provides a securing frame to the wandering of thoughts; the display shelves organize thinking, the antiquities promise reconstitution. The literalness of the address anchors the potentially endless drifting of the mind in a referential setting;[2] the body is held in place and secured on the couch. This function of the architectural, specifically the house, is not peculiar to H.D.'s text; rather, it is typical. The figure of the four walls contains, outlines, holds. Yet H.D.'s text itself unwalls one of its walls while denying its absence.[3] The unwalled wall hints at what escapes the violence of the four walls, what eludes the reconstituted understanding of analysis. What eludes announces itself as the contingent, the accidental: the limit of meaningful experience, the contingency of setting. "I was annoyed because I heard someone laughing outside the door," H.D. writes; "I seldom hear or register what is going on in the waiting room or the hall." The rumbling of excess intrudes, it moves about like unwanted neighbors, drawing attention to a positioned body, to distraction, to what interrupts sense. "The Professor said, 'so the memories are faded?' Perhaps he felt that I was really trying too hard

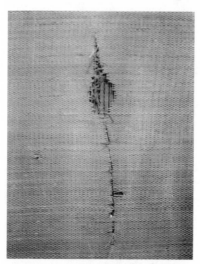

to make a dramatic sequence of this story that was all 'an atmosphere' . . . I snapped at him rather, 'No—not faded'" (162).

Recollection bears with it the possibility or the implied reality of loss of self, its dissolution beyond what is held fast in the foyer and made present again, reworked, and metabolized. The materiality and incidental quality of the house mark the double function of preservation and loss. This alternating movement between gathering and dissemination, controlled organization and dispersion, describes not only H.D.'s text and the analytic experience she presents, nor the psychoanalytic experience alone, but rather characterizes a wider movement or process of reading. H.D.'s text pushes against a limit of legibility, a limit experienced as a failure of the mind. "That is in myself too," she writes, "—a wonder as to the seemliness, or the safety even, of continuing this experience or this experiment" (47). H.D.'s psychoanalytic poiesis follows no clear genre definitions or standards; she describes not only the difficulty of psychoanalysis but

also the threat of incoherence with the absence of disciplinary definitions and genre stability. The field of H.D.'s writing here has no fence. The writing ploughs on through various textures, hitting rocks and stubborn old roots, but this metaphor fails to enclose the nature of the project. Its field is torn open, unbounded. "For my head, although it cannot have taken very long in clock-time for these pictures to form there, is already warning me that this is an unusual dimension, an unusual way to think, that my brain or mind may not be equal to the occasion" (47).

In countermovement to this fissure, H.D. reinvests Freud as the figure of authority. "Perhaps in that sense the Professor was right (actually, he was always right, though we sometimes translated our thoughts into different languages or mediums)" (47). He was always right. In tandem with the stability of Freud as pillar, H.D. installs her own stability over time through furniture. "But there I am seated on the old-fashioned Victorian sofa in the Greek Island hotel bedroom, and here I am reclining on the couch in the Professor's room, telling him this, and here again am I, ten years later, seated at my desk in my own room in London" (47). The subject stays seated.

Freud's Couch

The couch is both one and many; it holds together and threatens dissolution at once. It presents a kind of dissolving solidity. In reassuring, the couch invokes anxiety. The ambivalent function of Freud's couch in H.D.'s *Tribute* is very much like that of the couch one can see today in Maresfield Garden 20, Hampstead, the home in which Freud died in 1939. In both H.D.'s tribute and Freud's house, the couch marks out a position in the installation of the house, a founding, laying out, and setting up meant to shelter and preserve.

Ten days before Freud emigrated from Vienna to London, in March 1938, his student August Aichorn enlisted Edmund Engelman to photograph Freud's home at Berggasse 19. As Engelman describes it:

> The historical apartment [*Wohnung*] and the practice would be emptied out, the furnishings [*Einrichtung*] partly stored, partly sent on after them. We agreed that it was of the utmost importance for the history of psychoanalysis to hold fast its birthplace in all of its details—so that, in Aichorn's words, "a museum can be created when the stormy years have passed." (98)

The house is supplemented by the photograph to assure the seemingly self-evident connection between the placement of furniture, the *Einrichtung*, and the birth of psychoanalysis. Engelman's narrative connects the interior of the Viennese apartment, the conception of thought, and the presence of the man himself: "I was nearly overwhelmed at the prospect of seeking out and photographing the place of the emergence [*Entstehungsort*] of psychoanalysis, of working in Freud's practice and home and seeing the spots where he had written his many books—but above all, at the prospect of meeting Freud himself" (94). Step by step the photographer moves from housing to the generation of psychoanalysis to writing to the origin, Freud, himself. Engelman's photographs are indeed poignant, largely owing to the aura of future-anteriority lent them by the narration of their history, which shadows Engelman's own survival story. When he emigrates to the United States, Engelman leaves the negatives in Vienna with Aichorn, who will be dead by the end of the war. Engelman returns to Europe after the war to retrieve them and finds them finally safe in Anna Freud's hands in London. The haunting quality of these photos is anything but a self-contained immediate quality exuding from the images themselves. The absencing feature of the photographic medium itself expands into a narrative of imminent loss that tells of a twilight moment between presence and absence—a prolonging of the sense of "this will have been."[4] The photographic negatives, like Freud himself, make the arduous journey across the Channel and become almost a living shadow of the Freud home. The science or practice of psychoanalysis is anthropomorphized and given a "birthplace" in the home, a grounding in a surrounding to hold it fast in face of the general threat of destruction.[5]

In a letter to Wilhelm Fliess on June 12, 1900 (included in a footnote in the Strachey edition of *The Interpretation of Dreams*), Freud projects the future memory of the origin of psychoanalysis as a plaque on a building. Describing a visit to his family retreat in Bellevue, where he wrote much of the *Traumdeutung*, Freud writes:

> Do you suppose that some day a marble tablet will be placed on the house, inscribed with these words:
>
> > "In this House, on July 24th, 1895
> > the Secret of Dreams
> > was Revealed to Dr. Sigmund Freud."
>
> At the moment there seems little prospect of it.[6]

The scriptural area of Freud's tablet and the photographic quadrilaterals of Engelman's representations mark off places that emerge as preserving a sense of presence or proximity to an origin. The house is not merely incidental to this representational structure but is its very condition of possibility—the space that contains, the facade that supports.

I would like to recall briefly some of Freud's remarks about topology in chapter 7 of *The Interpretation of Dreams*. Here he makes clear that part of the function of the dream is to lay out a representational theater, a *Schauplatz*, that activates wish-fulfillment by the mere fact of presentation. Freud calls this scene or place a "psychic locality" (*GW* 2/3:541). While the spatial model can be seen as a stand-in for temporal interactions between systems, they retain a "constant spatial orientation." This locality, of course, is not grounded in anatomy; Freud exhorts us: *Wir bleiben auf psychologischem Boden* (*GW* 2/3:541), "we remain on psychological ground." Freud supports his use of spatial imagery in these famous passages with another housing image: "I can see no harm in it. We are justified, in my view, in giving free rein to our speculations so long as we do not mistake the scaffolding for the building" (575; "*das Gerüst für den Bau halten*," *GW* 2/3:541).

The effort to mark and preserve the point of origination—whether Freud's plaque, Engelman's photos, or H.D.'s room—undermines the sense of presence it strives to extend. Psychoanalysis itself is uncanny, Freud says, precisely because it destabilizes the difference between past and present through the dynamic of repression and renders mobile the contours around visibility. The integrity of the visible (that is, the empirical) is challenged in the Freud House Museum in Hampstead, presented as one of the places of the discovery of the unconscious. Among its discoveries of course is the thought that "discovery" is not really possible: that the "truth" cannot shine forth revealed in undistorted presence. This thought challenges the very principles of display.[7] Around this destabilization of presence, anxiety gathers. The threat to wholeness or plenitude exerted as the past intrudes upon the present, as absence punctuates presence, evokes castration anxiety. In the essay on the uncanny, Freud talks about the multiplication of substitute phallic signs that are meant to ward off the anxiety yet also stand as "harbingers" of the very dread against which they have been installed. Likewise, as described in "Fetishism," the fetish object both reinforces and disavows the castration anxiety that generated it. The wholeness of objects splits, the integrity of subjectivity dissolves, the past and the present do not remain in a stable linear relationship, presence and absence commingle.

The same instabilities occur in Freud's essay "Das Unheimliche." The
failure of the law of noncontradiction comes forth strongly in his etymo-
logical analysis. Freud writes:

> What interests us most in this long extract is to find that among its differ-
> ent shades of meaning, the word "*heimlich*" exhibits one which is identical
> with its opposite, "*unheimlich*." What is *heimlich* thus comes to be *unheim-
> lich*. . . . Thus *heimlich* is a word the meaning of which develops in the direc-
> tion of ambivalence, until it finally coincides with its opposite, *unheimlich*.
> (*SE* 17:224–26/ *GW* 12:235–37)

The oscillation between the familiar and the strange comes forth in the
peculiarity of the signifier *heimlich* (canny, homey or homelike, close to
heimisch, as well as secret or hidden), which harbors within itself the opposing definitions of the *heimlich/heimisch* and the *unheimlich*, the uncanny, or literally the unhomely. Freud implies that a certain "prehistory"
of the uncanny comes to light to disturb any full understanding of a present. The past intrudes into the present, the repressed returns in a disguised
form to haunt the present and bear witness to its lack of wholeness. The
ingression upon integrity and wholeness enacted by the uncanny opens
upon the "psychic floor, *auf psychologischem Boden*." The floor remains
irreducible here. Its ambiguity and reversibility are characteristic of the
house. The floor and the house are not metaphoric vehicles for the uncanny or for a psychic reality; rather, the house is the irreducibly alien
location or frame for the psyche, whose reality can only be exposed within
the grid of the house.

Jacques Derrida develops this ambivalence as an oscillation between
opposites in *Mal d'archive* (*Archive Fever*), which was first delivered as
a paper at the Freud House in London. Derrida situates his text in the
Freud House as a museum, a space, an archive that can hold all sorts of
contradictions. He writes:

> *Every* archive . . . is at once *institutive* and *conservative*. Revolutionary and tra-
> ditional. An *eco-nomic* archive in this double sense: it keeps, it puts in reserve,
> it saves, but in an unnatural fashion. . . . A moment ago we called it nomo-
> logical. It has the force of law, of a law which is the law of the house (*oikos*), of
> the house as place, domicile, family, lineage, or institution. Having become a
> museum, Freud's house takes in all these powers of economy.[8]

While asking the question of "where the outside begins," Derrida focuses on the role of exteriority in archivization that he draws from Freud's topological interpretation of the psyche:

> This *exterior*, thus archival, model of the *psychic* recording and memorization apparatus, does not only integrate the inaugural concepts of psychoanalysis. . . . Taking into account the multiplicity of regions *in* the psychic apparatus, this model also integrates the necessity, inside the *psyche* itself, of a certain outside, of certain borders between insides and outsides . . . [a] *domestic outside.* (18–19/37)

The archive marks the passage from the animating principle of the *archons* to the necessary external place that shelters them. Derrida writes: "The meaning of 'archive,' its only meaning, comes to it from the Greek *arkheion*: initially a house, a domicile, an address, the residence of the superior magistrates, the *archons*, those who commanded" (2/12–13). This passage parallels that from the living memory, *mneme*, to the mechanical or technical memory of the writing apparatus or mark, *hypomnema*, that supplements it.[9]

> [T]he archive . . . will never be either memory or anamnesis as spontaneous, alive and internal experience. On the contrary: the archive takes place at the place of originary and structural breakdown of the said memory. *There is no archive without a place of consignation, without a technique of repetition, and without a certain exteriority. No archive without outside.* (11/26)

Moreover, the archive does not simply receive and record but in fact shapes and conditions what is archived there (17/34). The house as archive—as "an internal substrate, surface, or space without which there is neither consignation, registration, impression nor suppression, censorship, repression" (19/37)— functions as a *"prosthesis of the inside"* (19/38). It remains irreducible and cannot be absorbed into the interiority of a subject.[10]

The Freud House houses *Archive Fever*. Likewise, housing houses what Derrida calls a "domestic outside." Housing is not an embodiment of a meaning; instead, it continues to devolve outwardly to the limits of its capacity to be theorized. At these limits it may seem as if we speak of the empirical, but perhaps the house is also just the limit of articulation, the medium that allows it to come forth, to dwell. *Archive Fever,* another quadrangle (the book or page), marks the threshold between the feverish divisions between inside and outside that establish "psychic locality," on the one hand, and Maresfield Garden 20 on the other. The scholarship of archive fever borders on the empirics of tourism. For archive fever is the desire to return to and reanimate an origin that the archive itself occludes. What is archive fever? Derrida writes:

> It is to burn with a passion. It is never to rest, interminably, from searching for the archive right where it slips away. It is to run after the archive, even if there's too much of it, right where something in it anarchives itself. It is to have a compulsive, repetitive, and nostalgic desire for the archive, an irrepressible desire to return to the origin, a homesickness, a nostalgia for the return to the most archaic place of absolute commencement. (91/142)

The establishment of house museums is undoubtedly in part a product of archive fever.

In 1938 many of Freud's signature possessions—his famous collection including pieces such as the Gradiva and his etching of Abu Simbel, as well as "the couch"—were relocated to Maresfield Garden 20.[11] The famous couch probably draws the most attention. It "stands" for the "standing in for" of all the things in the museum—each of which stands in for its original owner, a prior story, or an invisible cultural and historical context. There is a moment of surprise for the unsuspecting at the heavy oriental carpets spread on the stubby couch with a slightly inclined end and the oriental rug hanging on the wall behind it. The couch presents a bit of turn-of-the-century Vienna and its orientalism, also evoked by the collection of antiquities.[12] The couch in fact does not resemble its stereotype, the now prototypical icon of the brown leather couch, slightly inclined, a bit like a Napoleonic camp bed, a more minimalist kind of design reminiscent of a medical examining table. It is this icon that comes to mind in the metonymy "the couch," understood to stand in for the whole process and profession of psychoanalysis.

When one looks at this couch in Maresfield Garden, what is it that one actually "sees"? What can one possibly actually "see" there? Of course we see a convergence of historical factors; we also see both a divergence and a convergence between general and particular, between "the couch" understood as a general sign for Freudian-style psychoanalysis and this very couch upon which so many very Freudian-style analyses must have taken place. Freud himself did not say much about the use of the couch.

The positioning of Freud's chair out of the patient's sight at the head of the couch establishes the relationship of transference by blocking out the particularity of the analyst. The chair was placed to provide a direct view of the desk, giving Freud a clear view of many of his favorite antiquities that were arranged there (many consider it crucial to analyze which ones were "at the desk" with Freud).[13] As many have noted, Freud said little about the use of the couch and the now-classic positioning of furniture that have been canonized in psychoanalytic practice. Freud's explains his justification for this technique in the short text "Zur Einleitung der Behandlung"("On Beginning the Treatment"):

> I must say a word about a certain ceremonial which concerns the position in which the treatment is carried out. I hold to the plan of getting the patient to lie on a sofa [*Ruhebett*] while I sit behind him out of his sight. This arrangement has a historical basis; it is the remnant of the hypnotic method out of which psycho-analysis was evolved. But it deserves to be maintained for many reasons. The first is a personal motive, but which others may share with me. I cannot put up with being stared at by other people for eight hours a day (or more). (*SE* 12:133–34/ *GW* 8:467)

This positioning is supposed to stabilize the patient-analyst relation and block the reversibility of vision. This installation of a subject-object relation aims to protect the analyst's position so that he will not become the patient, the one looked at and scrutinized. At the same time the removal of the analyst from the patient's view is meant to put the transference relationship in the place of that of influence or suggestion: the power relationship that held together the patient-doctor relationship in treatment by hypnosis or, earlier, by magnetism. The couch is a remnant of the very practice of hypnosis from which psychoanalysis distinguishes itself. The couch thus reconnects these two historical periods while the positioning ought to hold them apart.

The reversible subjective-objective genitive "Freud's couch" harbors the same possibility. Freud, patient, discovery of the unconscious, birthplace of psychoanalysis: origin, foundation, influence, and indebtedness—all vaguely commingle on the couch. The reversal of position actually does take place. In 1938 (March 21, before the German invasion), Freud writes to Arnold Zweig: "Four weeks ago, one of my usual operations was followed by unusually severe pain so that I had to put aside my work for twelve days, and, in pain and with a hot water bottle, I lay on the couch that is destined for others."[14] The couch thus also marks Freud's decline (through reversal, marked as *ungewohnt*, unusual), pointing to the fact of

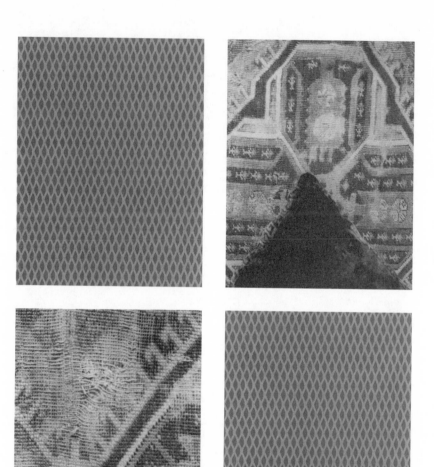

mortality, sickness, old age and death, finitude, limitations. The couch is the bed of past and future.

Most agree that the reclining position is conducive to a regressive state that allows the unconscious to come forth; the infantilizing position encourages transference. Waugaman writes: "Lying on the couch promotes a preoedipal maternal transference, with unconscious fantasies of being held in the analyst's arms or womb" (343).[15] The "womb-like setting" provides what Winnicott terms a "holding environment" (282),[16] in which the analysand can relax censorship. This interpretation is comforting, but the same author reports cases in which the couch was identified with a coffin; "death meant lying down," said another patient (Waugaman, 348). "Winnicott had a patient who associated lying on the couch to feeling in his early adolescence that lying on his back meant death—'being helpless, lying in a coffin'" (Waugaman, 348). The couch opens up a kind of ripple in time regressing into the womb and pointing forward into the grave. It also opens the one lying on it to the scrutiny of the analyst; Waugaman writes: "Patients view the couch as the place where their secrets will be revealed" (349). The couch flickers between past and present, conscious and unconscious, here and elsewhere—that is, it is both a piece of furniture and something else. To the same extent that the couch supports the patient, it also protects the doctor from "being looked at." One analyst writes:

> When placing the patient on the couch, the analyst is provided with a protective shield that allows for the maintenance of a private space or domain which cannot be easily invaded by the patient. . . . As Freud recognized, the traditional psychoanalytic setup constitutes a protective barrier for the analyst that facilitates the analyst's capacity to deal in private with his or her own senses of anxiety, frustration, anger, disillusionment, and other affective states generated by the analytic process while addressing the patient's demands.[17]

This is a strangely reduced notion of "private space" as "not being looked at."[18] We might extend it in fact to all the space behind the closed doors, the muffled signs of life in the analyst's home, so often adjacent to the office—all the mysterious suggestions of another world of which the patient often gains a faint odor or glimpse, but into which he is never invited. This private space—"the feelings of the analyst" (or we could easily say "the feelings of the philosopher")—are likewise obliquely expressed by the couch. It thus marks a limit or frontier to the analytic discourse;

it lays out its foundation. Lichtenberg encapsulates this strange meeting point in the following anecdote: "A patient who came to me after two unsuccessful attempts at psychotherapy began her first use of the couch by pouring out a vituperative denunciation of me, my fee, and my furniture, with particular emphasis on my 'hard ugly couch'—a custom-built, extra-wide Danish import of which I am especially proud" (284). The refusal to lie down enacts resistance to the analysis; sitting up is a symptom that interrupts free association and puts a halt to analysis. In these moments of defiance, the analyst is looked at, his methods and competence questioned. The "protective shield" set up by the couch allows the analyst to avoid this kind of scrutiny.

The couch lays out a place demarcating the parameters of what is meaningful in the analytic discourse. On the edges—somewhere in the "private space" in the chair beyond the couch, or in the awkward transition from the door to the couch—is static that threatens to "contaminate" the transference, to bring in what is unanalyzable or haphazard or what "properly" belongs to the analyst and not to the patient. But this very distinction is made impossible by the fact of the furniture: where the patient touches the analyst's taste, where the analyst's pride is extended to hold the patient.

The couch summarizes the beginning and the end of analytic ambition, as Lichtenberg writes:

> I was drawn by the lore of the Freudian revolution to become a pioneer explorer of the new frontier of the psyche. I intended to be a scientist, a doctor, and a psychoanalyst. The couch was to be my laboratory table for dissection and study, my operating table for surgical cure, and my magical bed for day and night dreams. When I began my personal analysis while a medical student, I approached the couch with awe; I envisioned it as a shrine for the realization of my ambitions. (280)

Perhaps this is some of the awe that resonates at the house in Maresfield Garden before that "horizontal slab," at once birth and the grave, the analyst's cover, but the place where he most concretely comes forth—the place where patient and analyst are closest. The couch condenses all the properties of fetishizing commemoration, the dream of a proximity now lost but once present, that can be supported by all sorts of other personal objects as well—the lone shoe or coat, the hat and cane, the gloves, the desk, the pen. The musealization of the couch creates a veil of authenticity that covers over this thing that is both seen and not seen. This dualism invokes the scenario in "Fetishism" of the original viewing of the mother's genitals in which the little boy sees what is not there. The couch becomes a fetish, allowing us to both see and not see. Like all museums of this kind, the Freud House presents a fluttering vision of contact and union with the original scene, with the man himself: his personal belongings, his furniture, his clothes, his collections. All these are invoked to create a sense of connection while at the same time drawing the contour of absence. The exposure of this absence generates castration anxiety and recalls the irrecoverable loss of the source of power (Freud or the author), the ineffectiveness of these signs to convey the man or the meaning, or to put us at the site of the discovery of the unconscious.

The couch subtends a quadrilateral space that defines the conditions of analytic discourse. This area begins with the surface contact between body and upholstery, but does not end there. The magic triangle between couch, chair, and door traces a dislocation in the structure of presentation (*Darstellung*/*Vorstellung*, presentation/representation, *Schauplatz*, stage or place of presentation); it parallels another triangle: between London, Vienna, and Engelmann's photographs. The very placement of the museum in London not only recalls Sigmund Freud, but also stands as a memorial to the Holocaust. While there is not always much direct discourse about the Holocaust within the physical parameters of the house, its very situation underlines Freud's situation. The presence of the London home brings forth the absence of the Viennese home at the same time as the monument to Freud becomes a generalized monument to the Holocaust. The more we see in London, the less we are present or in the present.

While the London museum tries to preserve the Freud rooms "as they were," the Vienna apartment at Berggasse 19, where Freud lived and worked for forty-seven years, is another story.[19] The entrance hall and the waiting room have been restored, but the crucial furniture and Freud's other belongings were moved to London. In their places the Vienna apartment houses a display of photographs, etchings, first editions, and other documents about Freud's life and work. Each item is accompanied by a small text on the wall. These include detailed descriptions of the objects; generally, the texts quote from Freud's letters and works to draw interesting connections of various kinds between the object or image displayed and the Freudian corpus. The exhibit displays a huge amount of informative cross-referencing (also available in the catalogue). Here and there, between portraits, diplomas, mementos, and first editions, are a few personal objects that belonged to Freud: a brush, a napkin ring, a cigar box.

On the lower half of the wall, large prints of Engelman's photos are superimposed over the places they depict. The angles, relative proportions, and positions shift, creating a disconcerting effect of doubling and disorientation. It is easy to forget where you are exactly. Through these prints the story of departure and the future anterior angle of the photographs return home. As the apartment at Berggasse 19 splits apart, the many strands of Freud's dwelling come together: the Vienna home, the house in London, the household displacement, and its photographic aspect. The

 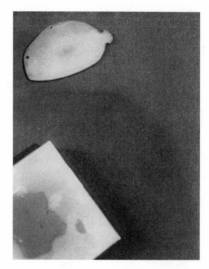

space displayed in these photographs is a "Freud House" that cannot be visited, that has no "interior." As such, as Freud's house it only comes into existence in this multiple context. This version of space itself is indebted to the topology of Freud's *Traumdeutung*. The place here differs from itself. Freud's house, like his couch, is not one, not two.

Exposition Rooms

This examination of the Freud museums has put into question the apparent self-evidence of an empirical site. On the other hand, my logic here displays a crass sort of reliance on the empirical, from the couch to the house address. The inclusion of what is merely empirical is meant to signal a textual heterogeneity, a point of contact with an "exteriority" no longer properly so-called. Freud's houses present the strange "domestic outside" Derrida describes in *Archive Fever*. As in the uncanny, inside and outside do not function as binary opposites but rather coarticulate each other. This relationship structures two housing scenes Freud describes in his correspondence with Martha Bernays, his fiancée. Freud imagines even the bliss of marital union in terms of furniture. Freud's engagement was rather lengthy, largely because of financial difficulties. In a letter dated August 1882, Freud addresses the problem of their poverty.[20] Here, furnishings are installed in a house of desire that binds and collects life forces:

> O my dear Märthchen, how poor we are! . . . [but] we need only two or three rooms, to live in and to eat in, and in which to receive a guest, and have a stove in which the fire for making meals does not go out. And everything that should be in them. Tables and chairs, beds, mirrors, a clock that reminds the happy ones of the passage of time, a reclining chair for an hour of happy reverie, rugs so that the housewife can keep the floors clean . . . and there are so many things to enjoy, the bookshelves, and the sewing table and the trusty lamp [*vertrauliche Lampe*], and everything must be kept in good condition. . . . And this thing [*dies Ding*] must bear witness to the earnest work that holds the house together, that thing to the sense for art, to dear friends whom one gladly remembers, to cities one has seen, to houses one would like to call back. All of this, a little world of happiness, of mute friends and witnesses of noble humanity, it is all still yet to come, the foundation of the house has not yet been laid, there are only two poor human beings there who love each other so unspeakably. (*Briefe*, 37)

I quote this passage at length to convey the sense of housing in it and its call to the future. Freud prophesies not only his marriage but also the processes of preservation and display that ground the house and hold together its structure and its functioning. The faithful lamp stands as an immanent unifying light. Placed among the heap of domestic items, it helps to bind the combining forces of the silent friends and witnesses, the work and passage of time, that constitute housing—what Martin Heidegger might call *wohnen* or dwelling. In "Bauen Wohnen Denken," "Building Dwelling Thinking," Heidegger presents the fundamental unity of these three verbs which are conventionally held apart. He develops these three axioms: "1. Building is really [*eigentlich*] dwelling. 2. Dwelling is the manner is which mortals are on earth. 3. Building as dwelling unfolds into the building that cultivates growing things and the building that erects buildings."[21]

In the mythic unfolding and convergence of the etymologies of these terms, Heidegger casts a bit of a magic spell over the image of the hearth that prevents it from falling apart into an inside and an outside. The opposition of inside and outside is avoided in this more "originary" kind of dwelling. Still, the opening of a space, an *Ort*, takes place in contrast to our usual understanding (*das Gewohnte*): "We work in the city, but dwell outside it. We travel, and dwell now here, now there. Dwelling so understood is always merely the occupying of a lodging" (*PLT* 215/183).[22] Both "dwelling" and "building," for Heidegger set up a double genealogy, giving rise both to this more "authentic" way of being and to the series of terms based on the verb *stellen*. This second group includes *Vorstellung, Darstellung, Bestellung, Ge-stell*, and many others.[23] These terms belong to the sphere of technology that sets up subject-object oppositions and differentiates between animate and inanimate. The full house, gathered around the burning hearth, is played off against the empty apartment up for rent. Heidegger's dichotomies line up with the disparagement of what is called "the empirical" that continues to produce excluded exteriors.

Like Heidegger's hearth, Freud's wish-house opens a space that would hold together life, work, identity, possessions, and love, but his desire for housing is exposed and turned inside out in another letter to Martha written about a year later. Dated August 22, 1883, Freud's letter describes his visit with a friend to the *elektrische Ausstellung*, the electrical exposition in Vienna. The show has not quite opened yet and much of the technology is in a state of disarray. Besides, he writes, most of what is displayed there can only be understood with the help of technical explanations and prior study. He is struck most of all, though, by some incidental furnishings that become the means of articulating his desire for his fiancée:

> So far, there is nothing exciting to see except for a set of small rooms which, as a pretense for the electrical illumination, display the most charming furniture from Jaray's [a well-known Viennese furniture house]. At the sight of these rooms all of my philosophy was done in. Herzig [Freud's companion at the exposition] remained cold, saying he was through with this kind of thing and knew that he would never call such things his property; I was in ecstasy as I imagined your joy at such a charming nest. (*Briefe*, 49)

After a few moments of grief that his wife will never have such furniture, Freud reminds himself that one can be very unhappy on a "wonderful sofa" and very happy on a good old leather armchair in the right com-

pany, and that "the woman must always be the most beautiful thing about the house and that all of these rooms are empty and lifeless, since their mistress isn't there" (*Briefe*, 49–50). The desire for furnishing is displaced onto the animating principle of the wife. The domestic interior appears in this letter outside and in public, as part of a technologically malfunctioning display case to be illuminated by electric light. The magic illumination

of the trusty lamp is replaced by desired fusion through consumption and interiorization (that is, possession). The flatness of possession is signaled by the malfunctioning electric light. The source of light stands outside the frame of the furnished room, which serves as both a random object to be lit up, and an incidental advertisement.

The doubling of Freud's dream house in the electrical exposition shows how display in space subtends the animating metaphor organizing furniture around a seemingly meaningful center: the woman or perhaps the analytic discourse between couch and chair. Yet the same display disarticulates and dismembers the fantastic friendship of furniture. Additionally, the exterior-interior raises the question of anti-Semitism and Freud and Herzig's "outsider" status; they stand as onlookers at a disarticulated display fair under the open sky. The synthesizing elements of the home are stranded, spread out across the representational field.

These readings might give a broader perspective on some of Freud's interpretations of symbols. *Zimmer* (room) stands for *Frauenzimmer* (woman) along with "*Haus* (house), . . . *Stadt* (city), *Burg, Schloß, Festung* (city, castle, fortification)" (*GW* 11:165). Women are allied with wood, thus with *Tische, gedeckte Tische und Bretter* (tables, laid out tables, and boards). Freud works out a connection between wood, *hyle* (material), and woman by way of the name of the island of Madeira, "wood, in the Portuguese" (*GW* 2/3:360). "Since 'bed and board' [*Tafel und Bett*, literally, 'table and bed'] constitute marriage," Freud writes, "in dreams often the former stand in for the latter" (*GW* 11:360). Sex is displaced onto furniture in this odd example of "table-turning": "The woman says about her husband: I set the table for him, but he overturned it. Lame children are supposed to come from the husband's *overturning* the table" (*GW* 11:164). [*Die Frau sagt von ihrem Manne: Ich ordnete ihm den Tisch, er aber wendete ihn um. Lahme Kinder sollen dadurch enstehen, daß der Mann den Tisch umwendet.*][24] The Jaray room turned outward is a lame child of desire exposed, the table turned on the furniture of philosophy.

Goethehaus Revisited

H.D. concludes her *Tribute to Freud* with an interpretation of Goethe's poem "Mignon's Song" (*Kennst Du das Land, wo die Zitronen blühen?*), which appears in his novel *Wilhelm Meister's Apprenticeship*. The poem calls for a recollection and return to an originary and paradisial homeland identified with Italy. Mignon, we learn in the course of Goethe's novel, was snatched away from her homeland and lives on in an agony of long-ing—for her home, her native language, her master Wilhelm. Mignon is physically unfit for life in the north and resists assimilation into the culture of *Bildung*.

Despite the romantic thematics surrounding the character Mignon and this song, the poem itself is classically structured and provides a formal shelter from romantic demise under the heat of the Italian sun. The place of shelter appears most concretely in the second stanza: *Kennst Du das Haus . . . Es glänzt der Saal, es schimmert das Gemach* (Do you know the house . . . The hall gleams, the room shimmers). The image of the house gathers and safeguards the lost and dissolving subject. The longing for an absent origin, here suggesting Italy, of course becomes foundational to the Romantic structure of a lost or not yet accomplished identity; the longing for Italy, many would agree, is perhaps constitutive of German identity in general.[25] The ambivalent structure of the house helps to explain how displacement can become a foundational commonplace. Housing exposes the tension and alternation between dissemination and containment that is operative in Goethe's song of Mignon. While the subject Mignon is unable to stay in place—to grow, become part of society, and construct an identity—the image of the house in the second stanza installs a place of refuge for the lost subject. It is this quality of the poem, perhaps, that renders it interesting to H.D. in her *Tribute to Freud*.

H.D.'s reading of the second stanza in particular brings together many strands of her own text through the imagery of a house. In chapter 73, H.D. quotes the whole poem, of which I reproduce the second stanza here:

Kennst Du das Land, wo die Zitronen blühen?
Kennst Du das Haus? Auf Säulen ruht sein Dach,
Es glänzt der Saal, es schimmert das Gemach,
Und Marmorbilder stehn und sehn mich an:
Was hat man dir, du armes Kind getan?
Kennst du es wohl?
Dahin! Dahin
Möchte ich mit dir, o mein Beschützer, ziehn. (*HA* 7:145)

Know you the house? Roof pillars over it,
The chambers shining and the hall bright-lit,
The marble figures gaze at me in rue:
"You poor child, what have they done to you?"

You know it, yes? Oh there, oh there,
With you, O my protector, would I fare. (83)

The poem is introduced into H.D.'s text gradually through the repetition
of the phrase, *Kennst du das Land?*, "Do you know the land?" This questioning animates the marble statues, which then are able to ask about the
speaker's past life.[26] Likewise, the sympathetic questioning binds H.D. and
Freud in a recollected presence of an idyllic scene. "We have rested in the
pastures, we have wandered beside those still waters, we have sensed the
fragrance of the myrtle thickets beyond distant hedges, and the groves of
flowering citrons. Kennst du das Land? Oh yes, Professor, I know it very
well" (85). H.D. translates and interprets the poem, which brings together
many of the strands of her narrative, including her relationship to the analyst: "It is all there," H.D. writes,

> the lyrical interrogation and the implication that the answer is given with it.
> It is: do you know the Land—but you do know it, don't you? The House?
> The Mountain? . . . You do know the house, don't you? The roof of the house
> stood on pillars like the original roof or part-roof of the temple of Karnak or
> the Parthenon of Athens. But this house seems nearer in time; there is the
> great entrance-room or Saal, with its glowing lamps and candles, and beyond
> it is the brightly tapestried or painted inner-room or rooms, the Gemach or
> apartment. It is there that we find the statues, the Marmorbilder, even as I
> had found the little images in the room beyond the actual consulting room,
> on the Professor's table. The statues stare and seem to say, what has happened
> to you? (110)

The rooms—*Saal* and *Gemach*—house the analysis and its images, the
icons and historical figures that recall and bind associations, memories, and
cultural networks. The room houses the exposition of the unconscious.
H.D.'s text gives an interpretation of the whole poem, interweaving its images and her own. The phantasms of uncovering the past, preserving history, domestic containment, the lyric call and response of recognition: these
all house a host of guests in the house that I'm here calling "Freud's."

The quadrangle stands as a temporary shelter that allows interpretation,
gathering, perhaps even some kind of understanding, "an atmosphere."[27]
Yet we know that Freud's house does not abide, the sheltering room is
itself always already opening onto its own multiplicity. The house begins
to fall apart as transferences and superpositionings come forth. H.D. describes: "The boys in the dream are not recognizably the hotel pageboys.

They are ghosts. They are, that is, 'ghosting' for another or others; when the ghosts take the form as brothers or as uncle-fathers, it will no doubt be seen that they again are ghosting. Or rather if we pursue the dream context, the intermediate ghosts, should they manifest, would be seen to be a step between brothers or uncle-fathers. We are all haunted houses" (146). The haunted house, however, when placed in the center of attention, cannot maintain itself, cannot remain what it is. When it begins to dissolve, a larger structure emerges to contain it: "It is really the Cathedral that is all-important," H.D. continues. "Inside the Cathedral we find regeneration or reintegration. This room is the Cathedral. . . . Yes (I repeated), the Cathedral of my dream was Sigmund Freud.' 'No,' he said, 'not me—but analysis'" (146–47). Freud speaks here the dissolution of all anthropomorphic unity of house and subject, of self conceived as an inside and an outside, body and spirit. "It is, as he had said of my grandfather, 'an atmosphere.' . . . The gnomes or gargoyles, the Gothic dragons, bird, beast, and fish of the inner and outer motives, the images of saints and the heroes all find their replicas or their 'ghosts' in this room or in these two rooms" (147). H.D. tends to return to the unity and the shelter of the room; but the obdurate expanse of her text persistently asserts an opening, consistently presses the limit of the quadrangle. "In this room or in these two rooms." Wherever there is a room there are also two rooms.

The house, then, is more a poetic than an empirical house. What now appears to be a historical museum refers us to a network of texts rather than an architectural solidity. The replacement of place by text is apparent in Gérard de Nerval's poem "Delfica," which is clearly reminiscent of "Mignon's Song." Nerval, a translator of German poetry, included a translation of "Mignon's Song" in his *Les filles du feu*. Here is Nerval's "version" of Mignon's song:

Delfica

La connais-tu, DAFNÉ, cette ancienne romance,
Au pied du sycamore, ou sous les lauriers blancs,
Sous l'olivier, le myrthe ou les saules tremblants,
Cette chanson d'amour . . . [sic] qui toujours recommence!

Reconnais-tu le TEMPLE, au péristyle immense,
Et les citrons amers où s'imprimaient tes dents?
Et la grotte, fatale aux hôtes imprudents,
Où du dragon vaincu dort l'antique semence.

Ils reviendront ces dieux que tu pleures toujours!
Le temps va ramener l'ordre des anciens jours;
La terre a tressailli d'un souffle prophétique . . . [sic]

Cependant la sibylle au visage latin
Est endormie encore sous l'arc de Constantin:
—Et rien n'a dérangé le sévère portique.[28]

Richard Sieburth's prose translation retains the echo of Goethe's poem in the questions at the beginning of the first two stanzas:

Delphica

Do you know it, DAPHNE, this old romance, at the foot of the sycamore or the white laurel trees, beneath the olive, the myrtle or the trembling willows, this song of love . . . that always rebegins!

Do you recognize the TEMPLE with its immense peristyle, and the bitter lemons that bore the imprint of your teeth? And the grotto, fatal to its careless guests, where the vanquished dragon's ancient seed lies asleep?

They shall return, these gods you still bemoan! Time will bring back the order of the ancient days; the earth has shuddered with a prophetic breath . . .

Meanwhile the sibyl with the Latin face still sleeps beneath the Arch of Constantine—and nothing has unsettled the severe portico.

In the opening line, the land Mignon asks about in Goethe's poem is explicitly replaced by a romance or love song, place by text. Nerval's poem translates the sheltering structure of Goethe's poem into a series of enigmatic and disconnected architectural images: an immense peristyle, a severe portico, and a sibyl sleeping beneath Constantine's arch. "Delfica" opens an unbounded field strewn with incoherent monuments that recall but do not restore the ancient place.

H.D. knew Goethe's lyric text from a musical setting but, placed in the context of *Wilhelm Meister*, completely missing from H.D.'s perspective, her identification with Mignon is more problematic. The poet identifies with the figure who is a product of incest, whose handwriting is disturbingly cramped, and whose body is convulsed in mechanical spasms. While the inclusion of Goethe's lyric provides a stabilizing frame in H.D.'s text, the context in fact shows the dissolution, rather than the becoming whole, of Mignon, the speaker position with which H.D. identifies. The poem appears at the opening of book 3 in *Wilhelm Meister*, following Mignon's first convulsive display at the end of book 2 and her subsequent attachment to Wilhelm.

"Mignon's Song" opens with an invocation of an Italianate landscape:

> Kennst Du das Land, wo die Zitronen blühen,
> Im dunkeln Laub die Gold-Orangen glühn,
> Ein sanfter Wind von blauen Himmel weht,
> Die Myrthe still und hoch der Lorbeer steht,
> Kennst du es wohl?
>   Dahin! Dahin
> Möcht' ich mit dir, o mein Beschützer, ziehn!
> (*HA* 7:155)

The translation reads:

> Do you know the land where the lemon blossoms grow,
> And through dark leaves the golden oranges glow,
> A gentle breeze wafts from an azure sky,
> The myrtle's still, the laurel tree grows high—
> You know it, yes? Oh there, oh there
> With you, O my beloved, would I fare. (83)

Mignon's longing to return to her semitropical homeland is also a desire to return to a paradisial garden featuring plants not found in the German north. Goethe naturalizes the classical imagery of the laurel and the myrtle which, as we will see, can function in a more allegorical way as well. The song presents dreams of a fusion with the land and the restoration of the security and protection of a father figure—the one addressed here in the poem sequentially as lover, protector, and father. At the same time Mignon is ultimately condemned as a figure unable to adapt to the conditions of northern life who remains regressively attached to a lost origin: "'Italy!' said Mignon in a meaningful tone; 'if you go to Italy, take me with you. I'm freezing here'" (84/ *HA* 7:146).

Later in the novel we learn that Mignon in fact is the product of an incestuous union between a member of the clergy and a woman whom he did not know to be his sister. When the man's family tries to explain to him what has happened, Mignon's father simply refuses to believe it. He rejects what he calls the flames of Hell of the conventional world and believes instead in the union of pure love. He locates this love in a paradisial landscape reminiscent of the first stanza of Mignon's song.

He admonishes his family: "Come and meet us beneath those cypresses that extend gravely into the sky, visit us in those groves where lemons and pomegranates surround us, and the tender myrtle unfolds its delicate blossoms—and then try to frighten us with your dismal, gray, man-made entrapments!" (357/ *HA* 7:583). The citrus and laurel landscape thus holds primordial security, fusion, and incest together in one place, contrasted with the "man-made nets" of the northern world.

Goethe focuses in these passages on natural elements, and Freud later identifies these same Mediterranean hot spots as privileged *topoi* of the unconsciousness. His reliance on Greek cultural images hardly needs mentioning. Rome, too, which Freud calls "the eternal city," is invoked as a privileged model of the psyche in *Civilization and Its Discontents*. The knowledgeable visitor to Rome, Freud explains, is able to recognize, locate, and psychically restore the oldest remnants, to read traces and traces of traces that are buried or have been replaced by subsequent structures. If, however, we imagine Rome as a psychic entity in which nothing has been destroyed, rather than a geographical site, we get a sense of the strange landscape of the mind, coming forth in Piranesi-like images forcing the limits of the imagination. On the one hand, the image of Rome should suggest the multilayered nature of the unconscious and its history; on the other, the geographical itself gives way in its figurative function. Freud says of his own comparison: "It is obviously senseless to continue spinning this fantasy; it leads to the unimaginable, indeed, to the absurd!" (*GS* 14: 428).[29] The model-like security that Rome was supposed to grant leads instead to a confusion of representations, a doubling of space, and a general chaos similar to the incestuous landscape suggested above.

In *Tribute to Freud*, H.D. also brings together the themes of paternal idealization and return to the mother through the localities of Greece and Rome. She considers her meeting with Freud to be a kind of crowning achievement:

> I felt that to meet him at forty-seven, and to be accepted by him . . . seemed to crown all my other personal contacts and relationships, justify all the spiral-like meanderings of my mind and body. I had come home, in fact. And another poem comes inevitably to prompt me:
>
> > *On desperate seas long wont to roam,*
> > *Thy hyacinth hair, thy classic face,*
> > *Thy Naiad airs, have brought me home*

To the glory that was Greece
And the grandeur that was Rome. (44)

Quoting Poe, H.D. thematizes her desire for reunification with her now-dead mother. She writes: "This is, of course, Edgar Allan Poe's much quoted Helen, and my mother's name was Helen" (44). This kind of fusion destroys ego boundaries and is potentially dangerous. Indeed, H.D. comes to question the limit of her sanity during her trip to Corfu, where she has visions of figures cast in light that she calls "the writing on the wall." "The Professor translated the pictures on the wall, or the picture-writing on the wall of a hotel bedroom in Corfu, the Greek Ionian island, that I saw projected there in the spring of 1920, as a desire for union with my mother. I was physically in Greece, in Hellas (Helen). I had come home to the glory that was Greece" (44), a glory that is disarticulating, disarming, disorienting—a glory that is a hallucination. The warm place and the house in the south are meant to open spaces that can unify disparate experiences and losses over time. Structurally, they contain chaos, but they also bring about a fusion and lack of differentiation that is threatening.

The insinuation of Mignon disrupts the interpretive legibility gathering around H.D.'s "Writing on the Wall." For Mignon is a figure of literal disarticulation even at the level of handwriting. Mignon takes to copying out everything she knows "by heart" and showing her handiwork to Wilhelm for correction: "She was tireless at what she was doing, and did it quite well except that the letters were uneven and the lines not straight. In this too her body seemed to be at variance with her mind" (77/ *HA* 7:135).

H.D.'s text, like the Freud house, repeats the dissociative doubling that characteristically interrupts or obstructs the totalizing tendency exemplified in the structure of the room. This tendency is clearly manifest in several important rooms in *Wilhelm Meister* in which identities are revealed and the plot unraveled. They include the room that houses the uncle's art collection; the tower room in which Wilhelm is awarded his papers; and perhaps most strikingly, the *Saal der Vergangenheit* (the room of the past) in book 8, which opens a space in which time seems to be suspended. This is probably the room that most resembles H.D.'s portrait of Freud's room. The Egyptian-style iron door is flanked by sphinxes; there are sarcophagi, *Aschenkästchen und Gefässen . . . Kränzen und Zieraten*, ash boxes and urns . . . wreaths and ornamentation, all reminiscent of Freud's "circle

of Gods" and his collections. Its artistry overcomes the very thought of
death it contains. The perfection of proportion allows the image of a subject to come forth who is freed of finitude and fragmentation:

> The architectural elements were fashioned from fine yellow marble, which
> shaded over into reddishness, blue stripes of an ingenious chemical composi-
> tion reproduced the effect of lapis lazuli, and, pleasing the eye by the contrast,
> gave coherence and unity to the whole. All this splendor and decoration was
> achieved by purely architectural means, and everyone who entered felt up-
> lifted by the design of the whole, showing what man is and what he can be.
> (331/ *HA* 7: 540)

This power of the room asserts a denial of death. Goethe's narrative moves
through various rooms, none of which is a terminal station; and of course
the tower itself has already been discarded. Any unifying room produces
an outside, and it is only a matter of time until the narrative dissolves in
confusion and dissociation.

The alternation between synthesis and disarticulation is particularly
pointed in the scene in which Wilhelm first encounters Nathalie, the
Amazon. The scenes considered above allow bits of the narrative to come
together, and the identity of figures is revealed; the chamber walls make
possible these moments of illumination. The scene with the Amazon, in
contrast, is utterly un-domestic, taking place in the open field. The group
of actors with whom Wilhelm has been traveling has been attacked by
marauding robbers. Wilhelm has been shot. As he regains consciousness,
he looks about to establish the welfare of the others:

> Wilhelm noticed that she was leaning with her back against her trunk which
> appeared to be locked and quite undamaged. He asked whether the others
> had been as lucky in preserving their possessions. With a shrug of her shoul-
> ders, she pointed to the adjoining meadow, which was littered with broken
> boxes, smashed trunks, slashed knapsacks and every kind of small utensils.
> (133/ *HA* 7:225)

Violence has left its trace in the way these belongings are strewn over the
open field; likewise, the group has dispersed.

The Amazon approaches, but it is not yet time for her identity and her
relationship to Wilhelm to be made clear. On the one hand, her figure
becomes illuminated, as if it were a hint or prophecy of the wholeness
to come. When she takes off her coat and lays it on Wilhelm, he has this

vision: "Her head seemed to be surrounded with shafts of light and there was a glow spreading across her whole appearance" (135/*HA* 7:228). The tendency towards this illumination, like the motion towards the glowing inner room, is interrupted through a jarring contrast with his own body: "The surgeon was at that moment treating him rather less gently, he was about to extract the bullet that was still lodged in the wound. So the saint disappeared from his fainting sight; he lost all consciousness." (135/*HA* 7:228). The surgeon, also a recurring figure, draws attention to the mechanics rather than the mystification of synthesis. The boundary between inside and outside is transgressed through the knife, while the unity of body and mind is dislocated. This open field, between destinations, is a place of exposure bringing about the loss of consciousness. Housing re-emerges to try to gather together the dismembered pieces of languages, of fields, that tend towards dispersion and darkness.

§6 Heidegger's Housing Problem

Being-in

In the "Letter on Humanism," Martin Heidegger tells a story of Heraclitus warming himself at his oven. According to the anecdote, people seeking the great man's wisdom are let in only to be disappointed at the spectacle of the meager body displaying its needy finitude—its need for warmth and shelter:

> In this altogether everyday place he betrays the whole poverty of his life . . . .
> At this disappointing spectacle even the curious lose their desire to come any closer. What are they supposed to do here? Such an everyday and unexciting occurrence—somebody who is chilled warming himself at a stove—anyone can find any time at home.

Finally Heraclitus tells them: "Here too the gods come to presence."[1]

The presence of the gods—their proximity, their neighborhood—takes place in a sheltered zone, a house of some kind, as the philosopher dwells, tarries, warms himself. (Heidegger specifically mentions that the stove is not being used to bake anything.) The guests are impatient at the all-too-familiar scene, lost in the everyday. Heraclitus' speech exhorts them to see behind "what they would see at home"—the banal as opposed to the divine, the finite and mortal as opposed to the great and transcendent. The guests enter in the mode of *Verfallenheit*, fallenness, but how do they depart? Heidegger leaves this question unanswered.

We might say sympathetically that the scene illuminates the interconnection between dwelling, building, thinking, and ultimately *Sein* that

Heidegger gets at elsewhere. Being itself throws man into the finitude
implicit in the need for warmth:

> What throws in projection is not man but Being itself, which sends man
> into the ek-sistence of Da-sein that is his essence. This destiny propriates as
> the clearing of Being—which it is. The clearing grants nearness to Being. In
> this nearness, in the clearing of the *Da,* man dwells as the existing one. (*BW*
> 241/ *W* 334)

Finitude dwells in proximity or the neighborhood of Being; *ek-sistence*
itself means that nothing like *Sein* could be present as something in-the-
world. The *Da* of *Dasein* is a puncture, an "in" that "in"augurates (*stiftet*)
the opening towards . . . that characterizes *Dasein.*

In *Being and Time,* of course, Heidegger is greatly concerned with Being-
in-the-world. As a fundamental trait of *Da-sein, In-sein,* or Being-in, cannot be structured as the relation between two things existing side by side
in the world. The relation of Being-in is not like that of "the water is 'in'
the glass, or the garment is 'in' the cupboard."[2] These instances of Being-in
within the world (*innerweltlich*) are only possible because of the Being-in-
the-world of *Dasein* and cannot be derived from anything in the world
(*innerweltliches*). Notice in this passage a Pascal-like passage to infinity in
trying to ground the *In-sein* of what is in the world:

> Both water and glass, garment and cupboard, are "in" space and "at"a loca-
> tion, and both in the same way. This relationship of Being can be expanded:
> for instance, the bench is in the lecture-room, the lecture-room is in the uni-
> versity, the university is in the city, and so on, until we can say that the bench
> is "in world-space." All entities whose Being "in" one another can thus be
> described have the same kind of Being—that of Being-present-at-hand—as
> Things occurring "within" the world. (*BT* 79/ *SuZ* 43)

The public location at the university—where the lecture may be held—
cannot disclose Being-in.

In the next paragraph Heidegger explains that *In-Sein* does not mean
anything spatial. Instead, "'In' is derived from '*innan*'—'to reside,'
'*habitare*,' 'to dwell'. . . . '*An*' signifies 'I am accustomed,' 'I am familiar with,' 'I look after something.' It has the signification of '*colo*' in the
senses of '*habito*' and '*diligo*'" (*BT* 80/ *SuZ* 54). Thus the way in which
Dasein is "there," is open to the world, is through its dwelling, its habitual
hanging around—its staying, its *Aufenthalt* in a familiar place. Its being

at home. This hanging around is not abstract; rather it is grounded in the ontic experience, or at least vocabulary, of domesticity. *In* is not a spatial term nor one implying containment. *Die Weltlichkeit* is the essence of *in*, for it is the whole name for the relation signifying relations among things in their disclosure or hiddenness that makes any ontic understanding of *in* possible. Another scene, however, puts a halt to the infinite expansion of the first instance of "things in the world." In this example the room emerges to hold and maintain the scene that allows the *um-zu* of *Zeug*, the "in-order-to" of equipment, to appear, a relation of references by which all things are related to other things:

> Provisionally, it is enough to take a look phenomenally at a manifold of such assignments. Equipment—in accordance with its equipmentality—always is *in terms of* [*aus*] its belonging to other equipment: ink-stand, pen, ink, paper, blotting pad, table, lamp, furniture, windows, doors, room. These "Things" never show themselves proximally as they are for themselves, so as to add up to a sum of *realia* and fill up a room. What we encounter as closest to us (though not as something taken as a theme) is the room; and we encounter it not as something "between four walls" in a geometrical spatial sense, but as equipment for residing. (*BT* 97–98/*SuZ* 68)[3]

Heidegger moves here from Pascal to Descartes; we are reminded of his cozy chamber and the fire by the side of which he brackets out all of his experience to arrive at the one fundamental truth in his smoking jacket and slippers.

This isn't any old room, but a clearly bourgeois room of a scholar with all the usual accoutrements—nothing special about it. Yet it installs an ontic presupposition in the exposition of the ontological—an empirical, biographical shadow informing the deduction of the worldliness of the world. This might be the trace of *Verfallenheit*, fallenness or inauthenticity, and does not necessarily contradict Heidegger's argument; yet it points to a constitutive role of (here, the author's) house in the exposition even of fundamental ontology. The *habitus* of the room makes possible the "orientation" in "dimension"—the *Um-uns-herum*, the "round-about-us," of *In-sein* that has nothing to do with the abstract measurement of empty space (*Räumlichkeit*):

> The regional orientation of the multiplicity of places belonging to the ready-to-hand goes to make up the aroundness—the "round-about-us" [*das Um-uns-herum*]—of those entities which we encounter as closest environmentally

[*umweltlich*]. A three-dimensional multiplicity of possible positions which gets filled up with Things present-at-hand is never proximally given. This dimensionality of space is still veiled in the spatiality of the ready-to-hand. (*BT* 136/ *SuZ* 103)

It comes through in domestic detail as the ghostly presence of the chamber, which provides our original orientation: "The 'above' is what is 'on the ceiling'; the 'below' is what is 'on the floor'; the 'behind' is what is 'at the door'; all 'wheres' are discovered and circumspectively interpreted as we go our ways in everyday dealings; they are not ascertained and catalogued by the observational measurement of space" (*BT* 137/ *SuZ* 103). The near/far familiarity, but hiddenness, of the home becomes acute in the telephone. In the eyeglasses and the telephone,[4] near and far oscillate. "Umweltlich," "environmentally," the glasses on the end of my nose are "more remote . . . than the picture on the opposite wall" (*BT* 141/ *SuZ* 107). One expects almost to see Gregor's picture of the woman in furs cut out from a magazine. "Equipment for seeing—and likewise for hearing, such as the telephone receiver—has what we have designated as the inconspicuousness of the proximally ready-to-hand" (*BT* 141/ *SuZ* 107). Subtending the familiarity of spectacles and telephone is the opposite wall, the *gegenüber befindliche Wand*.

The uncanniness of *Dasein* comes from this simultaneity of the near and the far, the usual and the strange, the familiar and the hidden.[5] Uncanniness is also articulated through building features, most obviously the house. Housing features primarily *conceal* ontological features, and thus become "unhausing," or *unheimlich*. Housing presents an average or implicit (*verfallene)* scene in which the determinations of Being are hidden or occluded. Being-in discloses not cozy homeliness, but the singularized exposure of one not at home and points to the uncanniness of *Dasein*. "That *about which* anxiety is anxious reveals itself as that *in the face of which* it is anxious—namely, Being-in-the-world" (*BT* 233/ *SuZ* 188). Anxiety comes up around *In-Sein*:

> Being-in has been disclosed as a potentiality-for-Being which is individualized, pure, and thrown. . . . Anxiety individualizes Dasein and thus discloses it as "solus ipse." But this existential "solipsism" is so far from the displacement of putting an isolated subject-Thing into the innocuous emptiness of a worldless occurring, that in an extreme sense what it does is precisely to bring Dasein

face to face with its world as world, and thus bring it face to face with itself as Being-in-the-world. (*BT* 233/ *SuZ* 188)

In its thrownness, *Dasein* takes on the guise of an isolated individual—a subject—contained in a space. While the space at first seems to be the comforting totality of the house or room, anxiety breaks in and shakes the foundations of the figure to awaken *Dasein* to its interconnectedness, thus revealing its home to be unhomeliness. Before it is revealed, however, *Dasein* lives in the fallen world of *Gerede*, chatter or idle talk. While this inauthentic life conceals the ontological, it nevertheless holds *Dasein* in a state of suspension—a quivering or hovering—that holds up its possibility to connect to its true nature:

> Ontologically this means that when Dasein maintains itself in idle talk, it is—as Being-in-the-world—cut off from its primary and primordially genuine relationships-of-Being towards the world, towards Dasein-with, and towards its very Being-in. Such a Dasein keeps floating unattached [*in einer Schwebe*]; yet in so doing, it is always alongside the world, with Others, and towards itself. (*BT* 214/ *SuZ* 170)

The power of the usual, the unremarkable, the unnoticed, is strong enough to hide even this shaking ground and its anxiety: "Yet the obviousness and self-assurance of the average ways in which things have been interpreted, are such that while the particular *Dasein* drifts along towards an ever-increasing groundlessness as it floats, the uncanniness of this floating remains hidden from it under their protecting shelter" (*BT* 214/ *SuZ* 170). Some other kind of language is needed to wake *Dasein* up to its own *Bodenlosigkeit*, its groundlessness or lack of a *floor*. Even its own uncanniness is hidden from it by a *wall* that acts like a simile (*gleichsam*): "When seen correctly, however, this interpretation is only a fleeing in the face of the conscience—a way for Dasein to escape by slinking away from that thin wall by which the "they" is separated, as it were [*gleichsam*], from the uncanniness of its Being" (*BT* 323/ *SuZ* 278).

The wall is the (perhaps not explicit) limit that makes possible the play of near and far, of the spectacles and the telephone, in the homeliness of the room. It is also the last filmy remainder between *Dasein* and its true *In-sein*: the wall which, torn away, leaves *Dasein* not at home. With the quaking of the house or its dismemberment (wall, door, floor . . .) *Unheimlichkeit* breaks in to break apart the "house of Being." With this rupture, *In-Sein* is exposed as sheer exposure. Comfortable living in the world is disrupted by anxiety as the destabilization of the house itself. This long passage clarifies the uncanny:

In anxiety one feels "*uncanny*". . . . But here "uncanniness" also means "not-being-at-home" [*das Nicht-zuhause-sein*]. In our first indication of the phenomenal character of Dasein's basic state and in our clarification of the existential meaning of "Being-in" as distinguished from the categorical signification of "insideness," Being-in was defined as "residing alongside . . . ," "Being-familiar with. . . ." This character of Being-in was then brought to view more concretely through the everyday publicness of the "they," which brings tranquillized self-assurance—"Being-at-home," with all its obviousness—into the average everydayness of Dasein. On the other hand, as Dasein falls, anxiety brings it back from its absorption in the "world." Everyday familiarity collapses. Dasein has been individualized, but individualized *as* Being-in-the-world. Being-in enters into the existential "mode" of the "*not-at-home.*" Nothing else is meant by our talk about "uncanniness." (*BT* 233/ *SuZ* 188–89)

Anxiety breaks down the thin wall between man, or *das Man*, and his *Un-zuhause*, a more originary condition that, in that sense, is more of a being at home than being at home is. "That kind of Being-in-the-world which is tranquillized and familiar is a mode of Dasein's uncanniness, not the reverse. *From an existential-ontological point of view, the 'not-at-home' must be conceived as the more primordial phenomenon*" (*BT* 234/ *SuZ* 189).

This originary *Un-zuhause* can only be reached through a *Haus*/house, a contingent and factical feature passing by and passed by.

Like anxiety, the call (of conscience) pulls *Dasein* out of its comfortable domestic forgetfulness. Through the call a hearing is awoken in *Dasein* that interrupts its usual domestic noise. The call is also characterized as a "*Bruch*," an interruption that breaks in on *Dasein's* house:

> Losing itself in the publicness and the idle talk of the "they," it *fails to hear* [*überhört*] its own Self in listening to the they-self. . . . This listening-away must get broken off; in other words, the possibility of another kind of hearing which will interrupt it, must be given by Dasein itself. The possibility of its thus getting broken off lies in its being appealed to without mediation. Dasein fails to hear itself, and listens away to the "they"; and this listening-away gets broken by the call if that call, in accordance with its character as such, arouses another kind of hearing, which, in relationship to the hearing that is lost, has a character in every way opposite. (*BT* 315-16/*SuZ* 271)

The call comes from *Dasein's* own *Un-zuhause*, its own *Unheimlichkeit*, neither myself nor an other: "'it' does the calling. . . . The caller is Dasein in its uncanniness: primordial, thrown Being-in-the-world as the 'not-at-home'—the bare 'that-it-is' in the 'nothing' of the world" (*BT* 321/*SuZ* 276–77). The call is received through the telephone, or through the tearing down of the house's wall, or perhaps looking out the window, opening the door. Insofar as *das Un-zuhause* is an existential-ontological primordial condition, however, in some sense it is the state of most truly being at home. The difference between the caller and the called aims to prevent this reabsorption of the extra-homely into the home, of *Unheimlichkeit* as propriety or identity.

The House of Being

In the "Letter on Humanism," Heidegger indeed argues that housing is prior to either *Unheimlichkeit* or the relationship of container and contained, *Gehäuse*, housing or casing, that characterizes the technological era. Heidegger writes explicitly: "Only because language is the home [*die Behausung*] of the essence of man can historical mankind and human beings not be at home in their language, so that for them language becomes a mere container [*Gehäuse*] for their sundry preoccupations" (*BW* 262/*W* 357). The forgetfulness of Being sees in the house only a house, a frame, or a container that stands in a technological relationship to *Seiendes*, to what is. As Heidegger writes in "Bauen Wohnen Denken" ("Building Dwelling Thinking"), simply occupying a space is not genuine "dwelling" though it is made possible by the more primordial determination of dwelling. What is dwelling, *wohnen*? It has already been identified with "*in*" in *Being and Time*. In the "Letter," Heidegger specifies: "In this nearness, in the clearing of the *Da*, man dwells as the eksisting one without yet being able properly to experience and take over this dwelling" (*BW* 241/ *W* 334). Heidegger reads the equivalence of *Nähe des Seins*, nearness of Being, and *Da* in Hölderlin's "Heimkunft" and identifies it with the term *Heimat*, homeland. *Heimat* is not supposed to mean Germany, though it is surely impossible to avoid this association.[6] Instead Heidegger defines *Heimat* ontologically: "The homeland [*die Heimat*] of this historical dwelling is nearness to Being" (*BW* 242/ *W* 335). *Wohnen* is thus a dwelling, a tarrying, a holding-ground, in the proximity of *Sein*; genuine *ek-sistence* takes place in the instant of the *Da* as it intersects with the opening toward Being.

Heimatlosigkeit, translated as homelessness, is defined as a forgetful condition, as a negative rather than as the primordial state it was in *Sein und Zeit*. Heidegger invokes Hölderlin's term *Heimat* as part of the effort to recall a genuine proximity between historical dwelling and Being:

> Only thus does the overcoming of homelessness begin from Being, a homelessness in which not only man but the essence of man stumbles aimlessly about. Homelessness so understood consists in the abandonment of Being by beings. Homelessness is the symptom of oblivion of Being. Because of it the truth of Being remains unthought. (*BW* 242/ *W* 335)

Heimatlosigkeit would thus be overcome in a remembering of the relationship towards Being as a clearing of the opening. This neighboring proximity and clearing of the opening take place in and as language.

Here as elsewhere Heidegger argues against an instrumental, teleological view of language: "In its essence, language is not the utterance of an organism; nor is it the expression of a living thing. Nor can it ever be thought in an essentially correct way in terms of its symbolic character, perhaps not even in its character of signification. Language is the clearing-concealing advent of Being itself" (*BW* 230/ *W* 324). Language by definition allows Being to approach but never to settle definitively because language remains within the sphere of *Seiendes*, the ontic, and *Sein* can never be a *Seiendes*, or anything ontic. Language is not a dualistic thing composed of a material and a psychic part, but is instead a belonging and a hearing (*gehören*), a correspondence (*Entsprechung*) between thinking and being: "Said plainly, thinking is the thinking of Being. The genitive says something twofold. Thinking is of Being inasmuch as thinking, propriated by Being, belongs to Being. At the same time thinking is of Being insofar as thinking, belonging to Being, listens to Being" (*BW* 220/ *W* 313–14). Thinking is appropriated by Being, and thus Being takes place in thinking through this mutual listening and belonging. In the opening of the essay, Heidegger writes:

> Thinking accomplishes the relation of Being to the essence of man. It does not make or cause the relation. Thinking brings this relation to Being solely as something handed over to it from Being. Such offering consists in the fact that in thinking Being comes to language. Language is the house of Being [*Die Sprache ist das Haus des Seins*]. In its home [*in ihrer Behausung*] man dwells. Those who think and those who create with words are the guardians of this home. (*BW* 217/ *W* 311)

In submitting thinking to *Sein*, a relay is set up in which thinking allows a relationship to Being to manifest as an offering (*darbieten*). In the medium of thinking, Being comes to language, or speaks. It comes to the "*in*," the "*Da*," the instantaneous moment of inscription in the fabric of language. It hovers, arrives, becomes near, but is never fully present.

Being falls off from itself in appropriating language and forming itself into a house. This house becomes a shelter or a dwelling if it preserves its relation to Being, or it becomes a mere container, apartment, house, living place—*Gehäuse*—if that relation is occluded. The strange joint of housing links language and its form as a house, on one hand, and the housing it becomes for human beings on the other: "Thinking builds upon the house of Being, the house in which the jointure of Being fatefully enjoins the essence of man to dwell in the truth of Being" (*BW* 259– 60). The strangeness of the syntax here warrants a look at the German: "Das Denken baut am Haus des Seins, als welches die Fuge des Seins je geschickhaft das Wesen des Menschen in das Wohnen des Seins verfügt" (*W* 354–55). There is a joining seam between the house of being (subjective genitive) and the housing of man, which herds man into dwelling, that is, into the house of Being. If you live in the house of Being, you are protected, sheltered, and look out the windows and walk out the door toward . . . *Sein*. In the same paragraph comes Heidegger's strange claim: "The talk about the house of Being is no transfer [*keine Übertragung*] of the image 'house' to Being. But one day we will, by thinking the essence of Being in a way appropriate to its matter, more readily be able to think what 'house' and 'to dwell' are" (*BW* 260/ *W* 355). "*Keine Übertragung*": no poetic ornament or metaphoric substitution.[7] No analogy between the familiar (house) and the unfamiliar (Being), though technically the analogy or equivalence is set up between language and house. We can see how *wohnen* has come to be determined in the wake of the relationship of Being, house, housing, and man. Dwelling, or *Aufenthalt*, is defined as an *ek-sistence* open to being in the moment or spot of the *Da*, as an orientation or inclination to Being, to a transcendent level. We have seen, too, how thinking and language become defined as media through which this relation takes place. The disappearing element, though, is the house, which stands firm in the original formulation and serves as the hinge or joint between the ontic and the ontological, between Being and language, language and man. It is the one term taken for granted, with no meditation on its etymology or complex tropics. House remains house, the ontic presupposition, the everyday, expelled as it is built upon. Being does not come to earth as the inhabitant of the house of language. Yet this reading is surely possible. This is perhaps what Werner Hamacher means when he points to the fundamentally "bad reading" to which this phrase lends itself; it suggests that the figure of the house simply and easily makes Being immediately available as something present when, by definition, it can never be any entity.[8]

Heidegger sets up a kind of pastoral idyll in which the technological relationship to *Seiendes* is given up: "Man is not the lord of beings [*des Seienden*]. Man is the shepherd of Being" (*BW* 245/ *W* 338). The shift from "*Herr*" to "*Hirt*," from master to shepherd, shifts the relationship between two things that are (*Seiende*) to a something that is (*Seiendes*, namely, *Mensch*) and a something that is not, a *Nicht-seiendes* (*Sein*), and thus establishes a truer dwelling:

> He [*man*] gains the essential poverty of the shepherd, whose dignity consists in being called by Being itself into the preservation of Being's truth. The call comes as the throw from which the thrownness of Da-sein derives. In his essential unfolding within the history of Being, man is the being whose Being as ek-sistence consists in his dwelling in the nearness of Being. Man is the neighbor of Being. (*BW* 245/ *W* 338–39)

All the effort to establish *Sein* as something that marks, punctures, arrives, approaches, departs, retreats, and so forth, falls to naught here as it is trivialized as a *Nachbar*, neighbor, the owner of the next farm, perhaps,—and certainly a *Seiendes*. The biblical overtones of this relationship to Being are dramatized as a country pastoral between neighbors.[9] The neighbor is just another name for the anthropomorphic figure of (a) god:

> *Ēthos* means abode, dwelling place [*Aufenthalt, Ort des Wohnens*]. The word names the open region in which man dwells. The open region of this abode allows what pertains to man's essence, and what in thus arriving resides in nearness to him . . . . The fragment says: Man dwells, insofar as he is man, in the nearness of god. (*BW* 256/ *W* 351)

Housed, man holds himself open, steady, stable, with god. The body is the temple of the soul, the church is the house of god. *Aufenthalt* is a halting, a stopping, a standing, a stasis.[10]

The figuring of language as the house of being thus installs a theologically grounded stability. This is quite different from the quaking and quivering ground of *Dasein's Unheimlichkeit* and *Un-zuhause-Sein* in *Being and Time*, where the "*da*" and the "*in*" are only fleeting instants of incision, not enduring places of presence. To establish this durability, Heidegger points to a primordial law, a *Zuweisung*, that sets it up: "Only such dispatching [*Fügung*] is capable of supporting and obligating. . . . More essential than instituting rules is that man find the way to his abode in the truth of Being. This abode first yields the experience of something we can hold on to. The truth of Being offers a hold for all conduct [*den Halt für alles Verhalten verschenkt die Wahrheit des Seins*]" (*BW* 262/ *W* 357). The halting takes places through an arbitrary positing of identity between two different terms: "'Hold' in our language means protective heed ['*Halt* bedeutet in unserer Sprache die '*Hut*']. Being is the protective heed that holds man in his ek-sistent essence to the truth of such protective heed—in such a way that it houses ek-sistence in language. Thus language is at once the house of Being and the home of human beings" (*BW* 262/ *W* 357). The elision of "*Halt*" and "*Hut*" gathers—houses—*Ek-sistenz* in language and, as this housing, inclines it towards its truth. "*Hirt*" (shepherd), "*Halt*," and "*Hut*" are joined together here to set up a stable ground or floor for the house of Being. This stability takes places through a decree of identity, a denial of difference.

The establishment of the house as a place that denies alteration echoes the claim for identity in Nietzsche's *Also sprach Zarathustra*, where, as Hamacher has pointed out, the phrase "house of Being" also occurs. In the chapter "Der Genesende" ("The Convalescent"), the animals say: "Everything goes, everything comes back; eternally rolls the wheel of being. Everything dies, everything blossoms again; eternally runs the year of being. Everything breaks, everything is joined anew; eternally the same house of being is built. Everything parts, everything greets every other thing again; eternally the ring of being remains faithful to itself."[11] Sameness is enforced through the decree (*Fügung*) of the house, close in-

deed to the carpentry and joining work (*Fuge*) of building. As Hamacher shows, the oscillation between same and different, between proper and improper, that characterizes the uncanniness of being is shut down by the stabilizing figure of the house—the same figure that makes *Unheimlichkeit* possible. He writes:

> This has to do with the architecture of this uncanny house of being (unheimliches Hauses des Seins [sic])—that the improper position of the question of being cannot, strictly and definitively speaking, be disconnected from its proper position. . . . It always, and in a constitutive manner, lends itself to a false reading. (363)

The proximity of Being can be seen as both stabilizing (as *Nähe*, *Nachbar*, or truth), or as destabilizing: as the fluctuating proximity and approximation of the "*Da*" or the "*in*," as an ever-moving approach.

"Perhaps Heidegger himself read badly sometimes," Hamacher continues. "That is the case, for example, with this turn of speech [*cette tournure*]: the house of being" (363). The bad reading here is in fact no reading at all—or the obliteration of the distinctions between *Hirt*, *Halt*, and *Hut*. Hamacher notes that Heidegger cites this phrase in his book on Nietzsche without commenting upon it. The failure to comment and to read is a failure to allow the instabilities of difference, and, according to Hamacher on Heidegger, this is precisely Heidegger's critique of the doctrine of eternal return: "It is about the discourse of Zarathustra's animals on the doctrine of eternal return, a discourse which, Heidegger says, is repetitive and too easy—so one must conclude that it is this turn of phrase, 'the house of being,' that is 'too easy,' this phrase which is a part of this facile and chattering discourse" (363).

Hamacher rightly points to the falsely stabilizing effect of the figure of the house here as part of its fundamental architecture. Likewise "language is the house of being" is an underread phrase that can be taken simply to celebrate the importance of language or finitude in a way that ignores its complicity with an identity-enforcing and hyper-stabilizing ideology of the *Heimat*.

Hannah Arendt perhaps has in mind this tendency of the house in her essay, "Thinking and Moral Considerations."[12] She takes up the word "house" as an example of the way in which general concepts reify and make inaccessible that which they are supposed to name. The word "house," Arendt writes, "is a word that could not exist unless one presupposes thinking about being housed, dwelling, having a home. As a word, 'house' is shorthand for all these things, the kind of shorthand without which thinking and its characteristic swiftness . . . would not be possible at all. *The word 'house' is something like a frozen thought which thinking must unfreeze*, defrost as it were, whenever it wants to find out its original meaning" (172–73). Like Heidegger, Arendt allies thinking and dwelling. Dwelling, however, does not bring us into the neighborhood of Being. Instead Arendt suggests that the thinking of dwelling, that is, the defrosting of the concept, might open a new relationship to the realm of the everyday. She writes: "To use once more the example of the frozen thought inherent in the word 'house,' once you have thought about its implied meaning—dwelling, having a home, being housed—you are no longer likely to accept for your own home whatever the fashion of the time may prescribe; but this by no means guarantees that you will be able to come up with an acceptable solution for your own housing problems. You may be paralyzed" (176). The thinking of the house for Arendt does not necessarily liberate or release us, but may make possible a changed relationship to finitude.

Building Dwelling Thinking

In Heidegger's essay "Bauen Wohnen Denken" ("Building Dwelling Thinking") the coordinates opened up by the room in *Sein und Zeit* come into place as the axes of the quasi-mythological "fourfold," "das Geviert." In "Bauen Wohnen Denken," the point identified as the *"in"* or the *"Da"* of *Dasein* is called an *Ort*, a place or location. The bridge appears in this essay as the kind of "building" or construction—*Bau*—that makes room for the fourfold (*das Geviert*) and thus sets up a fundamental orientation. The *Ort*, a place opened up by the built thing, in turn makes possible the dimensions of space around it: "The spaces [*Räume*] through which we go daily are provided for by locations [*Orten*]; their nature is grounded in things of the type of buildings" (*PLT* 156/ *VuA* 151). The building (*Bauten*) makes room for room. Space and spaces—*Raum* and *Räume*—are abstract and everyday modes of the genuine space of the *Ort*, in which building and dwelling come together as "the same." "What, then, does *Bauen*, building, *mean*? The Old English and High German word for building, *buan*, means to dwell. This signifies: to remain, to stay in a place" (*PLT* 146/ *VuA* 140). Finally these come together, not surprisingly, with Being:

> That is, *bauen, buan, bhu, beo* are our word *bin* in the versions: *ich bin*, I am, *du bist*, you are, the imperative form *bis*, be. What then does *ich bin* mean? The old word *bauen*, to which the *bin* belongs, answers: *ich bin, du bist* mean: I dwell, you dwell. The way in which you are and I am, the manner in which we humans *are* on the earth, is *Buan*, dwelling. To be a human being means to be on the earth as a mortal. It means to dwell. (*PLT* 147/ *VuA* 141)

While this thetic definition might have some appeal in stressing finitude, it privileges the primordial as genuine meaning and sets up a mythological framework with the term "mortals," a term implying a relationship to a god or gods, to the immortal. The fourfold names the unity of the dimensions set up through the prior definitions of dwelling and building: "But 'on the earth' already means 'under the sky.' Both of these *also* mean 'remaining before the divinities' and include a 'belonging to men's being with one another.' By a *primal* oneness the four—earth and sky, divinities and mortals—belong together in one" (*PLT 149/VuA* 143). The walls of the room and the *Wohnzeug* in *Sein und Zeit* here take on the shape of mythic axes: the up and down of the ceiling and floor are replaced by the earth and the sky; Heraclitus warming himself at the fireplace is restated as the relation between mortals and gods.[13]

Building, or a building, is a kind of architectonic that allows things to come into place in their places: "Space is in essence that for which room has been made [*Raum ist wesenhaft das Eingeräumte*], that which is let into its bounds. That for which room is made is always granted and hence is joined, that is, gathered, by virtue of a location, that is, by such a thing as the bridge" (*PLT* 154/ *VuA* 149). This ordering and allowing to come into place—this making room for—makes rooms. It is housing. It makes room(s) for and shelters what comes into place through it. This is why Heidegger says that the bridge is a house:

> The bridge is a thing of this sort. The location [*der Ort*] allows the simple onefold of earth and sky, of divinities and mortals, to enter into a site by arranging the site into spaces. The location makes room for the fourfold in a double sense. The location *admits* the fourfold and it *installs* the fourfold. The two—making room [*Einräumen*] in the sense of admitting and in the sense of installing—belong together. As a double space-making, the location is a shelter for the fourfold or, by the same token, a house [*ein Huis, ein Haus*, Heidegger's gloss in the German text]. Things like such locations shelter or house men's lives [*behausen den Aufenthalt des Menschen*]. (*PLT* 158/ *VuA* 152–53, Heidegger's gloss)

The spatial relations of *Ort* rely on and presuppose the relations of housing. The mythic organization of the four retains the silhouette of the empirical house as a necessary condition of man's dwelling or tarrying on earth (*Aufenthalt*). The four are moved in like the cupboard and the table. The room with the "ink-stand, pen, ink, paper, blotting pad, table, lamp, furniture, windows, doors, room" recurs here—the professor's house which perhaps stands as the unspoken alternative to the idyll of the *Schwarzwaldhof,* to which, Heidegger admits, we cannot return.

The bridge—that which allows us to pass over to the other side—is essentially a house that stands stable. Building—of bridges and houses—crosses over from the *Bestand*, the "standing reserve," of technics to what lies beyond the technical. In "Die Frage nach der Technik" ("The Question Concerning Technology"), Heidegger contrasts the hydraulic energy plant with the bridge. The energy plant is built into the river in order to "order up" (*bestellen*) its energy, store it, and make it dispensable. The energy of the river is torn out of itself and set to work by and for man; it is the *Bestand* that answers to the *Bestellen* of the technical relation of subject and object. The river in a sense is "expropriated" from itself, is torn from its bed as its home: "The hydroelectric plant is not built into the Rhine River as was the old wooden bridge that joined bank with bank for hundreds of years. Rather, the river is dammed up into the power plant" (*BW* 321/ *VuA* 19). Genuine building is contrasted with technical construction in that it connects. The bridge is thus a *Bestandstück des Bestandes*—but also goes beyond the limits of the *Bestellen/Bestand* pair, beyond the totality of the technical. *Bauen* itself divides into two:

> The old word *bauen*, which says that man *is* insofar as he *dwells*, this word *bauen* however *also* means at the same time to cherish and protect, to preserve and care for, specifically to till the soil, to cultivate the vine. Such building only takes care [*hütet*]—it tends the growth that ripens into its fruit of its own accord. Building in the sense of preserving and nurturing is not making anything. Shipbuilding and temple-building, on the other hand, do in a certain way make their own works. Here building, in contrast with cultivating, is a constructing. Both modes of building—building as cultivating, Latin *colere, cultura*, and building as the raising up of edifices, *aedificare*—are comprised within genuine building, that is, dwelling. (*PLT* 147/ *VuA* 141)

Bauen on the one hand belongs to the *techné* of nature—its coming forth into something other than itself—and to the technics of modern society: the challenging forth, the establishing of a thing set up and against, a *Gegenstand* and *Bestandstück*. *Bauen* has the pliability to stretch between these two zones: the infratechnical *Bestand*, and the building that is a protecting, a sheltering, a housing, a dwelling. Likewise, the bridge can be understood as a mere object that connects one side to the other for various purposes, or it can be seen as a *Ding*, a thing, that first sets up the space of a "between."

In section 2 of "Bauen Wohnen Denken," Heidegger describes at length how the bridge, understood as a "thing," first allows the surrounding landscape to come into being:

> The bridge swings over the stream "with ease and power." It does not just connect banks that are already there. The banks emerge as banks only as the bridge crosses the stream. The bridge designedly causes them to lie across from each other. One side is set off against the other by the bridge. . . . The bridge *gathers* the earth as landscape around the stream. (*PLT* 152/ *VuA* 146)

The bridge, like the room and the house, is an *Ort*, that which first allows spaces, dimensions, and directions to emerge around it: "The bridge *gathers* to itself in *its own* way earth and sky, divinities and mortals" (*PLT* 153/ *VuA* 147). Associated with the fourfold, *das Geviert*, the bridge is not an object, but a thing, a thing connected to essence as that which gathers.

> Gathering or assembly, by an ancient word of our language, is called "thing." The bridge is a thing—and indeed, it is such *as* the gathering of the fourfold which we have described. To be sure, people think of the bridge as primarily and really *merely* a bridge; after that, and occasionally, it might possibly express much else besides; and as such an expression it would then become a symbol, for instance a symbol of those things we mentioned before. But the bridge, if it is a true bridge, is never first of all a mere bridge and then afterward a symbol. (*PLT* 153/ *VuA* 147–48)

Although Heidegger has said that both modes of building—cultivation as well as instrumental putting into place—genuinely belong to building, here we see that only one type of bridge is "*echt*," true or authentic, namely, the kind of "thing" that allows no instrumental organization of cause and effect or means and end. This understanding of being and dwelling is also a critique of that concept of metaphor that imagines a neutral literal sign as primary upon which extra meanings or traits are then overlaid. The house which is the house of being should not be modeled on a "mere" house, but rather should be built first of all as a gathering of the four, a more essential and authentic house that would ultimately allow for the limited sense of a plain old mere house. Building here thus presents a view of poetic language that is not structured along the lines of the dualism between literal and figurative.

   In ". . . dichterisch wohnet der Mensch . . ." (". . . Poetically Man Dwells . . .") Heidegger allies the poetic not with a type of language, but with measurement, or the taking of measure (*Maß-nahme*). Elaborating on the phrase *"dichterisch wohnet der Mensch,"* Heidegger understands this dwelling to mean a *Zwischen*, a between, that, like the bridge, gathers the four and opens up dimension as *Ort*:

> The upward glance passes aloft toward the sky, and yet it remains below on the earth. The upward glance spans the between of sky and earth. This between is measured out for the dwelling of man. We now call the span thus meted out the dimension. This dimension does not arise from the fact that sky and earth are turned toward one another. Rather, their facing each other itself depends on the dimension. Nor is the dimension a stretch of space as ordinarily understood; for everything spatial, as something for which space is made, is already in need of the dimension, that is, that into which it is admitted. (*PLT* 220/ *VuA* 189)

This poetic dwelling operates in the same way as the bridge. As a *Zwischen*, it crosses from the *"bloße"* or mere residence of *wohnen* to the opening of genuine space through the gathering, the coming forth of essence. Poetic dwelling is an alternative measure that does not fall into the *Bestand des Bestellens* of the technical:

> But dwelling occurs only when poetry comes to pass and is present, and indeed in the way whose nature we now have some idea of, as taking a measure for all measuring. This measure-taking is itself an authentic measure-taking, no mere gauging with ready-made measuring rods for the making of maps. Nor is poetry building in the sense of raising and fitting buildings. But poetry, as the authentic gauging of the dimension of dwelling, is the primal form of building. Poetry first of all admits man's dwelling into its very nature, its presencing being. Poetry is the original admission of dwelling. Nor is poetry building [*Bauen*] in the sense of raising and fitting buildings [*Bauten*]. (*PLT* 227/ *VuA* 196)

In "The Question Concerning Technology" Heidegger strives to maintain a vital link between the *Bauten* of the technical and that which is nothing technical at all. In contrast, here he opens and allows to persist a zone that is clearly identified as the more primordial and original, that which is beyond and escapes the technical. The poetic lies beyond the instrumental, or the region of cause and effect, that characterizes the technical. *Bauen*, identified with poetry and dwelling, also eludes instrumentality. Like poetic language, considered a wholly other language, this *Bauen* is not simply everyday *Bauen* with features added on to it. Instead,

Dichten, Wohnen, and *Bauen* are intertwined to convey a language that does not follow the dualism of cause and effect or instrumentality: "Poetry [*das Dichten*] first causes dwelling [*das Wohnen*] to be dwelling. Poetry is what really lets us dwell. But through what do we attain to a dwelling place? Through building [*das Bauen*]. Poetic creation, which lets us dwell, is building" (*PLT* 2153/ *VuA* 183, translation modified).

Despite Heidegger's efforts to evade dualism, two buildings still remain: the authentic one and the everyday technical one, the one in which we merely take up residence, or the bridge which we merely use to get to the other side: "To be sure, people think of the bridge as primarily and really *merely* a bridge" (*PLT* 153/ *VuA* 147). We are also given the opposition between "*das eigentliche Vermessen*" and "*kein bloßes Abmessen,*" "an authentic measure-taking, no mere gauging." In distinguishing the authentic building, dwelling, etc., the "mere" is produced and reproduced as degraded. Later in "Bauen Wohnen Denken," Heidegger returns to the question of the empirical remnant, reflecting upon the Heidelberg bridge. The event of thinking the bridge is described in a way that criticizes representational thinking as the division between subject and object, "internal consciousness" versus external object:

> If all of us now think, from where we are right here, of the old bridge in Heidelberg, this thinking toward that location is not a mere experience inside the persons present here; rather, it belongs to the nature of our thinking *of* that bridge that *in itself* thinking gets through, persists through, the distance to that location. From this spot right here, we are there at the bridge—we are by no means at some representational content in our consciousness. From right here we may even be much nearer to that bridge and to what it makes room for than someone who uses it daily as an indifferent river crossing. (*PLT* 156–57/ *VuA* 151)

While we may be sympathetic with Heidegger's effort to rethink thinking, he continues to reproduce two bridges between which there is no "bridge." Between them lies . . . an abyss? The bridge over this abyss is thinking. "What if," Heidegger concludes his essay,

> man's homelessness consisted in this, that man still does not even think of the *real* plight of dwelling as *the* plight? Yet as soon as man *gives thought* to his homelessness, it is a misery no longer. Rightly considered and kept well in mind, it is the sole summons that *calls* mortals into their dwelling. (*PLT* 161/ *VuA* 156)

Housing problems are recuperated as the predecessor of genuine dwelling; a bridge is crossed from the empirical to thought thanks to which homelessness is domesticated and becomes a condition of the true home, the true dwelling. The *Unzuhause-sein*, the not-being-at-home, from which man is called into dwelling, is itself a hidden home, a home by another name.

Identity and Difference

The status of the house does not, however, remain stable but rather stands at a kind of "crossroad" that can always be shaken up again. In *Identity and Difference*, Heidegger, as he often does, exhorts us to give up thinking of the relationship between Being and thinking as one of synthesis through mediation, as a "*nexio*" or "*connexio*"—the bond between two preexisting things joined by a copula, through predication or conceptual representational thinking (*Vorstellen*). Instead, we are to think of Being and thinking, or man, as being primordially interconnected through a *Zusammengehören*, a belonging together, that predates any possible dialectical synthesis or representational predication. Man, on the one hand, stands enumerated among a plurality of *Seiendes*: "Man obviously is a being. As such he belongs to the totality of Being—just like the stone, the tree, or the eagle. To 'belong' here still means to be in the order of Being."[14]

Man is distinguished from other *Seiendes* by being originally oriented towards Being: "But man's distinctive feature lies in this, that he, as the being who thinks, is open to Being, face to face with being; thus man remains referred to Being and so answers to it. Man *is* essentially this relationship of responding [*Bezug der Entsprechung*] to Being, and he is only this" (*ID* 31/ *IuD* 18). The italics of *is* indicate the connection to being that the statement is getting at. This correspondence between man and Being is a belonging and a kind of listening; the shift from the enumerated *Seiendes* to the ontological relationship of man to Being shifts the meaning of *Gehören*, belonging, to *hören*, hearing: "A belonging [*Gehören*] to Being prevails within man, a belonging which listens [*hört*] to Being because it is appropriated to Being" (*ID* 31/ *IuD* 18). Correspondingly, *Sein* understood as *Anwesen* can only come to present itself (*west an*) through the opening (*Lichtung*) created by man's orientation towards being: "Being is present and abides [*west und währt*] only as it concerns man through the claim it makes on him. For it is man, open toward Being, who alone lets Being arrive as presence" (*ID* 31/*IuD* 19).

Man and Being thus are linked not by *Einordnung*, the intercalated ordering of a series or the dovetail joints of ontic carpentry, but rather through this mutual belonging: the listening which corresponds to a demand and address. This understanding can only be reached by a release of "metaphysical," representational thinking that passes through mediation and predication. As long as we remain within this language,

> [w]e do not as yet enter the domain of the *belonging* together. How can such an entry come about? By our moving away from the attitude of representational thinking. This move is a leap in the sense of a spring. The spring leaps away, away from the habitual idea of man as the rational animal who in modern times has become a subject for his objects. Simultaneously, the spring also leaps away from Being, but Being, since the beginning of Western thought, has been interpreted as the ground in which every being as such is grounded. (*ID* 32/*IuD* 20)

To shift from *gehören* to *hören* is to shift from the relation of subject and object to a different relationship. This shift requires a distancing achieved through a leap away from the ground: ground understood as the conventional structure of ground/entity, as explanatory and ontological structure. What is demanded is a radical break from the concept of ground, or from any conventional concept at all:

> Where does the spring go that springs away from the ground? Into an abyss? [*Wohin springt der Absprung, wenn er vom Grund abspringt? Springt er in einen Abgrund?*] Yes, as long as we only represent the spring in the horizon of metaphysical thinking. No, insofar as we spring and let go. Where to? To where we already have access: the belonging to Being. Being itself, however, belongs to us [*gehört zu uns*]; for only with us can Being be present as Being, that is, become present. (*ID* 32–33/*IuD* 20)

The shifting of registers that opens a new possibility of thinking here cannot be counted under the rules of the technical world; *Einordnung* of entities is no longer in question. The cobelonging of man and being cannot be stated, but takes places as the event, the *Er-eignis*, translated here as (the event of) appropriation: "We must experience simply this owning in which man and Being are delivered over to each other [*dieses Eignen, worin Mensch und Sein einander ge-eignet sind*], that is, we must enter into

what we call *the event of appropriation*" (*ID* 36/*IuD* 24). The leap away
from the ground, viewed from the other side, is a turning in or towards—
Einkehr. "This spring is the abruptness of the unbridged entry into that
belonging which alone can grant a toward-each-other of man and Being,
and thus the constellation of the two. The spring is the abrupt entry into
the realm from which man and Being have already reached each other
in their active nature" (*ID* 33/*IuD* 20–21). With no architectural mediation, thinking moves into a new "area," *ein Bereich.* This moving into is
important: "Only the entry into the realm of this mutual appropriation
determines and defines the experience of thinking" (*ID* 33/*IuD* 21).

The experience of thinking is associated with this turning away from
conventional conceptual senses and is characterized as a movement, not
a result or a thesis. The *Ereignis* is thus the coming into the area itself as a
singular event, a performative shift of semantics: "The term event of appropriation here no longer means what we would otherwise call a happen-
ing, an occurrence. It now is used as a *singulare tantum.* What it indicates
happens only in the singular, no, not even any longer in any number, but
uniquely. [*Was es nennt, ereignet sich nur in der Einzahl, nein, nicht einmal
mehr in einer Zahl, sondern einzig*]" (*ID* 36, translation modified/*IuD* 25).
The *Einzahl* (singular) is *Keinzahl* (no number), the active self-interrup-
tion—*nein, nicht einmal mehr*, no, not even any longer—itself the disruption of the ordered series, itself the irruption of the *Ereignis.*

In some sense then it would be impossible to define the *Ereignis* or to
give sense to its results without falling back into conventional understanding. The new *Bereich*, or region, cannot be allowed to stabilize. Heidegger
writes: "The event of appropriation is that realm, vibrating within itself,
through which man and Being reach each other in their nature, achieve
their active nature by losing those qualities with which metaphysics has
endowed them" (*ID* 37/*IuD* 26). The vibrating, swinging movement is
associated with language itself. The turn into this *Bereich* threatens always
to stabilize; yet, Heidegger argues, the mobility of language can in fact
prevent this:

> To think of appropriating as the event of appropriation means to contribute
> to this self-vibrating realm [*heisst am Bau dieses in sich schwindenden Bereiches
> zu bauen*: literally, to build on the building of this self-vibrating realm].
> Thinking receives the tools for this self-suspended structure from language.
> For language is the most delicate and thus the most susceptible vibration
> holding everything within the suspended structure of the appropriation. We

dwell in the appropriation inasmuch as our active nature is given over to language. (*ID* 37–38/*IuD* 26)

"Building" and "event" would seem to be incompatible terms. Heidegger is relying on the always-possible semantic shifts of the *Sprung* to destabilize the stabilizing operation itself. Building comes in here almost as a compulsion to find a stabilizing element to offset the dizzying effects of the *Abgrund*. Heidegger summarizes:

> This principle in the sense of a statement has in the meantime become a principle bearing the characteristics of a spring that departs from Being as the ground of beings, and thus springs into the abyss. But this abyss is neither empty nothingness nor murky confusion, but rather: the event of appropriation. In the event of appropriation vibrates the active nature of what speaks as language, which at one time was called the house of Being. (*ID* 39/*IuD* 28)

The house of Being is shaken apart here, yet building remains as a vestige of the desire to stabilize a floor or ground on which things happen.

The leap, *der Sprung*, takes the place of the bridge to forge the relationship between two registers of language, two river banks, two bridges. In *Was heißt Denken?* Heidegger describes this leap to characterize the relationship to a blooming tree in ways other than representation (*Vorstellen*) and the inside/outside relationship of consciousness/object. In shifting language the example moves

> outside of science. Instead we stand before a tree [*Baum*] in bloom, for example—and a tree stands before us. The tree faces us. The tree and we meet one another, as the tree stands there and we stand face to face with it. As we are in this relation of one to the other and before the other, the tree and we *are*.[15]

The relationship is posed first within the terms of the technical, of the *Ge-stell*, within which everything is "placed," *gestellt*. Yet the slight twisting of terms alters the placement of subject and object into an animated relationship of introduction: the tree introduces itself to us, who stand across, ready to receive the introduction. In this mutual juxtapositioning, the italics of *sind* show that the terms are not simply related through predicative representation, in such a way that their Being "appears," tarries, or dwells in the emphasis of the italics. Heidegger continues:

> This face-to-face meeting is not, then, one of these "ideas" buzzing about in our heads. Let us stop here for a moment, as we would to catch our breath

before and after a leap. For that is what we *are* now, men who have leapt, out
of the familiar realm of science and even, as we shall see, out of the realm of
philosophy. (*Thinking*, 41/*Denken*, 26)

As the Being of beings marks itself in the italics of *sind*, the leap happens,
syncopating the *sind* into two which are yet "the same" (what Heidegger
would call *das Selbe*): "And where have we leapt? Perhaps into an abyss?
No! Rather, onto some firm soil [*Boden*]. Some? No! But on that soil
upon which we live and die, if we are honest with ourselves. A curious,
indeed unearthly [*unheimliche*, uncanny] thing that we must first leap
onto the soil on which we really stand" (*Thinking*, 41/*Denken*, 26).

With the leap, the language in this passage becomes increasingly performative in the form of questions and exclamations. The breathless moment of the leap alters the *Abgrund* into a ground, the soil or ground of
life upon which we stand without ever noticing it. *Boden—Abgrund* become connected here as "the same," *das Selbe*, through an uncanny alternation. The defamiliarizing of terms allows the genuine ground (*Boden*)
to come forth, but the *unheimlich*—the uncanny, the unhomely—is recuperated in the authenticity or homeliness of this same ground. The *Baum*
[tree] is a *Bau* [building].

Op(p)en/(heimer)

Is it possible to prevent the stabilization of the ground and the house
or to prevent the creeping in of identity and/as the safety of the native
home? Perhaps to do so it is necessary to look beyond Heidegger himself
to an interlocutor. *Dichten* and *Denken*, we know, form a pair that are "the
same," yet dwell in their difference. Avital Ronell has written eloquently
about this in "On the Misery of Theory Without Poetry: Heidegger's
Reading of Hölderlin's 'Andenken'": "When he attempted to give a face
to the cobelonging of poetry and thought," she writes, "Heidegger said
that poetry stretched upward, toward evanescent heights, while thought
reached into abysses, gaining depth. Elsewhere he figures poetry and
thought as twin summits" (17). Heidegger writes:

Poetry and thinking meet each other in one and the same only when, and
only as long as, they remain distinctly in the distinctness of their natures. The
same never coincides with the equal, not even in the empty indifferent oneness of what is merely identical. The equal or identical always moves toward

the absence of difference, so that everything may be reduced to a common denominator. The same, by contrast, is the belonging together of what differs, through a gathering by way of the difference. We can only say "the same" if we think difference. It is in the carrying out and settling of differences that the gathering nature of sameness comes to light. The same banishes all zeal always to level what is different into the equal or identical. (*PLT* 218-19/ *VuA* 187)

To heed this notion of difference, I turn to George Oppen, American poet and Pulitzer Prize winner. His relationship to Heidegger inscribes him in the poetic program not of a protofascist, right-wing high modernist, as we might expect, but of a committed leftist. Oppen gave up writing for twenty-five years because he found political activism and poetry incompatible but began to write again in the 1960s. He was clearly opposed to tendentious political writing. His poetry is in no way socialist-realist, but does have many political strands throughout it. He worked also as a carpenter.

Oppen refers directly to Heidegger in a few places in his poetry.[16] I am concerned here with a more or less direct quote that appears in the long poem "Route" in the book *Of Being Numerous* (1968) for which Oppen won the Pulitzer Prize. It would be difficult to offer a totalizing interpretation of this text, ten pages long and spanning fourteen numbered sections. The poem clearly takes up questions of the sense and possibility of poetry in a war-driven and technological world with direct references to World War II, in which Oppen fought in France.

In section 13, Oppen shares with Heidegger concerns about technology. It presents the image of a broken-down world—clearly one in which dwelling, in Heidegger's sense, is not possible:

13

Department of Plants and Structures————obsolete, the old name
In this city, of the public works
Tho we mean to entangle ourselves in the roots of the world
An unexpected and forgotten spoor, all but indestructible
    Shards

To owe nothing to fortune, to chance, nor by the power of
    his heart
Or her heart to have made these things sing
But the benevolence of the real

Tho there is no longer shelter in the earth, round helpless belly
Or hope among the pipes and broken works

"Substance itself which is the subject of all our planning"
And by this we are carried into the incalculable.[17]

The perspective of this section steps beyond the availability of the objective, the *Bestand*, standing reading to be ordered up and used. Because the plants and works are broken down, the operativity of the technical is still legible as a trace but reduced to fragments. In stepping beyond the technical to the *Ge-stell*, the human subject is no longer the master of these materials—"nor by the power of his heart / Or her heart to have made these things sing." The poet cannot resuscitate or reanimate this, but rather it is Being itself—what Oppen calls "the benevolence of the real"—that summons both voice and things into singing. Twice the poem seemingly denounces its own poetic capacity: "All this is reportage," a merely repetitive activity. Yet when the "I" is released, the world still can reveal something (section 11):

Tell of the life of the mind, the mind creates the finite.

All punishes him. I stumble over these stories—
Progeny, the possibility of progeny, continuity

Or love that tempted him

He is punished by place, by scene, by all the holds
all he has found, this pavement, the silent symbols

Of it, the word it, never more powerful than in this
moment. Well, hardly as epiphany, but there the thing
is all the same. (199)

Reminiscent of Baudelaire's stumbling on the pavement bricks of poetry, as the I is turned over to the third person, the "silent symbols" yield up something after all, revealing "it." The "small word," for which Oppen is famous, points to a minimal ability of language to point, to call attention to itself.[18] "In this moment"—the very slight interruption of the "mere reportage" that activates the performativity of language and draws it out of the broken rubble of plants and works. Similarly, following the quote from Heidegger, "Substance itself which is the subject of all our planning," Oppen's text breaks out of repetition and reportage, of the calculability of the technical: "And by this we are carried into the incalculable"—again by the very small performative presencing of "this," by this something happens in the present that interrupts the manipulation and calculation of the technical. This, the poetic, interrupts it.

In some sense, however, the interruption is no interruption. If we look in Heidegger's *Identity and Difference*, the text that Oppen was reading at the time of writing this poem, we find that the second clause, not in quotation marks, is also in Heidegger's text: "Im selben Maße wie das Sein ist der Mensch herausgefordert, d.h. gestellt, das ihn angehende Seiende als den Bestand seines Planens und Rechnens sicherzustellen und dieses Bestellen ins Unabsehbare zu treiben" (*IuD* 23).

The translation, which was all Oppen knew, poses some problems: "To the same degree that Being is challenged, man, too, is challenged, that is, forced to secure all beings that are his concern as the substance for his planning and calculating; and to carry this manipulation on past all bounds" (*ID* 35).

The word that Oppen especially noted as one he would not have used—"substance"—has no literal counterpart in Heidegger's German. It translates the equally strange *Bestand*. The passage suggests that calculation itself is driven beyond the calculable, through which the *Ge-stell*—the essence of the technical which is itself nothing technical—is glimpsed. In some sense perhaps Oppen and Heidegger are saying "the same."

Oppen is himself extremely concerned with his use of Heidegger's line. In a note to himself dated June 1, 1966, Oppen elaborates upon the importance of his experience with Heidegger's text, and also relates a set of confusing circumstances around his borrowing of the phrase. After reading *Identity and Difference*, Oppen sleeps in the afternoon and has "confused and elaborate dreams."[19] In his dreams, Oppen receives a call: "At one time in the dream—the only section I was able to remember clearly—I was sitting in a chair near a group of people gathered around a small card-table at a sort of conference. The phone had rung, and I had answered—there seemed to be a small telephone table at my left" (*SL* 134).

Already the message is double—Heidegger's voice on the line and the strange conference table. Oppen's body itself reaches from the factical—the conference room scene—to the ontological, the call out of the *Un-zuhause* that calls, like anxiety, and awakens *das Man* into his *Unheimlichkeit*. The dream / call follows Oppen's reading of *Identity and Difference*. Oppen describes:

> That night I sat up very late, very carefully reading the essay, and after many hours felt I had understood it—It was very difficult for me to grasp the

extreme Idealist assumption on which it was based. When I had grasped it, I turned it over and over in my mind for a long time, unable to accept the assumption, but convinced that a part of the statement was of crucial importance to me, of such importance as to alter the subjective conditions of my life, the conditions of my thinking, from that point in time. (*SL* 135)

This is quite a testimonial. The dream / call suggests a profound confusion between what has been invented and what has been received, whether the statement in question belongs to Heidegger or to Oppen. Convinced he has plagiarized the phrase, Oppen reads and rereads Heidegger, yet cannot find the stolen phrase: "Substance itself which is the subject of all our planning / And by this we are carried into the incalculable" (*NCP* 201). Oppen agonizes about whether to place the words in quotes, whether to use it as the climax of the poem, as he considers it "plagiarized," but then reaches the conclusion: "I have not been able to find it, tho the essay is only 19 pages long. . . . It seems necessarily true that I did not read those sentences" (*SL* 136; compare *IuD* 23: the sentence is not in Heidegger's text). Yet on page 35 of the translation of Heidegger's essay, we find:

> Is it that Being itself is faced with the challenge of letting beings appear within the horizon of what is calculable? Indeed. And not only this. To the same degree that Being is challenged, man, too, is challenged, that is, forced to secure all beings that are his concern as the substance for his planning and calculating; and to carry this manipulation on past all bounds. (*ID* 35)

The lines conclude a paragraph introducing the notion of the *Ge-stell* as that which challenges or sets forth (*heraustellt*) man and Being to face each other in the relation of calculation and manipulability—that is, no longer where man is viewed as the master-subject who manipulates, but where the relation of technology is viewed in terms of a characteristic of Being itself—where even calculation and technics will reveal something of the true call of being.

Oppen loses both himself and Heidegger in this situation of citation. Feeling at first he is simply "using" a phrase of Heidegger's, it then becomes impossible to "calculate" the order of priority or to clearly set up an instrumentalization of Heidegger's text. This might be possible if Oppen had simply read the text and then incorporated the line in his own poem, but strangely Oppen and Heidegger relate in a kind of syncopation that allows neither to be originary or simply to be used or appropriated by the other. Instead Oppen's reading is elaborated by his dream experience, which opens up a double reception. This double reception, like the anecdote from Heraclitus, begins in a house: "And I told Mary," Oppen writes, "the one thing I could remember out of what seemed to have been a long and complex dream. Mary and I were in a large country house. . . . I don't remember ever having seen that house before, and yet it was a kind of house very familiar to me, a large, light wooden house, a very large sitting room, very lightly and casually furnished; I have an impression of chintz-covered wicker chairs, and a vague familiarity about the carpet, for which reason I didn't visualize it clearly, and probably French windows—certainly not any other kind of window—an openness" (*SL* 134). While filled with domestic detail, the room here is characterized by openness—open / Oppen—as are many building structures and elements throughout Oppen's poetry. Thanks to this openness, two inputs are opened up: the surrounding conversation (ontic) and the call through the telephone line—Heidegger on the ontological connection. Interestingly, even the transcendent line is punctuated, alternating between language and silence: "I . . . was listening with the receiver held between my chin and shoulder and I was taking notes either of the telephone conversation—in which there were, for some reason, very long silence [sic] broken by short sentences in a rather low and rather rasping masculine voice . . . *or* I was taking notes on the decisions at the table—I don't know which. I was surprised that I could listen to two conversations at once, and pointed out to myself that the phone conversation contained those long silences. Explaining to myself that that made it possible" (*SL* 134). The two discourses are intercalated in a way that allows Oppen not just to *hear* (*hören*) Heidegger but for them to *belong together* (*zusammengehören*). The line from Heidegger is interrupted and repeated through its interconnection with the surrounding world—the conversation at the table and the house in which it takes place. Because the house opens outwards, it allows this connection to take place. The house does not hold fast, but opens. (Here we might note that the interest in the house does not in fact lead to a vocabulary of the homeland—and notice too Oppen's family name was originally Oppenheimer; his father dropped the second part.)

The opening of the house and the entrance of Heidegger take place in another confusion of Oppen and Heidegger. Consider this very early poem of Oppen's, written in 1929:

> The knowledge not of sorrow, you were
>   saying, but of boredom
> Is——aside from reading speaking
>   smoking——
> Of what, Maude Blessingbourne it was,
>   Wished to know when, having risen,
> "approached the window as if to see
>   what really was going on";
> And saw rain falling, in the distance
>   More slowly,
> The road clear from her past the window-
>   Glass——
> Of the world, weather-swept, with which one shared the century. (*NCP* 5)

Drawing on the force of a semi-citation from Henry James, Oppen has the woman look outward; the house opens out to connect with the world in its boredom. Reading Heidegger in the 1960s, Oppen discovered and became touched by Heidegger's use of the term "boredom": "I have a superstition concerning my relation to H. The poem which happens to be printed as the first poem in *Discrete Series*—my first book—was written in 1929. That, I've learned, was the year in which H. was giving his Inauguration Speech in which he spoke of the mood of boredom (in the translation I have) which leads, again in the translation I have, to 'the knowledge of what-is.' The poem . . . begins with the 'knowledge of boredom'. . . . And boredom was an odd word to use. I am touched by superstition remembering my hesitation over that word and the sense of having been given it" (*SL* 156). Oppen contrasts this "giving," which never "took place" but was perhaps an "event" in Heidegger's sense, with what he believes is the mistaken giving of the later phrase. He accepts the gift where there could have been no literal giving, and denies it where there is in fact an actual borrowing.

Thus there is a knowing and borrowing that is neither actual nor non-actual, for it takes place not in a simple repetition but in a re-saying of the same, in a relatedness: as Oppen says, "Not truth but each other" (*NCP* 183). This dissolution of subject-object poles and confusion of identities takes place through the window. The lines from Oppen's early poem are revised in "Route" to read: "approached the window as if to see . . . / The boredom which disclosed / Everything———" (*NCP* 186). The quotation this time could be seen as a self-quotation, thus a self-differing within the author himself.

To treat the confusion of transmission in "Route," Oppen returns to the ending of Heidegger's *Identity and Difference.* "Whatever and however we may think, we will think in the context of tradition. Tradition preponderates if we are liberated from afterthinking into anticipatory thinking which is no longer a planning. Not until we turn our thoughts toward what had already been thought, shall we be employed for what has yet to be thought" (*SL* 136). What may at first appear to be a kind of "anxiety of influence" scenario actually pierces right to the center of one of Heidegger's most important thoughts: that of the undoing of linear temporality through the thinking of the unthought. This kind of reading undoes arithmetical ordering; the turn into the unthought of what is thought also enacts the critique of the instrumental structure of language and no longer allows it to be seen as a vehicle that "contains" or "transmits" meaning. This structure, too, would order signifier and signified along the same lines as text and reader. The turn into the "unthought," or a certain kind of repetition that implies no originality or priority, overlaps with what Heidegger calls the *Einkehr* (turn inward) or *Sprung* (leap) in this essay. These both express the vibrating or humming—or for Oppen: "It is true the great mineral silence / Vibrates, hums, a process / Completing itself" (*NCP* 179)—of the difference crossed with no bridge, the missing link between "bridge" and "bridge." Trying once more to account for his "invention" of Heidegger's phrase in "Route," Oppen writes: "Reacting with shock to what he had written, my mind went on and said the rest, and I thought that he had said it? But the name of the essay is Identity and Difference / A thought which has not been greatly simplified by the event" (*SL* 137).

The event is itself the vibrating, the "verging on vertigo," the "dizzy incredulity" (*SL* 156) that connects and destabilizes *Identity and Difference.* With the destabilizing of the event, the house shakes and opens up. Housing elements remain as the very medium for this exchange between finitudes that opens a glimpse beyond the merely technical relationship between entities. Housing is itself the *Ge-stell* insofar as it has the potential both to obscure what lies beyond the relationships among *Seiendes* and to reveal the belonging together of man and being in the relation of the technical—*something which is itself not technical.* This latter is building.

Building, in a positive sense, would be a taking off from the technical that opens up onto something other than the technical. In this sense, too, it remains grounded in the finite, the everyday, the ontic; yet it operates in such a way as to create and reveal crevices in its own structuring. Let us return for a moment to this passage from *Identity and Difference*:

> To think of appropriating as the event of appropriation means to contribute [*bauen*] to this self-vibrating realm. Thinking receives the tools [*Bauzeug*] for this self-suspended structure from language. For language is the most delicate and thus the most susceptible vibration holding everything within the suspended structure of the appropriation. We dwell in the appropriation inasmuch as our active nature is given over to language. (*ID* 37–38/ *IuD* 26)

The phrase "*am Bau bauen*" (to build on the building, translated as "contributing to the realm") seems to describe a kind of linguistic thinking that can be reduced neither to the visible nor the invisible, the present nor absent, but is characterized by an alternation, a syncopation, a cooperation between both, with no finality. This kind of language would participate in truth not as a concept or a proposition, but as *aletheia*, a kind of revealing. Oppen writes: "I think that poetry which is of any value is *always* revelatory. Not that it reveals or could reveal Everything, but it must reveal something . . . and for the first time. The confusion of 'must not mean but be' comes from this: it is a knowledge which is hard to hold, it is held in the poem, a meaning grasped again on re-reading—." The holding that cannot be held is building or sometimes a house, a house whose window opens up upon re-reading, or reading the un-thought. Oppen continues: "One can seldom describe this meaning—but sometimes one has stumbled on the statement made in another way. As Parmenides' 'The Same is to think and to be' is Charles Reznikoff's 'the girder, still itself among the rubble'" (*SL* 133).[20] Oppen forms a simile—"as . . . [so] is . . ."—between the Parmenides fragment and a fragment of a poem that itself holds a fragmentary building element. The building fragment, the girder, remains itself, still, ready for building, even when lost among the rubble.

Postscript

On my desk to my left there is a rectangular green marble paperweight with the word "SALVE" engraved upon it; next to it is Adam Sharr's book, *Heidegger's Hut*, a monograph about Heidegger's cabin in the Black Forest. Sharr's book includes photographs of the "hut," detailed floor plans, models, and empirical descriptions of building, location, and Heidegger's dwelling practices, as well as thought-provoking speculations about the relation between thinking and place. *Housing Problems*, in contrast, is more about the problem of the connection between the paperweight and *Heidegger's Hut*—the possible contiguity between a bit of touristic memorabilia and a book meant to forge a link between empirical place and the messages and meanings one carries away from it. In some ways, *Housing Problems* is something of a parody, though it did begin with some belief in the possibility of its theme. If the inclusion of the empirical in this study is actually a feint, then its omission does not require justification. In the end, *Housing Problems* was constructed out of the pieces of the failure of the empirical model it both invokes and rejects. Every empirical detail disappears as it is analytically framed.

This disappearance points to the familiar figure of the remnant, the spectral remainder that always eludes presentation. Heidegger's cabin is perhaps this remnant, the empirical building whose omission disturbs the symmetry of this text's layout. This layout is not a footprint either of house or of subject; what it tracks is the effort or the wish to connect origin and trace. The photographs in *Housing Problems* reiterate this desire and its frustration. They point to multiple authorship and origin, to the persistence of facticity as it recedes, and to the spectacle of indexicality itself. They are the trace of conversation and research, of technology and tourism, of collaboration and coincidence. Just as *Housing Problems* arouses and disappoints the desire for an empirical ground, Suzanne Doppelt's photographs—taken on site at the Strasbourg Cathedral, the Goethe House in Weimar, and the Freud Museums in Vienna and London—both respond to and decline the demand for illustration and reference. The disjunction and parallel between the text and the images are an aftereffect of the architectural disjunction itself. Because of this disjunction, the tiny black worms that covered us as we walked out of the cremation chamber at Buchenwald, spookily emerging as if the last survivors still carrying the message of what happened, as if the very soot from the ovens, cannot make their way into this text.

If this were the place for confession, I would admit that Heidegger's cabin is also a blind spot, a place that perhaps should have been included here. I would admit that I avoided the weightiness of what Todtnauberg invokes: the problem of Heidegger's politics, studied so gravely in the encounter between Celan and Heidegger associated with that place; and in the face of this problem, an anxiety of influence and a feeling of inadequacy with respect to the many great personalities who have grappled with this issue, a fear of failing to grasp the enormity of the questions at stake, to face directly the massive conflict of Heidegger's position. Yet this dread, too, mythologizes the mountain retreat and reinforces the *genius loci*, imbuing the place with a spirit that almost speaks to us. It is perhaps also this referential collapse that would make the text into a diagram that suffocates, and Heidegger's hut a Gothic vault, a haunted house in the depths of the forest. Yet its location is not so deep after all; Sharr's book also shows us the tourist signs lately erected, directing one's way along the "Martin Heidegger Rundweg" ("Martin Heidegger footpath") in Todtnauberg. What might be gained or lost by walking that way remains an open question.

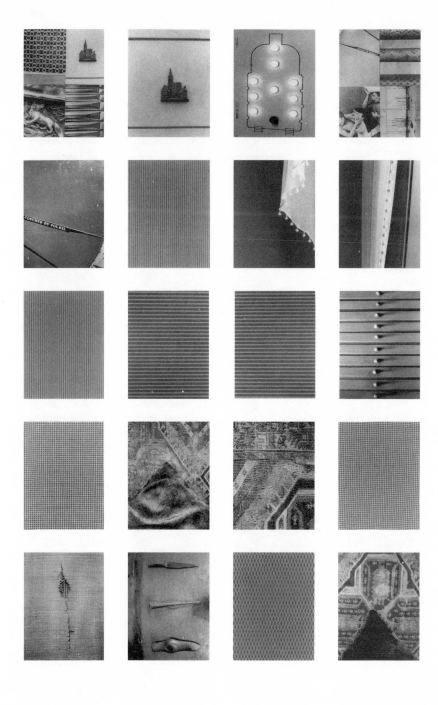

Notes

Introduction

1. Maul and Oppel, *Goethes Wohnhaus*, 29.

2. Kafka, *Sämtliche Erzählungen*, 359. English translations from *The Complete Stories*, 325. Page references to the English translation are followed by references to the German text.

3. Derrida elaborates on this function of architecture in *Psyché*, especially 511–12. Agacinski considers at length the foundational and law-giving function of architecture, especially in relation to politics, in *Volume*.

4. Hamon, in *Expositions* (1989), 28, also attributes to architecture the power of transfer.

5. See *Psyché*, 480.

6. In *The Architecture of Deconstruction* (10–11), Wigley outlines the "fundamental" role of architecture in philosophical discourse. For Wigley "architecture" does not indicate a referent outside of philosophy but names an internal difference or distance between truth and its "ground" or "foundation," between discourse and the material excess of writing and spacing that is the condition of its articulation. The hierarchy ordering structure, design, and ornament corresponds to the conception of buildings as a "decorated shed." See Harries, *The Ethical Function of Architecture*, especially 16–83. Payot also articulates the relation between architecture and philosophy as one of internal difference in his historically thorough study, *Le philosophe et l'architecte*. Lacour argues for the mutual interdependence of philosophy and architecture in her illuminating and rigorous *Lines of Thought*. She insists that the language of architectonics in Descartes is "not symbolic in the conventional sense. It was pragmatic and functional . . . it was active . . . a means of doing rather than a determined category, schema or concept." Descartes' *Discours*, Lacour argues, becomes possible in the oscillation between building and writing: "Descartes stated 'design' (*dessein*), his

intention or motive, is thus not the 'design' (*dessin*), outline or groundplan the architect draws 'à sa fantaisie.'. . . . Yet these two kinds of 'design' require each other. Viewed in terms of the 'discourse' which includes them both, Descartes' 'design'—by which I mean neither term alone but rather his use of and reliance on the two terms individually—takes place in the exchange between *dessein* and *dessin*, or discourse and architectonics, without which there would be no 'method'" (35).

7. Kant, *Kritik der reinen Vernunft*, 2:695 / *Critique of Pure Reason*, 653, translation modified. Page references to this English translation (modified if necessary) and to the German will be given parenthetically.

8. Lacour argues that the term "architectonics" deals with a *productive* gesture and seeks to understand the "language of architectonics" as something quite distinct from a thematization of architecture or from the "presence of architectural metaphors" (3). Likewise, Jacques Derrida (quoted by Lacour) writes: "Contrary to appearances, 'deconstruction' is not an architectural metaphor. The word ought and will have to name a thought of architecture, a thought at work" (quoted in Lacour, 2; see Derrida, *Psyché*, 517). In agreement with Derrida and Lacour, I also do not approach architecture as a metaphor, that is, as a representation or figurative expression of something other than itself. Lacour writes: "Architectonic form is instead another kind of writing which discursive writing, including the writing of metaphor, requires" (4–5). At the same time, the syntax of the term "architectonics" is difficult to pin down. While it clearly refers somehow to architecture, it also implies a generalizing movement or systematic overview of a set of relations involving construction. In "Phenomenality and Materiality in Kant," Paul de Man uses the term "architectonic" to describe a generalizing "poetic vision" that suspends teleology. Quoting a passage in Kant's *Kritik der Urteilskraft* in which the starry heaven is called a *weites Gewölbe*, a "vast vault," de Man writes: "The predominant perception, in the Kant passage, is that of the heavens and the ocean as an architectonic construct. The heavens are a vault that covers the totality of earthy space as a roof covers a house. Space, in Kant as in Aristotle, is a house in which we dwell more or less safely, or more or less poetically, on this earth" (*Aesthetic Ideology*, 81). De Man is clearly invoking Hölderlin's line *doch dichterisch wohnet / Der Mensch auf dieser Erde* ("yet poetically / Man dwells on this earth"), from a fragment sometimes called "In lieblicher Bläue" ("In lovely blue . . ."). Heidegger discusses the line in *Erläuterung zu Hölderlins Dichtung*, 33–48. For a definition of *architectonique* and references to Aristotle, Leibniz, and Kant, see Lalande, *Vocabulaire technique et critique de la Philosophie*, 77–78.

9. Hegel, *Vorlesungen über die Ästhetik*, Werke 14:269 / *Aesthetics*, 2:632. Page references to the English translation are incorporated parenthetically and followed by page references to the German text.

10. Likewise, huge numbers of sphinxes lined up form what is really an architectonic organization: "But all the same the sphinxes were set alongside one another in avenues, and this at once gives them a completely architectural character" (2:644/14:283).

11. The difficulty of beginning architecture is one of the main concerns of Hollier in *Against Architecture*. In his reading of Hegel and Bataille, Hollier focuses on the dominating and violent aspect of architecture as the imposition of a teleological form. In a similar vein, Payot makes the inaugural status of architecture his point of departure in *Le philosophe et l'architecte*. The problem of the beginning exemplifies the architectural disjunction in question. Payot writes: "Architecture is the beginning of thought. This assertion can be understood in two ways. It suggests that architecture is *only* the beginning, and therefore it is necessary to sublate it for knowledge to be established and for spirit to appropriate the image of itself in figurative sculpture; but it also says, at the same time, that architecture *is indeed* the beginning, that from which thought extracts itself. . . . These two teachings are connected: they confirm together the privileged relationship of architecture to presence-to-self—to knowledge, self-consciousness, the subject that appropriates itself, the organic truth—and they interpret this privilege as the effectivity of the negative: at the beginning, presence is delayed, deferred, in expectation and anxiety about itself; this shows the exteriority, the inadequacy, the sought-after quality of architecture" (48).

12. See Hollier, 3–6.

13. Heidegger derives the word *Ding* from the Germanic word for "thing," which he interprets to mean *Versammlung* (*Poetry, Language, Thought*, 153 / *Vorträge und Aufsätze*, 147). Further page references will be incorporated parenthetically and indicated as *PLT* and *VuA* respectively.

14. Harries gives a very helpful analysis of the problems of function and ornament in architecture within the context of the history of philosophy and particularly aesthetics in *The Ethical Function of Architecture*, especially Part One. He also gives a reading of Heidegger's "Bauen Wohnen Denken" in a discussion of Heidegger's critique of teleology in building and technology (part 3). The term "tactile" is borrowed from Benjamin, "Das Kunstwerk im Zeitalter seiner Reproduzierbarkeit" (*Gesammelte Schriften* 1.2), 504–5. Hereafter this work will be cited as *GS*.

15. Fuss focuses on the qualities of the bourgeois domestic interior and how they interact with the production of literary and psychological interiors in *The Sense of an Interior*. While making no totalizing claims, her methodology aims to "reconstruct the actual space of the literary interior as the writer experienced it" (8). She is particularly interested in the role of the senses in mediating between "literal and literary space." In contrast I am interested more in how this relationship is structured by disjunction rather than continuity. Her book also provides

a more historical approach to the notion of domestic interiority than I do here. For an interesting history of domestic space see also Rybczynski, *Short History of an Idea.*

16. Deleuze and Guattari associate this function of containment as a kind of reterritorialization with the photo (*Kafka*, 8–11).

17. In *Architecture from the Outside*, Grosz is also interested in destabilizing that aspect of architecture that I am aligning here with the house. She sees this possibility in Deleuze's philosophy: "There are a lot of different ways in which I think Deleuze's work could take off in architecture. . . . Take the idea, for example, of building as a fixed entity or a given, stable object (which is the standard notion of building today). A Deleuzian framework may help us transform these rather static ways of understanding construction. A building is made up of other spaces within it that move and change, even if its own walls remain fixed" (6). Additionally: "I am concerned here less with 'applying' Deleuzian concepts to the architectural field than with raising some questions inspired by the Deleuzian project of reconceiving thought in order to avoid coming up with recuperable answers, in order to unsettle or make architecture itself, if not stutter, then tremble" (61). The issue of stuttering and architectural trembling will become important below in my reading of *The Castle of Otranto*. Similarly influenced by the thinking of Deleuze, Rajchman also tries to envision a loosening of the relationship of means and ends in the modeling of architecture. This culminates in a notion of the "virtual house" resting on a "virtual plan." This is an interesting, if perhaps utopian, notion: "The virtual plan is thus not a general, abstract, or master plan; yet neither is it an empty or deconstructed one, functioning by unbuilding, undoing, or collapse alone. It is free just because it is neither ideal nor impossible. That is why the virtual house is the most intense house, the one to most 'affect' in ways that surprise us, obliging us to go beyond what normally seems possible" (*Constructions*, 120). McLaughlin also develops the notion of "virtual place" as part of a critique of the interpretation of aesthetic content as a stable substance, especially in "Virtual Paris: Benjamin's *Arcades Project*." See also McLaughlin's *Paperwork*, especially 18–28, on virtuality. McLaughlin's understanding of virtual place depends more on divisibility than on a conventional concept of possibility. Drawing on Benjamin's study of early German Romanticism, McLaughlin outlines "a virtual theory of aesthetic mediacy that defies the classic aesthetic categories based on substantial self-presence, whether of the work or art of the subject" (27).

Chapter 1

1. See Scheurmann and Bongaerts-Schomer, eds., "*. . . endlich in dieser Hauptstadt der Welt angelangt!*"

2. The relation between aesthetic production and critical theory is the main

issue throughout de Man's *Aesthetic Ideology*. In his introduction Andrzej War-minski gives an illuminating analysis of the term "aesthetic ideology" in de Man's work and stresses the way in which "ideology" is not simply an object to be demystified by "critique" but rather is itself generative of critical discourse. For an account of aesthetic ideology in relation to general problems of theory, see Redfield's *Phantom Formations: Aesthetic Ideology and the Bildungsroman*. This study is extraordinarily clear and demonstrates great historical depth. References to the enormous field of work on the *Bildungsroman* can also be found in Redfield. Other helpful works include Hardin, Kontje, Mayer, Moretti, and Sammons.

3. See especially 27–37.

4. *Goethe on Art*, 118. Some translations from this source have been modified. See also *Goethes Werke—Hamburger Ausgabe*, 12:177. All references to the German texts herein refer to this edition as *HA*.

5. Calhoon reads Goethe's experience of unity in the cathedral as an instance of fantasmatic identification in terms of Jacques Lacan's mirror-stage in "The Gothic Imaginary."

6. Kant, *Kritik der Urteilskraft*, paragraph 23ff.

7. In his account of the Strasbourg Cathedral experience in *Dichtung und Wahrheit*, the anxiety of the sublime and its mastery through representation is presented even more explicitly: "The more I considered the façade, the more was that first impression strengthened and developed, that here the sublime has entered into alliance with the pleasing. If the vast [*das Ungeheuere*], when it appears as a mass before us, is not to terrify; if it is not to confuse, when we seek to investigate its details,—it must enter into an unnatural, apparently impossible, connection, it must associate to itself the pleasing. But now, since it will be impossible for us to speak of the impression of the minster except by considering both these incompatible qualities as united, so do we already see, from this, in what high value we must hold this ancient monument; and we begin in earnest to describe how such contradictory elements could peaceably interpenetrate and unite themselves" (*Autobiography*, 416/ *HA* 9:382–83).

8. See Boisserée, *Briefwechsel / Tagebücher* and *Tagebücher 1808–1854*. For a historical treatment of the architecture of the Cologne Cathedral including reproductions of Boisserée's sketches and engravings of the cathedral at various points of completion, see Clemen.

9. Haischer also reads the two essays as autobiography limited to a sense of a linear history in "Ruine oder Monument? Goethes Lebenswerk im Spiegel seiner Gotik-Studien."

10. Apel et al., *Goethe als Sammler*, 14.

11. *Wilhelm Meister's Apprenticeship*, 3 / *Wilhelm Meisters Lehrjahre*, *HA* 7:12.

Chapter 2

1. In his *Teutsche Academie der Edlen Bau- Bild- und Mahlerey-Künste*, quoted in Robson-Scott, 7–9.

2. Jane and Marshall Brown read Goethe's *Faust* particularly in the context of the Gothic novel. They also document Goethe's references to Walpole and other Gothic literature in "*Faust* and the Gothic Novel."

3. *The Castle of Otranto* was translated into German in 1768 and again in 1794. Many German "versions" of the novel were also published. See Hall and Oppel. Oppel states that A. W. Schlegel was a fan of Walpole.

4. A. W. Schlegel and others sometimes entertained the possibility that Gothic had Saracen or Indian origins. See Frankl, 455–57, and Robson-Scott, 146.

5. Aristotle, 69.

6. For a trenchant analysis of barbarism see McLaughlin, "Virtual Paris."

7. Many of the German or Gothic traits praised in the eighteenth century go back to Tacitus' descriptions in his *Germania* (A.D. 97–98); for example: "It is a well-known fact that the peoples of Germany never live in cities, and will not even have their houses set close together. They live apart, dotted here and there, where spring, plain or grove has taken their fancy" (114). Interestingly Tacitus attributes this possibly to the fact that "they are such inexpert builders."

8. Herder praises folk poetry, including *alten gotischen Gesängen*, old Gothic songs, in these terms in his "Briefwechsel über Ossian" (1773, originally published along with Goethe's text "Von deutscher Baukunst" in *Von deutscher Art und Kunst. Einige fliegende Blätter*). Popular verse is alive, full of leaps and turns, virile, natural, and spontaneous. Though a proponent of the vitality of the "German," Herder did not approve of Gothic architecture. At the end of the correspondence Herder uses the term *gotisch* in the negative sense of overly ornate and artificial (234).

9. I am outlining here simply the negative treatments of barbarism in association with Gothic. Also allied with the variety and the movement of terms like "picturesque," the Gothic is simultaneously celebrated and sometimes considered a mode as "harmonious" as any classical model of beauty. See Frankl, 459, and Robson-Scott, 135. Both cite Friedrich Schlegel's reactions to the cathedrals of Louvain and Cologne in *Grundzüge der gotischen Baukunst*.

10. Chris Brooks considers seventeenth century university building in the "old style" to be Gothic revival because the style, especially fan vaulting, is consciously used. Most notably he considers the fan vault of 1659 in the chapel of Brasenose College an instance of revival because it is trompe l'oeil. It is, he writes, "architecturally an illusion. For it is of plaster, mimicking a structural form but without structural function, not a vault at all but a ceiling that looks like a vault. In one of the defining acts of revivalism—to be repeated endlessly over the next two centuries—Jackson shifted categories in his handling of the

gothic, from the constructional to the visual. Abstracted in this way, the chapel's fan-vault reveals itself as cultural spectacle and cultural sign, its purpose to impress and evoke, to summon the validating spirit of the medieval past into the present—and the presence—of seventeenth-century Anglican worship" (31–32). The point is simply that Gothic revival had beginnings in the seventeenth century though clearly it did not become widespread until the eighteenth century.

11. Thus "Gothic revival" implies a conscious (re)turn to an earlier style rather than a "survival" of building assimilating itself to older surroundings, though this also continued to occur. Clark specifically refutes the notion of Gothic survival, though he points out that Gothic did not cease to be a prevalent (though minor) style in England until the sixteenth century. Like Brooks, he points to the moment at which the Gothic style is named as the point at which it becomes an artificially invoked, thus ideologically laden, style; see Clark, 3–16. Gothic revival implies a positive reevaluation of Gothic and a new interpretation or "rediscovery" of the historical period. Ellis writes: "In the eighteenth century, the term gothic was revised and transformed from a term connoting the unfavourable, unhappy and ruined, to a more positive and confident understanding. The emergence of gothic fiction represents one of the defining moments when an older chivalric past was idealised at the expense of a classical present. The gothic is then a conscious anachronism, presented not as an error of taste or a corrupting influence, but as a positive attribute" (23).

12. Walpole bought what was called Chopped Straw-Hall from the "toy-woman" Mrs. Chenevix (Iddon, 1).

13. Leopold Friedrich Franz of Anhalt-Dessau, who built it, visited England in 1763 and 1766. Earlier examples of what Robson-Scott calls "Rococo Gothic" in Germany include: the Magdalenenkapelle in the park of the Nymphenburg Palace in Munich (1725–28); the Nauener Tor in Potsdam (1755); and the Schloss on the Pfaueninsel, Berlin (1794–97). Scharabi refers to *Wiedererweckung* and *Wiederentdeckung der Gotik* as well as *Neugotik*, 11.

14. While Varma might be considered somewhat outdated, Hogle likewise begins his definition of the Gothic genre with a list of spatial markers: "Though not always as obviously as in *The Castle of Otranto* . . . a Gothic tale usually takes place (at least some of the time) in an antiquated or seemingly antiquated space—be it a castle, a foreign palace, an abbey, a vast prison, a subterranean crypt, a graveyard, a primeval frontier or island, a large old house or theatre, an aging city or urban underworld, a decaying storehouse, factory, laboratory, public building, or some new recreation of an older venue, such as an office with old filing cabinets, an overworked spaceship, or a computer memory" ("Introduction: The Gothic in Western Culture," in *The Cambridge Companion to Gothic Fiction*, 2). Marshall Brown is an exception; he considers the Gothic machinery

and props rather superfluous in Walpole's text and sees its innovation instead in the introduction of "psychonarration." See *The Gothic Text*, 32.

15. Here Varma echoes Summers's remark in his preface to the 1924 edition of *The Castle of Otranto*: "It is the Castle itself which is the centre of Walpole's romance" (xx–xxi).

16. Frank argues that Walpole's ambivalence about his authorship mirrors the overall ambivalence characteristic of the novel, which, she suggests, is grounded in the sociohistorical context.

17. In pointing to research proposing that there were real historical precedents to Walpole's novel, Wein suggests that Walpole had done more historical research than he would like his readership, up to the present day, to believe. Wein argues that Walpole had an ambivalent relationship to history that the dual nature of Strawberry Hill would support.

18. Morrissey cites these passages to detail Walpole's construction of a historical forgery (both Strawberry Hill and *The Castle of Otranto*), 123–24. See also Barthes on *l'effet de réel*, in *Essais critiques IV*. He defines this as the effect of signs, especially of seemingly superfluous detail and narrative description, that draw attention to themselves as "the real" (174).

19. In *Gothic*, Botting surveys ambivalent contemporary reviews of Walpole's novel. He writes, for example: "The ambivalent reactions produced by *The Castle of Otranto* of a wider audience concerning the eighteenth century's relation to its Gothic past and its changing present . . . in failing to offer an overriding and convincing position, *The Castle of Otranto* leaves readers unsure of its moral purpose. Its uncertain tone and style, between seriousness and irony, is perhaps the novel's cardinal sin and one that is visited in various forms on all its literary offspring" (53). The novel seems to reinforce and restore patriarchal order; at the same time, "The style of writing itself works against reason and propriety and led critics of the time to baulk at its absurdities, lack of morality and false taste" (51). These stylistic features characterize Walpole's house as well. Ellis documents contemporary critical uncertainty: "*The Critical Review* . . . concluded with an air of jaded insouciance that 'whether he speaks seriously or ironically we neither know nor care'" (28). Ellis suggests that the novel is "structurally unstable" in following conventions of both the novel and the romance.

20. Clery associates this imagery of the letter with the threat of fiction in Walpole's time to "present fears concerning the addictive, pathological nature of the pleasures of fiction, and the powers wielded by the novelist over the sensibilities of her or his reader" (65).

21. This follows the sense of allegory suggested in Dante's "Letter to Can Grande": the literal level of the narrative is interpreted in terms of a biblical story or moral or anagogical counterpart. Preminger and Brogan, eds., *The New Princeton Encyclopedia of Poetry and Poetics* explains as follows: "Perhaps the

dominant attitude in current classifications is that there are degrees of allegorical compositions, depending on the extent to which a text displays two divided tendencies. One tendency is for the elements of the text to exhibit a certain fictional autonomy. The other tendency is for these elements to imply another set of actions, circumstances, or principles. . . . Insofar as a composition is allegorical, it tends to signal the ambivalence or allusiveness of its language and to prescribe the directions in which a reader should interpret it" (31–32). More recent work on allegory has tended to stress its foundation in the temporality of the text rather than its resolution in a moral or other meaning. In other words emphasis is on the impossibility of an "immediate" connection between sign and sense; allegory underscores, instead, the production of meaning through the repetition of mechanical signs related to one another. De Man's reading of allegory in "The Rhetoric of Temporality" stresses the distended temporality of reading over the synchronicity of an interpreted sense in allegory: "We have . . . a relationship between signs in which the reference to their respective meanings has become of secondary importance. But this relationship between signs necessarily contains a constitutive temporal element; it remains necessary, if there is to be allegory, that the allegorical sign refer to another sign that precedes it. The meaning constituted by the allegorical sign can then consist only in the *repetition* (in the Kierkegaardian sense of the term) of a previous sign with which it can never coincide, since it is of the essence of this previous sign to be pure anteriority" (207). Spacing is just as crucial as the temporal extension de Man identifies in allegory here. Benjamin articulates the coextension of temporality and spacing in allegory in his *Ursprung des deutschen Trauerspiels* (*The Origin of German Tragic Drama*), especially in dealing with the ruin (*GS* 1.1). Allegory has a double action that yields, on the one hand, a "fable" and, on the other, the debris of signifiers left behind in the field of finitude (history, temporality): "But it will be unmistakably apparent, especially to anyone familiar with allegorical textual exegesis, that all of the things which are used to signify derive, from the very fact of their pointing to something else, a power which makes them appear no longer commensurable with profane things, which raises them onto a higher plane, and which can, indeed, sanctify them. Considered in allegorical terms, then, the profane world is both elevated and devalued. This religious dialectic of content has its formal correlative in the dialectic of convention and expression. For allegory is both: convention *and* expression; and both are inherently contradictory" (175/ *GS* 1.1:350–51). This semiotic polemic plays itself out in *Otranto* in the tension between the interpretive claim in the preface and the digressive qualities of the text. For Benjamin, these qualities, which enforce the uninterpretable facet of allegorical writing, tend towards the opacity and illegibility of the image: "Both externally and stylistically—in the extreme character of the typographical arrangement and in the use of highly charged metaphors—the written word tends towards the visual. It is not possible to conceive of a starker opposite to the artistic symbol, the plastic symbol, the image of organic totality, than this amorphous fragment which is seen in the form of allegorical script" (175–76/ *GS* 1.1:351–52). The isolated body parts can be seen as this kind of fragments; likewise, Frederic's knights arrive as strangely mute guests who communicate only through gestures. The same is true of the gigantic inscribed but undecipherable sword they carry—literally a *Schriftbild*. Their refusal to speak—the fusion of their bodily gestures and their language—infuriates Manfred, who sees it as a violation of decorum and hospitality. Receiving the knights, Manfred "put several questions to them, but was answered only by signs. They raised their vizors but sufficiently to feed themselves, and that sparingly. Sirs, said the prince, ye are the first guests I ever treated within these walls, who scorned to hold any intercourse with me: nor has it oft been customary, I ween, for princes to hazard their state and dignity against strangers and mutes" (99). The knights cannot be assimilated into the story line until they begin to speak and draw the spirit up out of the letter; likewise, the sword remains bound to the ground and incomprehensible until the eventual coming together of the giant.

22. Clery makes the connection between Walpole's phrase and Adam Smith's economic "invisible hand" (66). She reads *The Castle of Otranto* in the context of the contradictions arising in eighteenth century England between the systems of aristocratic inheritance and the rising interests of bourgeois capitalism, "founded on contract rather than genealogy" (76). An interesting variant appears in her quotation of Henry Home's critique of landed property: "Home's rhetorical antithesis, by which the integrity of an insentient object [property] is raised to a highest principle, becoming 'in effect a mortmain,' a dead hand potentially endangering human life and freedom" (77). Clery interprets the agency of objects, such as the helmet, body parts, and enormous sword in *The Castle of Otranto*, as part of this alienation (77–78).

23. These terms are important in the distinction often made between the "male" and "female" Gothic. Williams suggests that male Gothic is characterized by the hero / villain's transgressive acts and punishment, while in female Gothic, order is restored, usually through marriage (103). Both, I would add, are characterized by a resolution of mystery, usually a repentance, and a restoration of order through explanation, even if this includes supernatural elements. Williams writes: "The male Gothic protagonist, however, fails and dies. The hero / villain is an isolated overreacher punished for his hubris, his violation of the Law. He destroys himself. . . . The female Gothic heroine experiences a rebirth" (103). Moreover, Williams views fiction as a kind of house; pointing out that many historians of literature pay little attention to Gothic fiction, she adds: "Or a Realism-centered critic may, less often, admit Gothic into the House of Fiction under a new name" (2). While considering the functions of fiction in

architectural terms, Williams does not question the operativity of these terms, themselves put into place through Gothic fiction. Later she also describes the process of revelation and resolution in terms of architecture: "Like that of the Freudian analysand, the heroine's 'hysterical misery' may be alleviated by exploring the dark corridors, opening the closed doors, lifting the black veil" (171). By accepting the house as ground, she covers over the question of the grounding of the house.

24. Napier makes a similar argument. See especially chapter 1, "Techniques of Closure and Restraint" (9–43) and chapter 2, "Techniques of Destabilization and Excess" (44–72).

Chapter 3

1. Todorov identifies the suspension of resolution with the fantastic, rather than the uncanny. The fantastic is characterized by a "hesitation" about whether or not the rules of reality apply; if they do, the result is "uncanny," if not, "marvelous." See *The Fantastic*, 41.

2. Freud, "The Uncanny," *The Standard Edition of the Complete Psychological Works of Sigmund Freud* 17:224 / "Das Unheimliche," *GW* 12:236. *The Standard Edition* is cited in text as *SE*.

3. I have developed this interpretation of the uncanny at length in "It Walks: The Ambulatory Uncanny." See this for full bibliography on the topic as well. In *Victorian Hauntings*, Wolfreys gives a succinct account of "spectrality" and the uncanny as the blurring of the distinction between presence and absence.

4. See again "It Walks," 1119 and note 14. On the analogy between walking and reading, see also McLaughlin, "Virtual Paris," 214–17.

5. The invocation of this biblical model raises questions about the "age" of the uncanny. Vidler, for example, in *The Architectural Uncanny* considers the uncanny to be a strictly modern postindustrial phenomenon of alienation. While I would not necessarily date the uncanny to the biblical texts on letter and spirit, these terms can help elucidate its articulation in the Western tradition insofar as it is informed by this model. On the other hand, because I am arguing that the uncanny comes about with the destabilization of oppositions and the violation of the law of contradiction, there is potential for it wherever these take place or wherever inside and outside are organized in a relationship of opposition; this suggests that architecture, as a primordial distinction between interior and exterior, is coeval with the possibility of the uncanny, or vice versa. In *Victorian Hauntings*, Wolfreys seems to agree in arguing that the uncanny, or "spectrality," as a deconstituting constitutive feature of representation, is "present" wherever there is narrative and representation: "Haunting remains in place as a powerful force of displacement, as that disfiguring of the present, as the

trace of non-identity within identity, and through signs of alterity, otherness, abjection or revenance. Indeed, according to Derrida, haunting is not simply a thing of the past or, indeed, something from the past" (1). At the same time, though, he privileges modernity as the most haunted place: "Another way to approach this question of haunting might therefore be to suggest that all forms of narrative are spectral to some extent"; but, "A spectre haunts modernity, and the spectral is at the heart of any narrative of the modern" (2–3). It is not clear how he makes the step from a generalized model of representation to one delimited to modern narrative.

6. On the Gothicism of reading, see also Hustis.

Chapter 4

1. Many argue that what I am identifying as a generic struggle here represents a historical paradigm shift of sorts from a feudal to a capitalist economy. Wellbery, for example, understands the "historical-cultural process" of the novel as the collapse of the symbolic, in "Die Wahlverwandtschaften (1809)." Vogl argues that the novel represents a conflict between two types of "economy": a domestic economy and that of *Kameralismus*. This conflict likewise accounts for "deregulation" and the removal of clear limits and borders.

2. Breithaupt argues that *Die Wahlverwandtschaften* is principally "about" the production of culture through the limitations of imagistic representation; Edward grates against this process of limitation in his struggling towards infinity. Wellbery interprets Edward's outward movement as an effect of the opening up of unlimited commercial expansion (307).

3. J. Hillis Miller gives a reading of the *Gleichnisrede* in sympathy with mine in his excellent essay, "Anastomosis," in *Ariadne's Thread*, especially 209ff. Miller stresses the role of catachresis in his interpretation to name the ungrounded naming of the first element in a set of substitutions (198–99). See also Brodsky, "The Coloring of Relations."

4. For Hegel the house is defined by having four walls, either square or oblong, governed by right angles; see *Vorlesungen über die Ästhetik*, in *Werke*, 14:296, 306ff. The emphasis on squaring, enclosing, and the perpendicular has to do with the dominance of purposiveness in architecture.

5. Benjamin refers to Goethe's letter to Zelter, June 1, 1809: *Ich hoffe, sie sollen meine alte Art und Weise darin finden. Ich habe viel hineingelegt, manches hinein versteckt. Möge auch Ihnen dies offenbare Geheimnis zur Freude gereichen* (*GW* 6:638). [I hope you will find in it my old ways. I have put much into it, and hidden some. May this open secret afford some pleasure to you too.]

6. On Benjamin's very difficult essay, see Stanley Corngold, "Genuine Obscurity Shadows the Semblance Whose Obliteration Promises Redemp-

tion: Reflections on Benjamin's 'Goethe's Elective Affinities,'" in Richter, ed., *Benjamin's Ghosts*; Gasché, especially 60–102; Leacock; Menninghaus, especially 73–94; Beatrice Hannsen, "' Dichtermut' and 'Blödigkeit'—Two Poems by Friedrich Hölderlin, Interpreted by Walter Benjamin," and Sigrid Weigel, "The Artwork as Breach of a Beyond: On the Dialectic of Divine and Human Order in Walter Benjamin's 'Goethe's Elective Affinities,'" both in Hannsen and Benjamin, eds., *Walter Benjamin and Romanticism*; and Tantillo.

7. Miller reaches similar conclusions. His essay includes thorough insightful readings of the problem of mimesis in these multiplying examples, which economy requires I only mention here. For a careful analysis of problems of mimesis and representation, see Peucker.

8. Schneider reads this, along with the larger problem of ungrounding, as part of a general "mobilization" or even "virtualization" of space characteristic of a historical moment of alienation from nature definitive of modernity (289–90).

Chapter 5

1. H.D. traveled in modernist circles in both the U.S. and Europe. In her very thorough study *H.D.'s Freudian Poetics*, Chisholm reads H.D.'s oeuvre as a radical intertextuality with a feminist agenda. The book also provides an extensive bibliography. For insightful readings of H.D.'s work as a decentering textual practice, see also Riddel. Pound originally coined the term "Imagiste" and its three-point agenda to launch H.D.'s poetry; see *Literary Essays of Ezra Pound*, 3–15. See also the works of Kenner and Waldrop.

2. Winter invokes the famous address in noting the difficulty of locating an institutional origin for psychoanalysis. She writes: "We cannot identify psychoanalysis with an academic department or a particular hospital or asylum like the Salpêtrière or the Allgemeines Krankenhaus. Instead, when we attempt to locate Freud, we may think first of a city, Vienna, and a local address there, Berggasse 19, where he both lived and had his consulting rooms from 1891 until he was forced to flee from Nazi-controlled Austria to England in 1938. 'Freud' [sic] and psychoanalysis seem simultaneously to inhabit domestic and public spaces: the couch, the middle-class household, the psychotherapist's office, the city, the world" (7).

3. The image is interestingly evocative of the dream-house described by Rainer Maria Rilke in *Die Aufzeichnungen des Malte Laurids Brigge*.

4. I can only gesture here towards the literature on photography implicit in my reading. In the classic *On Photography*, Sontag indicates this quality: "Photography is an elegiac art, a twilight art. . . . All photographs are *memento mori*. To take a photograph is to participate in another person's (or thing's) mortality, vulnerability, mutability. Precisely by slicing out this moment and freezing

it, all photographs testify to time's relentless melt. . . . A photograph is both a pseudo-presence and a token of absence" (15–16). Barthes locates the photo on the cusp between presence and absence, present and past; see *La chambre claire*, 120. He also connects it with the future anterior (150). Benjamin, in contrast, developed the thought that the photo offers something that was not available in the present or presence of the thing photographed, giving us the concept of the "optical unconscious" (*GS* 2:1:371). Like Barthes he considers the contingency of photography one of its primary features (371). With reference to August Sander's photographs, which present a "physiognomic gallery" of heads, Benjamin quotes Goethe to describe the kind of observation that the non-empirical yet materially bounded space of photography makes possible: *Es gibt eine zarte Empirie, die sich mit dem Gegenstand innigst identisch macht und dadurch zur eigentlichen Theorie wird* [There is a tender empiricism that makes itself inwardly identical with the object, and in this way becomes genuine theory] (2:1:380). Goethe's notion of *zarte Empirie* might be relevant to the desire for indexicality in both photography and housing. In *Spectral Evidence*, Baer argues compellingly that photography need not be assimilated to a narrative model but in fact can give rise to something wholly new that was never experienced in any "original" form. He writes: "My effort to reorient photography criticism away from a narrative model of experienced time is also an attempt to acknowledge that for uncounted numbers of individuals, significant parts of life are not experienced in sequence but as explosive bursts of isolated events. This book explores photography's tremendous potential to capture such experiences without integrating them into a mitigating context and thus denying their force" (6).

5. For an interesting reading of the ways in which the psychoanalytic process is installed in Freud's apartment and the experience of the museum, see Fuss and Sanders, "Berggasse 19: Inside Freud's Office" and Fuss, *The Sense of an Interior*.

6. The passage is added in a footnote to the Strachey translation of *The Interpretation of Dreams*, 154. Thanks to Jeffrey Wallen for pointing this out to me. The original can be found in Freud's *Briefe*, 254.

7. I am greatly indebted here to Weber's unparalleled reading of the dissolution of observation, the dislocation of place, and the "crisis of phenomenality" of castration (222) and related problems in Freud in *The Legend of Freud*.

8. *Mal d'archive*, 20 / *Archive Fever*, 7. Further references will be incorporated parenthetically to the English translation and the French text.

9. Derrida works out this relationship in detail in "Freud et la scène de l'écriture" in *L'écriture et la différence*. A mark of the finitude of memory, the archive or document preserves the finitude it seeks to evade; it thus will always be haunted by the death drive and vulnerable to destruction (11–12/26–27).

10. In *Paperwork*, McLaughlin works out very insightfully the logic of the

"scene of writing," the irreducibility of the withdrawing substrate, and the dissolution of a self-contained subject with reference to Derrida and Freud. McLaughlin writes: "But the key rapport is one of a psyche that is not self-contained to dynamic writing material or support that is not simply a self-present *aide-mémoire*. If this scene is in part one of psychic exteriorization—a spatialization of the mind in the figure of an inorganic graphic support—it is also, again reciprocally, one of the interiorization of the inorganic matter of the writing machine in the psyche (what Derrida calls 'death and finitude *within* the psyche')" (9). I suggest that housing plays a role similar to that of paper for McLaughlin—a necessary material support that withdraws as it supports.

11. It is generally noted that Freud began to collect antiquities following his father's death, thus as a kind of compensation for loss, just as Goethe immediately replaced his dead wife's rooms with cabinets for his collections. For an analysis of Freud's collection as homologous to the "collecting" features of psychoanalysis, see John Forrester, "'Mille e tre': Freud and Collecting," in Elsner and Cardinal, eds., *The Cultures of Collecting*; and Lynn Gamwell, "The Origin of Freud's Antiquities Collection," in Gamwell and Wells, eds., *Sigmund Freud and Art*. See also Fuss, 78.

12. Fuss describes the historical context of Viennese orientalism well and likens the atmosphere in Freud's office to that of the "late Victorian fantasy of the opium den" in *The Sense of an Interior*, 90.

13. Fuss analyzes carefully what Freud could see both when seated in his study (especially 80–87) and while seated next to the couch (87–99). Gamwell also analyzes the objects visible from the desk as Freud's "audience" (27). See also Forrester in Elsner and Cardinal, eds., 227.

14. Quoted in Inge Scholz-Strasser's introduction to Engelman's *Sigmund Freud*, 8.

15. Waugaman, 338–57. Issue 15:3 of *Psychoanalytic Inquiry* was devoted to the question of the couch. Thanks to William M. Bernstein for bringing this to my attention.

16. Joseph D. Lichtenberg, M.D., draws this term from Winnicott in his essay "Forty-Five Years of Psychoanalytic Experience On, Behind, and Without the Couch," *Psychoanalytic Inquiry* 15:3 (1995), 280–93.

17. George Moraitis, M.D., "The Couch as a Protective Shield for the Analyst," *Psychoanalytic Inquiry*, 15:3 (1995), 406–12; quote on pages 407–8.

18. Interestingly, Fuss notes that Engelman was not able to photograph the view from Freud's chair, as it was too narrowly positioned to allow for the tripod, and concludes: "The consulting room chair stands as a fundamentally uninhabitable space, a tribute to the imposing figure of the analyst who remains, even to the searching eye of the camera, totally and enigmatically other" (99). Barthes also connects private space with not being seen: "'Private life' is nothing

but this zone of space, of time, in which I am not an image, an object" (*La chambre claire*, 32).

19. Forrester also contrasts the two museums. Of the Vienna museum, he writes: "It was dominated visually by blown-up-to-life-size photographs of how it once had been, photographs that stood in for all the objects that had been removed to London when the Freuds escaped from the Nazis. It had a derisible atmosphere, perhaps one deliberately induced to remind visitors of yet one more loss that the war had visited on Vienna; but it still prompted the thought that a museum of fake souvenirs is a fake museum—a screen museum, the Freudian might say." He contrasts this with the "real furniture" and objects in the London museum, which he calls a "perfect souvenir-world" (246–47). Fuss suggests that the photographs, "originally taken for the postwar construction of a Freud museum, have themselves *become* the museum—miniature sites of preservation and display" (73). It seems to me important that both the Freud museums exist and that neither can really be considered more "authentic" or truer than the other.

20. See Gay's biography of Freud for details.

21. Heidegger, *Poetry, Language, Thought*, 148. Further references to *PLT* will be incorporated parenthetically. Compare *Vorträge und Aufsätze*, 142. Further references to *VuA* will be incorporated parenthetically.

22. There are some interesting passages in Benjamin's *Passagen-Werk* that bring together many of the same images. See I4,4 and I4,5 especially, for example: "'To dwell' as a transitive verb—as in the notion of 'indwelt spaces'; herewith an indication of the frenetic topicality concealed in habitual behaviour. It has to do with fashioning a shell for ourselves" (*The Arcades Project*, 221/1:292).

23. On the interworkings of these terms I am especially indebted to Lacoue-Labarthe, for example in "Typographie," in Agacinski, Derrida, et al., *Mimesis des Articulations*.

24. Is this meant to suggest the "impropriety" of anal sex? *Tisch und Bett* standing for marriage is formulaic, while this phrase of overturning the table is less clear. Thanks to Rosemarie Waldrop for help with these German phrases. This table-turning may be linked to the figure in Marx's *Kapital* on *Ware* that describes the form of the commodity, inverting the Hegelian dialectic. (There the tables *tanzen*). The figure also invokes the scene of nineteenth-century séances.

25. Lienhard writes, for example, that the longing for Italy is virtually an "inborn" characteristic, and quotes Emrich as saying that the German without it is no German at all (28).

26. For an interesting reading of the historical context of these marble figures, see MacLeod.

27. The appearance of the quadrangle is suggestive of Heidegger's term *das Geviert*, the fourfold, but remains to be understood. In his *Aesthetics*, Hegel also privileges the establishment of four corners, four right angles (compare 2:46),

in the establishment of the house as the fundamental type of architecture. He understands it primarily as a social division between inside and outside: "Now of course a house as such is built principally as a dwelling, as a protection against wind, rain, weather, animals, and men, and it requires a complete enclosure where a family or a larger community can assemble, shut in by themselves, and pursue their needs and concerns in this seclusion" (2:664/14:307).

28. Nerval, *Oeuvres completes* 3:647. The poem was published first in 1845 as "Vers dorés," which later became the title of another poem originally entitled "Pensée antique." Nerval included "Delfica," with some differences in diction and punctuation, in *Les chimères* (3:1784). I reproduce that version here.

29. Gay points out Freud's ambivalence about Rome, which he first associated with incestuous desires (132). He describes Freud's love of the Mediterranean south in terms reminiscent of Goethe.

Chapter 6

1. Heidegger, *Basic Writings*, 257 / *Wegmarken*, 352. Further references will be indicated parenthetically as *BW* and *W*, respectively.

2. Heidegger, *Being and Time*, 79 / *Sein und Zeit*, 54. Further references will be indicated parenthetically as *BT* and *SuZ*, respectively.

3. For a very helpful analysis of space, place, and regionality in Heidegger, see Casey, *The Fate of Place*, especially chapter 11, "Proceeding to Place by Indirection: Heidegger," 243–84.

4. The importance of the figure of the telephone was discovered by Ronell in her highly original text, *The Telephone Book*. Ronell treats the problem of the call as well as questions of the uncanny, the house of Being, and "not being at home." I am indebted to her work here.

5. For an in-depth discussion of Heidegger and the uncanny, as well as the problem of *heimisch* and *unheimisch-sein*, see Weber, "Uncanny Thinking," in *The Legend of Freud*, and "Le repatriement inquiétant et l'expérience de l'irremplaçable," unpublished manuscript. Thanks are due here to Ronell, *The Telephone Book*, 62–70, on the uncanny and the call. For an interesting discussion of Derrida's reading of the uncanny in Heidegger, see also Wigley, especially chapter 4, "The Domestication of the House," 97–121.

6. Lacoue-Labarthe comments on the references to *Heimat* and points out how the question of *Heimat* becomes the question of German identity in *Heidegger: La politique du poème*, 127. He also discusses what I am calling here Heidegger's pastoralism and its alliance with what Lacoue-Labarthe calls Heidegger's "archi-facism" (41). Heidegger develops the problematic of *Heimat* in his late essay "Sprache und Heimat." While working his way towards a definition of *Heimat* as the proximity to Being, Heidegger nevertheless notes the

historical specificity both language and *Heimat* imply (*Aus der Erfahrung des Denkens*, 156). Thanks to Avital Ronell for bringing this text to my attention. Here Heidegger investigates poetry in terms of its *Gebild* (176) which, I suggest, is parallel to the term *Gestalt*. Lacoue-Labarthe has devoted much attention to this problematic term in Heidegger, which ultimately underpins Heidegger's appeal to myth and thus that aspect of his thinking that makes it compatible with fascism. See additionally Lacoue-Labarthe's *Le sujet de la philosophie*; *L'imitation des modernes*; *La fiction du politique*; and his essay with Jean-Luc Nancy, *Le mythe nazi*, as well as his "Typographie" in Agacinski, Derrida, et al., *Mimesis des articulations*.

7. For more on this critique of the notion of metaphor as ornament or substitution, see Derrida, "La mythologie blanche" in *Marges de la philosophie*. For his comments on this turn of phrase in Heidegger, see "Le retrait de la métaphore" in *Psyché*, especially 81–87. Derrida stresses that this phrase operates neither metaphorically nor literally, since it first establishes the familiarity of the house as that which would be transferred to something less familiar. On Derrida's reading of the house, see my "The Gift of Metaphor." In *The Paths of Heidegger's Life and Thought*, Pöggeler devotes a subchapter to the question, "Is Language the House of Being?" For the most part, he contextualizes the question within the history of theories of language. Referring to Emmanuel Lévinas, he points to the incommensurability between the contingency of the house and the absolute nature of Being. He writes: "By abstractly surveying the common view of the world, we can theoretically postulate a linguistic community; but language does not thereby become a self-enclosed view of the world and certainly not a house, but rather something full of houses between which communication goes forth and back" (258). Thanks also to Lacour's work on this question.

8. In "Peut-être la question" in *Les fins de l'homme*, Hamacher makes the latter point very clearly: "Being is never . . . simply present in language. Being is not home [*n'est pas à la maison*]" (361).

9. The term "neighbor" calls out for further understanding. Since the writing of this chapter, I have begun to reconsider my reading here in terms of the work of Emmanuel Lévinas and Edmond Jabès, suggesting a more positive potential for neighbor, but this must be deferred here.

10. This stabilizing points to the conservative and containing function of the house. Wigley considers Heidegger's use of the house to be reactionary. Interestingly, he suggests a link between the house and Heidegger's politics. In a note he comments: "In the late essays, his argument that the familiar sense of the house is a cover of a double violence acts as his own cover. Just as the figure maintains his allegiance to the tradition of metaphysics it is supposedly deployed to displace, it also maintains his allegiance to what he still referred to in the

1935 *Introduction to Metaphysics* as the 'inner truth' of the party, the truth from which the party itself is seen to have fallen" (*Architecture of Deconstruction*, 240, note 46). In contrast Casey points to the moment of "breaking out" of borders, breaking out of the containment of the house, as the celebration of violence and expansion characteristic of Heidegger's connection with Nazism. See *The Fate of Place*, 262–65. In *Of Hospitality*, Derrida points out how the stabilization of the house or home takes place as a reaction to a fundamental porousness between the inside and outside: "Wherever the 'home' is violated, wherever at any rate a violation is felt as such, you can foresee a privatizing and even familialist reaction, by widening the ethnocentric and nationalist, and thus xenophobic, circle" (53). The security of the interior space of the house will always entail an exclusionary violence: "No hospitality," Derrida writes, "in the classic sense, without sovereignty of oneself over one's home, but since there is also no hospitality without finitude, sovereignty can only be exercised by filtering, choosing, and thus by excluding and doing violence" (55).

11. Nietzsche, *The Portable Nietzsche*, 329 / *Also sprach Zarathustra*, *Kritische Studienausgabe*, 4:272–73.

12. "Thinking and Moral Considerations," in Arendt, *Responsibility and Judgment*. Thanks to Michael Gottsegen for bringing this passage to my attention.

13. Harries analyzes Heidegger's writing on building and dwelling in *The Ethical Function of Architecture*. He particularly poses the question of the "archaism" of Heidegger's terminology, associated in part with Heidegger's Nazi sympathies. Harries tries to find a middle way between a resurrection of a mythic past and a necessary questioning of the conditions of modernity. See especially 152–66. It is necessary, writes Harries, to see the connections between Heidegger's efforts to "recover the archaic truth of pre-Socratic Greece" as well as the "seductive simplicity of Heidegger's Black Forest farmhouse" and Nazi ideology and aesthetics but concludes: "Still, as long as we recognize that such farmhouses lie irrecoverably behind us, they help us understand more clearly what Heidegger calls the plight of our own dwelling, even as the failure of Heidegger's disastrous attempt to reappropriate the archaic in the modern age speaks to the threat of idolatry. We still must learn to dwell" (166).

14. Heidegger, *Identity and Difference*, 31 / *Identität und Differenz*, 18. Further references will be incorporated parenthetically as *ID* and *IuD*, respectively.

15. Heidegger, *What Is Called Thinking?* 41 / *Was heißt Denken?* 25–26. Further references will be incorporated parenthetically as *Thinking* and *Denken*, respectively.

16. For a discussion of Oppen's references to Heidegger, see Thackrey, especially 33–45.

17. Oppen, *New Collected Poems*, 200–201. This collection is cited in text as *NCP*.

18. Thanks to Forrest Gander for this attention to the "small word." I am generally indebted to him for my reading of Oppen and refer also to his "Finding the Phenomenal Oppen" in *A Faithful Existence*, 135–44.

19. *The Selected Letters of George Oppen*, 134. This collection is cited in text as *SL*.

20. Heidegger discusses this fragment in *Identität und Differenz*, 14.

Bibliography

Agacinski, Sylviane. *Volume: philosophies et politiques de l'architecture.* Paris: Galilée, 1992.

———, Jacques Derrida, et al. *Mimesis des articulations.* Paris: Aubier-Flammarion, 1975.

Apel, Helmut, Jochen Klauß, Margarete Oppel, and Werner Schuber, eds. *Goethe als Sammler: Kunst aus dem Haus am Frauenplan in Weimar.* Zürich: Offizin, 1989.

Arendt, Hannah. *Responsibility and Judgment.* New York: Schocken, 2003.

Aristotle. *Poetics.* Translated by James Hutten. New York: Norton, 1982.

Armstrong, Nancy. *Fiction in the Age of Photography: The Legacy of British Realism.* Cambridge, Mass.: Harvard University Press, 1999.

———. *How Novels Think: The Limits of Individualism from 1719–1900.* New York: Columbia University Press, 2005.

Austen, Jane. *Northanger Abbey.* Ware, Hertfordshire, England: Wordsworth Editions, 1993.

Bachelard, Gaston. *La poétique de l'espace.* Paris: Presses Universitaires de France, 1957.

Baer, Ulrich. *Spectral Evidence—The Photography of Trauma.* Cambridge, Mass.: MIT Press, 2002.

Barthes, Roland. *Le bruissement de la langue. Essais critiques IV.* Paris: Éditions du Seuil, 1984.

———. *La chambre claire: Note sur la photographie.* Paris: Gallimard, Le Seuil, 1980.

Benjamin, Walter. *The Arcades Project.* Translated by Howard Eiland and Kevin McLaughlin. Cambridge, Mass.: Belknap Press, 1999.

———. *Gesammelte Schriften.* Edited by Rolf Tiedemann and Hermann Schweppenhäuser. Frankfurt am Main: Suhrkamp, 1991. 7 vols.

———. *Das Passagen-Werk*. Edited by Rolf Tiedemann. Frankfurt am Main: Suhrkamp, 1982. 2 vols.

———. *Selected Writings, Vol. 1. 1913–1926*. Edited by Marcus Bullock and Michael W. Jennings. Cambridge, Mass.: Harvard University Press, 1996.

Bennett, Tony. *The Birth of the Museum: History, Theory, Politics*. London: Routledge, 1995.

Bernstein, Susan. "The Gift of Metaphor." *Differences* 16:3 (fall 2005): 76-86.

———. "It Walks: The Ambulatory Uncanny." *Modern Language Notes* 118:5 (December 2003): 1111–39.

Boisserée, Sulpiz. *Briefwechsel/Tagebücher*. Göttingen: Vandenhoeck & Ruprecht, 1970. 2 vols.

———. *Tagebücher 1808–1854*. Darmstadt: Eduard Roether Verlag, 1978. 2 vols.

Bolz, Norbert W., ed. *Goethes Wahlverwandtschaften: Kritische Modelle und Diskursanalysen zum Mythos Literatur*. Hildesheim: Gerstenberg Verlag, 1981.

Botting, Fred. *Gothic*. London: Routledge, 1996.

Breithaupt, Fritz. "Culture of Images: Limitation in Goethe's *Wahlverwandtschaften*." *Monatshefte* 92:3 (2000): 302–20.

Brodsky, Claudia. "The Coloring of Relations: *Die Wahlverwandtschaften* as *Farbenlehre*." *Modern Language Notes* 97:5 (1982): 1147–79.

Brooks, Chris. *The Gothic Revival*. London: Phaidon, 1999.

Brooks, Peter, and Alex Woloch, eds. *Whose Freud? The Place of Psychoanalysis in Contemporary Culture*. New Haven: Yale University Press, 2000.

Brown, Marshall. *The Gothic Text*. Stanford, Calif.: Stanford University Press, 2005.

Brown, Jane K., and Marshall Brown. "*Faust* and the Gothic Novel." In Jane K. Brown, Meredith Lee, and Thomas P. Saine, eds., *Interpreting Goethe's* Faust *Today*. Columbia, S.C.: Camden House, 1994, 68–80.

Cadava, Eduardo. *Words of Light: Theses on the Photography of History*. Princeton: Princeton University Press, 1997.

Calhoon, Kenneth S. "The Gothic Imaginary: Goethe in Strasbourg." *Deutsche Vierteljahresschrift für Literaturewissenschaft und Geistesgeschichte* 75, no. 1 (March 2001): 5–14.

Casey, Edward S. *The Fate of Place: A Philosophical History*. Berkeley: University of California Press, 1997.

Chisholm, Diane. *H.D's Freudian Poetics: Psychoanalysis in Translation*. Ithaca, N.Y.: Cornell University Press, 1992.

Clark, Kenneth. *The Gothic Revival: An Essay on the History of Taste*. Hammondsworth, England: Penguin Books, 1964.

Clemen, Paul. *Der Dom zu Köln*. Düsseldorf: Schwann, 1980.

Clery, E. J. *The Rise of Supernatural Fiction, 1762–1800*. Cambridge, England: Cambridge University Press, 1995.

Crews, Frederick, ed. *Unauthorized Freud: Doubters Confront a Legend.* New York: Viking Penguin, 1998.

Deleuze, Gilles, and Félix Guattari. *Kafka: pour une littérature mineure.* Paris: Éditions de Minuit, 1975.

De Man, Paul. *Aesthetic Ideology.* Edited and with an introduction by Andrzej Warminski. Minneapolis: University of Minnesota Press, 1996.

———. *Blindness and Insight: Essays in the Rhetoric of Contemporary Criticism.* Introduction by Wlad Godzich. Minneapolis: University of Minnesota Press, 1983.

Derrida, Jacques. *Archive Fever: A Freudian Impression.* Translated by Eric Prenowitz. Chicago: University of Chicago Press, 1996.

———. *L'écriture et la différence.* Paris: Éditions du Seuil, 1967.

———. *Khôra.* Paris: Galilée, 1993.

———. *Mal d'archive.* Paris: Galilée, 1995.

———. *Marges de la philosophie.* Paris: Éditions du Seuil, 1972.

———. *Of Grammatology.* Translated by Gayatri Chakravorty Spivak. Baltimore: Johns Hopkins University Press, 1998.

———. *Of Hospitality: Anne Dufourmantelle Asks Jacques Derrida to Respond.* Translated by Rachel Bowlby. Stanford, Calif.: Stanford University Press, 2000.

———. *Psyché: inventions de l'autre.* Paris: Galilée, 1987.

Descartes, René. *Discours de la méthode.* Paris: Garnier-Flammarion, 1966.

———. *Discourse on Method and the Meditations.* Translated by F. E. Sutcliffe. London: Penguin Books, 1968.

———. *Méditations métaphysiques.* Paris: Garnier-Flammarion, 1979.

Doolittle, Hilda. *Collected Poems, 1912–1944.* New York: New Directions, 1983.

———. *Helen in Egypt.* New York: New Directions, 1961.

———. *Tribute to Freud.* New York: New Directions, 1974.

Ellis, Markman. *A History of Gothic Fiction.* Edinburgh: Edinburgh University Press, 2000.

Elsner, John, and Roger Cardinal, eds. *The Cultures of Collecting.* London: Reaktion, 1994.

Engelman, Edmund. *Sigmund Freud: Wien IX. Berggasse 19.* Vienna: Verlag C. Brandstätter, 1993.

Ferris, David S., ed. *Walter Benjamin: Theoretical Questions.* Stanford: Stanford University Press, 1996.

Foucault, Michel. "What Is an Author?" In James D. Faubion, ed., *Aesthetics, Method, and Epistemology.* Translated by Robert Hurley and others. New York: New Press, 1998. 205–22.

Franck, Didier. *Heidegger et le problème de l'espace.* Paris: Éditions de Minuit, 1986.

Frank, Marcie. "Horace Walpole's Family Romance." *Modern Philology* 100:3 (February 2003): 417–35.

Frankl, Paul. *The Gothic: Literary Sources and Interpretations Through Eight Centuries.* Princeton: Princeton University Press, 1960.

Freud, Sigmund. *Briefe, 1873–1939.* Frankfurt am Main: S. Fischer Verlag, 1968.

———. *Gesammelte Werke.* Frankfurt am Main: Fischertaschenbuch Verlag, 1999. 18 vols.

———. *The Interpretation of Dreams.* Translated by James Strachey. New York: Basic Books, 1955.

———. *The Standard Edition of the Complete Psychological Works of Sigmund Freud.* Translated by James Strachey. London: Hogarth Press, 1973–74. 24 vols.

Friedman, Susan Stanford, ed. *Analyzing Freud: Letters of H.D., Bryher, and Their Circle.* New York: New Directions, 2002.

Fuss, Diana. *The Sense of an Interior: Four Writers and the Rooms that Shaped Them.* New York and London: Routledge, 2004.

———, and Joel Sanders. "Berggasse 19: Inside Freud's Office." In Joel Sanders, ed., *Stud: Architectures of Masculinity.* New York: Princeton Architectural Press, 1996. 112–39.

Gamer, Michael, intro. and ed. *The Castle of Otranto,* by Horace Walpole. London: Penguin Books, 2001.

———. *Romanticism and the Gothic: Genre, Reception, and Canon Formation.* Cambridge and New York: Cambridge University Press, 2000.

Gamwell, Lynn, and Richard Wells, eds. *Sigmund Freud and Art: His Personal Collection of Antiquities.* Introduction by Peter Gay. Binghamton, N.Y.: SUNY Press, 1989.

Gander, Forrest. *A Faithful Existence: Reading, Memory, and Transcendence.* Washington, D.C.: Shoemaker & Hoard, 2005.

Gasché, Rodolphe. *The Honor of Thinking: Critique, Theory, Philosophy.* Stanford, Calif.: Stanford University Press, 2007.

Gay, Peter. *Freud: A Life for Our Time.* New York: Norton, 1998.

Goethe, Johann Wolfgang von. *The Autobiography of Johann Wolfgang von Goethe.* Translated by John Oxenford. University of Chicago Press, 1974. 2 vols.

———. *Elective Affinities.* In David E. Wellbery, ed., *The Collected Works,* vol. 11. Translated by Judith Ryan. Princeton: Princeton University Press, 1995.

———. *Goethe on Art.* Translated by John Gage. Berkeley and Los Angeles: University of California Press, 1980.

———. *Goethes Werke.* Hamburg: Christian Wegner Verlag, 1958. 14 vols.

———. *Wilhelm Meister's Apprenticeship.* Translated by Eric A. Blackall and Victor Lange. Princeton: Princeton University Press, 1989.

Grosz, Elizabeth. *Architecture from the Outside: Essays on Virtual and Real Space.* Cambridge, Mass.: MIT Press, 2001.

Haischer, Peter-Henning. "Ruine oder Monument? Goethes Lebenswerk im Spiegel seiner Gotik-Studien." *Goethe-Jahrbuch* 122 (2005): 215–29.

Hall, Daniel. "The Gothic Tide: Schauerroman and Gothic Novel in the Late Eighteenth Century." In Susanne Stark, ed., *The Novel in Anglo-German Context: Cultural Cross-Currents and Affinities.* Amsterdam and Atlanta: Rodopi, 2000. 51–60

Hamacher, Werner. "Expositions of the Mother: A Quick Stroll Through Various Museums." In *The End(s) of the Museum/Els limits del museu.* Curators John G. Hanhardt and Thomas Keenan. Barcelona: Fundació Antoni Tàpies, 1996. 81–134.

———. "Peut-être la question." In Philippe Lacoue-Labarthe and Jean-Luc Nancy, eds., *Les fins de l'homme: à partir du travail de Jacques Derrida.* Paris: Galilée, 1981. 345–65.

Hamon, Philippe. *Expositions: literature et architecture au XIXe siècle.* Paris: José Corti, 1989.

———. *Expositions: Literature and Architecture in Nineteenth-Century France.* Translated by Katia Sainson-Frank and Lisa Maguire. Introduction by Richard Sieburth. Berkeley: University of California Press, 1992.

Hannsen, Beatrice, and Andrew Benjamin, eds. *Walter Benjamin and Romanticism.* New York and London: Continuum, 2002.

Hardin, James, ed. *Reflection and Action: Essays on the Bildungsroman.* Columbia, S.C.: University of South Carolina Press, 1991.

Harries, Karsten. *The Ethical Function of Architecture.* Cambridge, Mass.: MIT Press, 1997.

Hegel, G. W. F. *Aesthetics: Lectures on Fine Art.* Translated by T. M. Knox. Oxford: Clarendon Press, 1975. 2 vols.

———. *Vorlesungen über die Ästhetik. Werke,* vols. 13–15. Frankfurt am Main: Suhrkamp, 1986.

Heidegger, Martin. *Aus der Erfahrung des Denkens, 1910–1976.* Frankfurt am Main: Vittorio Klostermann, 1983.

———. *Basic Writings.* Edited by David Farrell Krell. Harper Collins, 1993.

———. *Being and Time.* Translated by John Macquarrie and Edward Robinson. New York: Harper and Row, 1962.

———. *Erläuterung zu Hölderlins Dichtung.* Frankfurt am Main: Vittorio Klostermann, 1981.

———. *Identität und Differenz.* Stuttgart: J. G. Cotta'sche Buchhandlung, 1957.

———. *Identity and Difference.* Translated by Joan Stambaugh. New York: Harper and Row, 1969.

————. *Poetry, Language, Thought.* Translated by Albert Hofstadter. New York: Harper and Row, 1971.

————. *Sein und Zeit.* Tübingen: Max Niemeyer Verlag, 1977.

————. *Vorträge und Aufsätze.* Stuttgart: Verlag Günther Neske, 1954.

————. *Was heißt Denken?* Stuttgart: Reclam, 1992.

————. *Wegmarken.* Frankfurt am Main: Vittorio Klostermann, 1978.

————. *What Is Called Thinking?* Introduction by J. Glenn Gary. New York: Harper and Row, 1968.

Herder, Johann Gottfried von. *Von deutscher Art und Kunst. Einige fliegende Blätter.* Edited by Joseph Bernhart. Munich: Albert Langen, n.d.

Hogle, Jerrold E., ed. *The Cambridge Companion to Gothic Fiction.* Cambridge, England: Cambridge University Press, 2002.

Hölderin, Friedrich. *Werke und Briefe.* Edited by Friedrich Beißner and Jochen Schmidt. Frankfurt am Main: Insel Verlag, 1969. 3 vols.

Hollier, Denis. *Against Architecture: The Writings of Georges Bataille.* Translated by Betsy Wing. Cambridge, Mass.: MIT Press, 1989.

Hustis, Harriet. "'Reading encrypted but persistent': The Gothic of Reading and Poe's 'The Fall of the House of Usher.'" *Studies in American Fiction* 27:1 (1998): 3–20.

Iddon, John. *Horace Walpole's Strawberry Hill: A Historic Guide from Walpole's Time to the Present.* Twickenham, London: St. Mary's University College, 1996.

Kafka, Franz. *The Complete Stories.* Edited by Nahum N. Glatzer. New York: Schocken, 1971.

————. *Sämtliche Erzählungen.* Frankfurt am Main: Fischer Taschenbuch Verlag, 1970.

Kant, Immanuel. *Critique of Pure Reason.* Translated by Norman Kemp Smith. New York: St. Martin's Press, 1965.

————. *Kritik der reinen Vernunft.* Frankfurt am Main: Suhrkamp Taschenbuch Verlag, 1974. 2 vols.

————. *Kritik der Urteilskraft.* Frankfurt am Main: Suhrkamp Taschenbuch Verlag, 1974. 2 vols.

Kenner, Hugh. *The Pound Era.* Berkeley: University of California Press, 1971.

Kontje, Todd. *The German Bildungsroman: History of a National Genre.* Columbia, S.C.: Camden House, 1993.

Lacoue-Labarthe, Philippe. *La fiction du politique: Heidegger, l'art et la politique.* Paris: Christian Bourgois, 1987.

————. *Heidegger: la politique du poème.* Paris: Galilée, 2002.

————. *L'imitation des modernes.* Paris: Galilée, 1986.

————. *Le sujet de la philosophie.* Paris: Aubier Flammarion, 1979.

————, and Jean-Luc Nancy, *Le mythe nazi*. La Tour d'Aigues: Éditions de l'Aube, 1991.

Lacour, Claudia Brodsky. "Architectural History: Benjamin and Hölderlin." *Boundary 2* 30:1 (2003): 143–68.

————. *Lines of Thought: Discourse, Architectonics, and the Origin of Modern Philosophy*. Durham, N.C., and London: Duke University Press, 1996.

Lalande, André. *Vocabulaire technique et critique de la Philosophie*. Paris: Presses Universitaires de France.

Leach, Neil. *Rethinking Architecture: A Reader in Cultural Theory*. London: Routledge, 1997.

Leacock, N. K. "Character, Silence, and the Novel: Walter Benjamin on Goethe's *Elective Affinities*." *Narrative* 10:3 (2002): 277–306.

Lefebvre, Henri. *La production de l'espace*. Paris: Anthropos, 1974.

Lienhard, Johanna. *Mignon und ihre Lieder, gespiegelt in den Wilhelm-Meister-Romanen*. Zürich and Munich: Artemis Verlag, 1978.

Lyotard, Jean-François. *The Postmodern Condition: A Report on Knowledge*. Translated by Geoff Bennington and Brian Massumi. Minneapolis: University of Minnesota Press, 1984.

MacLeod, Catriona. "Floating Heads: Weimar Portrait Busts." In Burkhard Henke, Susanne Kord, and Simon Richter, eds., *Unwrapping Goethe's Weimar: Essays in Cultural Studies and Local Knowledge*. Rochester, N.Y.: Camden House, 2000. 64–84.

Mandelarzt, Michael. "Bauen, Erhalten, Zerstören, Versiegeln. Architektur als Kunst in Goethe's 'Wahlverwandtschaften.'" *Zeitschrift für Deutsche Philologie* 118:4 (1999): 500–17.

Maul, Gisela, and Margarete Oppel. *Goethes Wohnhaus*. Munich: Carl Hanser Verlag, 1996.

Mayer, Gerhart. *Der deutsche Bildungsroman. Von Aufklärung bis zur Gegenwart*. Stuttgart: J. B. Metzlersche Verlagsbuchhandlung, 1992.

McLaughlin, Kevin. *Paperwork: Fiction and Mass Mediacy in the Paper Age*. Philadelphia: University of Pennsylvania Press, 2005.

————. "Virtual Paris: Benjamin's *Arcades Project*." In Gerhard Richter, ed., *Benjamin's Ghosts: Interventions in Contemporary Literary and Cultural Theory*. Stanford, Calif.: Stanford University Press, 2002. 204–25.

Menninghaus, Winfried. *Schwellenkunde: Walter Benjamins Passage des Mythos*. Frankfurt am Main: Suhrkamp, 1986.

Miles, Robert. *Gothic Writing, 1750–1820: A Genealogy*. Manchester and New York: Manchester University Press, 2002.

Miller, J. Hillis. *Ariadne's Thread: Story Lines*. New Haven: Yale University Press, 1992.

Miller, Norbert. *Strawberry Hill: Horace Walpole und die Ästhetik der schönen Unregelmäßigkeit.* München: Carl Hanser Verlag, 1986.

Moraitis, George. "The Couch as a Protective Shield for the Analyst." *Psychoanalytic Inquiry* 15:3 (1995): 406–12.

Moretti, Franco. *The Way of the World. The Bildungsroman in European Culture.* London: Verso, 1987.

Morrissey, Lee. *From the Temple to the Castle: An Architectural History of British Literature, 1660–1760.* Charlottesville and London: University of Virginia Press, 1999.

Napier, Elizabeth R. *The Failure of Gothic: Problems of Disjunction in an Eighteenth-century Literary Form.* Oxford: Clarendon Press, 1987.

Nerval, Gérard de. *Oeuvres complètes.* Edited by Jean Guillaume and Claude Pichois. Paris: Éditions Gallimard, 1989. 3 vols.

———. *Selected Writings.* Translated by Richard Sieburth. Penguin Books, 1999.

Nietzsche, Friedrich. *Kritische Studienausgabe.* Edited by Giorgio Colli and Mazzino Montinari. Munich and New York: Deutscher Taschenbuch Verlag/de Gruyter, 1988. 15 vols.

———. *The Portable Nietzsche.* Edited and translated by Walter Kaufmann. New York: Viking Penguin, 1968.

Oppel, Horst. *Englisch-deutsche Literaturbeziehungen.* Vol. 1, *Von der Romantik bis zur Gegenwart.* Berlin: Erich Schmidt Verlag, 1971.

Oppen, George. *New Collected Poems.* New York: New Directions, 2002.

———. *The Selected Letters of George Oppen.* Edited by Rachel Blau DuPlessis. Durham, N.C., and London: Duke University Press, 1990.

Payot, Daniel. *Le philosophe et l'architecte: Sur quelques determinations philosophiques de l'idée d'architecture.* Paris: Aubier Montaigne, 1982.

Peucker, Brigitte. "The Material Image in Goethe's *Wahlverwandtschaften.*" *Germanic Review* 74:3: 195–213.

Poe, Edgar Allan. *Complete Tales and Poems.* New York: Vintage Books, 1978.

Pöggeler, Otto. *The Paths of Heidegger's Life and Thought.* Translated by John Bailiff. Atlantic Highlands, N.J.: Humanities Press, 1997.

Pound, Ezra. *Literary Essays of Ezra Pound.* Edited by T. S. Eliot. New York: New Directions, 1968.

Preminger, Alex, and T. V. F. Brogan, eds. *The New Princeton Encyclopedia of Poetry and Poetics.* Princeton: Princeton University Press, 1993.

Punter, David. *The Literature of Terror: A History of Gothic Fictions from 1764 to the Present Day.* New York: Longman, 1980.

Rajchman, John. *Constructions.* Cambridge, Mass.: MIT University Press, 1998.

Readings, Bill. *The University in Ruins.* Cambridge, Mass.: Harvard University Press, 1996.

Redfield, Marc. *Phantom Formations: Aesthetic Ideology and the Bildungsroman.* Ithaca, N.Y.: Cornell University Press, 1996.

Richter, Gerhard, ed. *Benjamin's Ghosts: Interventions in Contemporary Literary and Cultural Theory.* Stanford, Calif.: Stanford University Press, 2002.

Riddel, Joseph. "Decentering the Image: The 'Project' of 'American' Poetics?" In Josué V. Harari, *Textual Strategies.* Ithaca, N.Y.: Cornell University Press, 1979. 322–58.

———. "H.D.'s Scene of Writing: Poetry as (and) Analysis." *Studies in the Literary Imagination* 12:1 (1979): 41–59.

Robson-Scott, W. D. *The Literary Background of the Gothic Revival in Germany: A Chapter in the History of Taste.* Oxford: Clarendon Press, 1965.

Ronell, Avital. "On the Misery of Theory Without Poetry: Heidegger's Reading of Hölderlin's 'Andenken.'" *PMLA* 120:1 (January 2005): 16–32.

———. *The Telephone Book: Technology, Schizophrenia, Electric Speech.* Lincoln: University of Nebraska Press, 1989.

Rosenheim, Shawn, and Stephen Rachman, eds. *The American Face of Edgar Allan Poe.* Baltimore: Johns Hopkins University Press, 1995.

Roth, Michael S., ed. *Freud: Conflict and Culture.* New York: Alfred A. Knopf, 1998.

Rybczynski, Witold. *Home: A Short History of an Idea.* New York: Penguin Books, 1987.

Sabor, Peter, ed. *Horace Walpole: The Critical Heritage.* London: Routledge, 1987.

Sammons, Jeffrey. "The Mystery of the Missing Bildungsroman, or What Happened to Wilhelm Meister's Legacy?" *Genre* 14 (1981): 229–46.

Scharabi, M. *Architekturgeschichte des 19. Jahrhunderts.* Tübingen and Berlin: Ernst Wasmuth Verlag, 1993.

Scheurmann, Konrad, and Ursula Bongaerts-Schomer, eds. " . . . *endlich in dieser Hauptstadt der Welt angelangt!" Goethe in Rom.* Mainz: Verlag Philipp von Zabern, 1997.

Schneider, Helmut J. "Wahllandschaften: Mobilisierung der Natur und das Darstellungsproblem der Moderne in Goethes *Wahlverwandtschaften.*" In Martha B. Helfer, ed., *Rereading Romanticism.* Amsterdam: Rodopi, 2000. 285–300.

Schorske, Carl E. *Fin-de-Siècle Vienna: Politics and Culture.* New York: Vintage, 1981.

Sharr, Adam. *Heidegger's Hut.* Cambridge, Mass.: MIT Press, 2006.

Sherman, Daniel J., and Irit Rogoff, eds. *Museum Culture: Histories, Discourses, Spectacles.* Minneapolis: University of Minnesota Press, 1994.

Sontag, Susan. *On Photography.* New York: Picador, 2001.

Sulzer, Johann Georg. *Allgemeine Theorie der schönen Künste in einzeln, nach alphabetischer Ordnung der Kunstwörter auf einander folgenden, Artikeln abgehandelt.* Leipzig: In der Weidmannschen Buchhandlung, 1792–99.

Summers, Montague. Introduction. *The Castle of Otranto and the Mysterious Mother* by Horace Walpole. London: Chiswick Press for Constable and Company, 1924. xi–lvii.

Tacitus. *On Britain and Germany.* Translated by H. Mattingly. Baltimore: Penguin Books, 1948.

Tantillo, Astrida Orle. *Goethe's Elective Affinities and the Critics.* Rochester, N.Y.: Camden House, 2001.

Thackrey, Susan. *George Oppen: A Radical Practice.* San Francisco: O Books and the Poetry Center and American Poetry Archives, 2001.

Todorov, Tzvetan. *The Fantastic: A Structural Approach to a Literary Genre.* Translated by Richard Howard. Ithaca, N.Y.: Cornell University Press, 1975.

Tschumi, Bernard. *Architecture and Disjunction.* Cambridge, Mass.: MIT Press, 1996.

Twenty Maresfield Gardens: A Guide to the Freud Museum. London: Serpent's Tail, 1998.

Varma, Devendra P. *The Gothic Flame.* Metuchen, N.J., and London: Scarecrow Press, 1987.

Vergo, Peter, ed. *The New Museology.* London: Reaktion Books, 1989.

Vidler, Anthony. *The Architectural Uncanny: Essays in the Modern Unhomely.* Cambridge, Mass.: MIT Press, 1992.

Vogl, Joseph. "Nomos der Ökonomie. Steuerungen in Goethes *Wahlverwandtschaften.*" *Modern Language Notes* 114 (1999): 503–27.

Völker, Werner, ed. *Bei Goethe zu Gast: Besucher in Weimar.* Frankfurt am Main: Insel Verlag, 1996.

Waldrop, Keith. "A Reason for Images: One Key to Modernism." *Modern Language Studies* 15:3 (1985): 72–84.

Walpole, Horace. *The Castle of Otranto.* In Peter Fairclough, ed., *Three Gothic Novels.* London: Penguin Books, 1968.

———. *A Description of the Villa of Mr. Horace Walpole, at Strawberry-Hill near Twickenham.* Strawberry Hill, England: 1784.

———. *Selected Letters.* Edited by W. S. Lewis. New Haven and London: Yale University Press, 1973.

Watt, James. *Contesting the Gothic: Fiction, Genre and Cultural Conflict, 1764–1832.* Cambridge, England: Cambridge University Press, 1999.

Waugaman, Richard M. "The Couch as Transference Object." *Psychoanalytic Inquiry* 15:3 (1995), 338–57.

Weber, Samuel. *The Legend of Freud.* Stanford, Calif.: Stanford University Press, expanded edition, 2000.

————. "Le repatriement inquiétant et l'expérience de l'irremplaçable," unpublished manuscript.

Wein, Toni. "Tangled Webs: Horace Walpole and the Practice of History in *The Castle of Otranto.*" *English Language Notes* 34:4 (June 1998): 12–22.

Wellbery, David E. "Die Wahlverwandtschaften (1809)." In Paul Michael Lützeler and James E. MacLeod, eds., *Goethes Erzählwerk.* Stuttgart: Reclam, 1985: 291–318.

Wigley, Mark. *The Architecture of Deconstruction: Derrida's Haunt.* Cambridge, Mass.: MIT Press, 1993.

Williams, Anne. *Art of Darkness: A Poetics of Gothic.* Chicago: University of Chicago Press, 1995.

Winter, Sarah. *Freud and the Institution of Psychoanalytic Knowledge.* Stanford, Calif.: Stanford University Press, 1999.

Wittkower, Rudolf. *Architectural Principles in the Age of Humanism.* New York: Norton, 1971.

Wolfreys, Julian. *Victorian Hauntings: Spectrality, Gothic, the Uncanny and Literature.* London: Palgrave, 2002.

Wyschogrod, Edith. "Autochthony and Welcome: Discourses of Exile in Levinas and Derrida." In Yvonne Sherwood and Kevin Hart, eds., *Derrida and Religion: Other Testaments.* New York: Routledge, 2005. 53–61.

Index

MERIDIAN

Crossing Aesthetics

Louis Marin, *Of Representation*

J. Hillis Miller, *Speech Acts in Literature*

Maurice Blanchot, *Faux pas*

Jean-Luc Nancy, *Being Singular Plural*

Maurice Blanchot / Jacques Derrida, *The Instant of My Death / Demeure: Fiction and Testimony*

Niklas Luhmann, *Art as a Social System*

Emmanual Levinas, *God, Death, and Time*

Ernst Bloch, *The Spirit of Utopia*

Giorgio Agamben, *Potentialities: Collected Essays in Philosophy*

Ellen S. Burt, *Poetry's Appeal: French Nineteenth-Century Lyric and the Political Space*

Jacques Derrida, *Adieu to Emmanuel Levinas*

Werner Hamacher, *Premises: Essays on Philosophy and Literature from Kant to Celan*

Aris Fioretos, *The Gray Book*

Deborah Esch, *In the Event: Reading Journalism, Reading Theory*

Winfried Menninghaus, *In Praise of Nonsense: Kant and Bluebeard*

Giorgio Agamben, *The Man Without Content*

Giorgio Agamben, *The End of the Poem: Studies in Poetics*

Theodor W. Adorno, *Sound Figures*

Louis Marin, *Sublime Poussin*

Philippe Lacoue-Labarthe, *Poetry as Experience*

Ernst Bloch, *Literary Essays*

Jacques Derrida, *Resistances of Psychoanalysis*

Marc Froment-Meurice, *That Is to Say: Heidegger's Poetics*

Francis Ponge, *Soap*